INDIGENOUS YOUTH AND MULTILINGUALISM

"… a much-needed exploration of language practices, policy implementation, and advocacy efforts among Indigenous youth living in the United States and around the world. The ethnographies will challenge readers to engage in socially conscious ethnographic research and consider their responsibility to support ongoing language revitalization efforts around the globe."

Guadalupe Valdés, Stanford University, USA

"Finally, scholars and students have a resource that accounts for the vitality and massive diversity of Indigenous youth communicative repertoires. This path-breaking volume tackles the important and neglected work of exploring the relationship between ever-morphing Indigenous youth cultural practice and the traditional goals of language policy and planning."

Betsy Rymes, The University of Pennsylvania, USA

"This book raises important questions about existing conceptualizations of language maintenance and language shift. It fills a gap in our knowledge of Indigenous youth and provides important insights about language and identity."

Ariana Mangual Figueroa, Rutgers University, USA

"Throughout the book, young people's love of their language expresses itself, whether that love is there from the beginning or learned later. The future of their Indigenous languages is in their hands. Thanks to the editors and authors in this volume, the literature on language loss and revitalization now includes the voices of this critical young generation."

f California-Berkeley, USA,
from the Foreword

Bridging the fields of youth studies and language planning and policy, this book takes a close, nuanced look at Indigenous youth bi/multilingualism across diverse cultural and linguistic settings, drawing out comparisons, contrasts, and important implications for language planning and policy and for projects designed to curtail language loss and promote intergenerational learning and understanding.

Within the book, Indigenous and non-Indigenous scholars with longstanding ties to language planning efforts in diverse Indigenous communities examine language policy and planning as *de facto* and *de jure*—as covert and overt, bottom-up and top-down. This approach illuminates crosscutting themes of language identity and ideology, cultural conflict, linguistic survivance, continuance, and linguistic human rights as youth negotiate these issues within rapidly changing sociolinguistic contexts. A distinctive feature of the book is its chapters and commentaries by Indigenous scholars writing about their own communities.

This landmark volume stands alone in offering a look at diverse Indigenous youth in multiple endangered language communities; related theoretical, empirical, and methodological insights; and lessons for intergenerational language planning in dynamic sociocultural contexts.

Leisy T. Wyman is Associate Professor in the Language, Reading and Culture Program, and affiliate faculty in the American Indian Studies and Second Language Acquisition and Teaching Programs at the University of Arizona, USA.

Teresa L. McCarty is the George F. Kneller Chair in Education and Anthropology at the University of California, Los Angeles, and the Alice Wiley Snell Professor Emerita of Education Policy Studies at Arizona State University, USA.

Sheilah E. Nicholas (Hopi) is Assistant Professor in the Language, Reading, and Culture Program, and affiliate faculty in the American Indian Studies and Second Language Acquisition and Teaching Programs at the University of Arizona, USA.

INDIGENOUS YOUTH AND MULTILINGUALISM

Language Identity, Ideology, and Practice in Dynamic Cultural Worlds

Edited by

Leisy T. Wyman, Teresa L. McCarty,
and Sheilah E. Nicholas

Routledge
Taylor & Francis Group

NEW YORK AND LONDON

First published 2014
by Routledge
711 Third Avenue, New York, NY 10017

Simultaneously published in the UK
by Routledge
2 Park Square, Milton Park, Abingdon, Oxon OX14 4RN

Routledge is an imprint of the Taylor & Francis Group, an informa business

© 2014 Taylor & Francis

Library of Congress Cataloging in Publication Data
Indigenous youth and bi/multilingualism : language identity, ideology, and practice in
    dynamic cultural worlds / edited by Leisy T. Wyman, Teresa L. McCarty, and Sheilah
    E. Nicholas.
    pages cm.
    Includes bibliographical references and index.
    1. Indians of North America—Languages. 2. Indian youth—North America—
    Languages. 3. Bilingualism—North America. 4. Multilingualistm—North America. 5.
    Language shift—North America. 6. Language renewal—North America.
    7. Anthropological linguistics—North America. I. Wyman, Leisy Thornton.
    PM206.I54 2013
    497—dc23
    2013004960

ISBN: 978-0-415-52242-7 (hbk)
ISBN: 978-0-415-52243-4 (pbk)
ISBN: 978-0-203-12143-6 (ebk)

Typeset in Bembo and Stone Sans
by EvS Communication Networx, Inc.

Printed and bound in the United States of America by Publishers Graphics,
LLC on sustainably sourced paper.

To Indigenous youth everywhere, who, through their innovative language practices and activism, are shaping the future of Indigenous languages and communities.

CONTENTS

FOREWORD

Leanne Hinton

The last two decades have seen the flowering of a new kind of literature. The literature spans a number of academic fields—linguistics and applied linguistics, anthropology and linguistic anthropology, sociology, education, and Indigenous studies—and goes beyond the academy as well, into advocacy and local practice, with authors and readers ranging from researchers to teachers to families. This is the literature on endangered languages, and it is about, by, and for both university researchers and the communities of people whose languages they are.

Many interesting trends can be seen in the study of endangered languages over time. One trend is in the practices of linguistic documentation. Generations of linguists have documented endangered languages, but earlier generations, spanning much of the 20th century, were primarily documenting them for the posterity of linguistic science. Now, although that agenda is still a partial guide, the needs and demands of the language communities have taken on a much larger role. Documentation is more massive, with trends toward a greater emphasis on data over analysis, and on the broad documentation of different genres and styles of speaking (Hill, 2006; Himmelmann, 2006). Documentation is more interdisciplinary, more collaborative, and more user-friendly, with an understanding that both the data and its analysis will be used by the community for their own needs (Austin, 2003; Flores Farfán & Ramallo, 2010; Gippert, Nikolaus, Himmelmann, & Mosel, 2006; Woodbury, 2003, 2011). This gives documentary linguistics more features of applied linguistics and humanism than it did in the past (Mosel, 2006). This has also led to new ethical standards for linguistic documentation, with new responsibilities to community defined, and a change in the researchers' attitudes away from the notion of speaker as subject to speaker as research partner (Dwyer, 2006; Mato Nunpa,

2006). The importance of archiving linguistic data has also received much more attention in recent years, along with the development of technology and markup conventions increasing archival accessibility, and related issues of privacy vs. availability, and intellectual property ownership (Conathan, 2011; Nathan, 2006; Trilsbeek & Wittenburg, 2006).

Another linguistic trend has been the study of what is happening to languages within the context of endangerment. Some powerful research, starting in the 1970s and pioneered by Nancy Dorian, has been done on language death, defined as changes in the structure of a language in the last generations of speakers during the process of language shift (Austin & Sallabank, 2011; Dorian 1973, 1981, 1989; Nettle & Romaine, 2000). More recently, we see the beginnings of a change toward studying the language not of the last speakers, but rather the first speakers of a new generation as part of the language revitalization process (Hinton, 2000; Holton, 2009; Reid, 2010).

Much attention in the last two decades has focused on language reclamation and revitalization, and the positive steps being taken by members of communities whose languages are endangered (Fishman, 1991, 2001; Grenoble & Whaley, 2006; Hinton & Hale, 2001; Hobson, Lowe, Poetsch, & Walsh, 2010). And, as language revitalization and reclamation have become a worldwide trend in speech communities, new and more applied research has followed on how to teach and learn endangered languages, and how people can bring their heritage languages back into use (Coronel-Molina & McCarty, 2011; Grenoble & Whaley, 2001; Hinton & Hale, 2001; Sallabank, 2011).

Much of the recent research has been not just on language form but also on the social processes of language shift, and the human processes of language ideology and language reclamation (Meek, 2010; Schieffelin, Woolard, & Kroskrity, 1998; Tsunoda, 2006). Although much has been written from a point of view from outside the speech communities about the global importance of language diversity and the public ideologies that are part of the endangerment process (Hale et al., 1992; Harrison, 2007), currently the point of view is increasingly community-internal, and becomes more about the issues of human language rights and of community-based views of their languages (Skutnabb-Kangas, 2008; Skutnabb-Kangas, Phillipson, & Rannut, 1994).

The academy and the community trade ideas back and forth, and the difference between them is shrinking. The expansion of authorship and readership into the community is another important trend. An increasing number of researchers are themselves members of endangered language communities, and many of those use their work for community benefit. Many of the authors now are the local practitioners themselves, writing to record and critique the history and methods of language work in their community, and to help other practitioners (Arviso & Holm, 2001; Cantoni, 1996; Platero, 2001; Supahan & Supahan, 2001; Wilson & Kamanā, 2001; Yunkaporta, 2010; and most of the chapters in Reyhner, 1997).

Within the field of language revitalization, there has been a good deal of focus on schools, with special attention to bilingual and immersion schooling (Holm, 2006; Poetsch & Lowe 2010; Wilson & Kamanā, 2001). The study of language revitalization in practice has also researched the venues of community (Amery, 2010; Goodfellow, 2009a, 2009b; McNaboe & Poetsch, 2010; Olawsky 2010), family (Hinton, 2013), and individual initiatives (Hinton, Vera, Steele, & Advocates for Indigenous California Language Survival, 2002; Williams, 2006).

In all of these areas of research, the agency for language shift and revitalization has been with the adult generations—the elders who are the knowledge-keepers, yet who might not have passed on the language to their children, and the professional-age adults who established and taught in bilingual and immersion schools, made community policy, learned their heritage language on their own, or made a decision for their family to use—or not—their language at home. Nowhere in the literature have the young people themselves been seen as the agents within the processes of language change, shift, and revitalization, until Wyman, McCarty, Nicholas, and their colleagues began their work on this topic. This volume fills that gap.

In this book, the focus is on the youth—on their own practices and beliefs about language, and as the agents of change, in both form and use of their heritage tongues. In some of the chapters we see a young generation in the grip of language shift, yet trying to manage the process by developing strategies to participate in their heritage culture and contribute to their community even while not being fully able to participate linguistically. We see young people struggling with complex and competing ideologies about language, making their way between them to come to their own conclusions and find their own place within the processes of shift and shift reversal. We hear the stories of youth with strong heritage language socialization through immersion schools, contrasted with others where the language is not supported. In others, we see the younger generations who are seizing the reins of their languages' future and developing projects of language planning, learning and use. We see the fresh and different views of language from youthful eyes, without some of the conservative ideologies of older generations. We see the struggles they go through for their identity and how language fits into it.

In this book, we see language as a living thing even among youth who know very little of their heritage tongue, but still use what they know of it and of English itself in creative ways that allow them to claim their Indigenous identity and represent it to others. Throughout the book, young people's love of their language expresses itself, whether that love is there from the beginning or learned later. The future of their Indigenous languages is in their hands. Thanks to the editors and authors in this volume, the literature on language loss and revitalization now includes the voices of this critical young generation.

References

Amery, R. (2010). Monitoring the use of Kaurna. In J. Hobson, K. Lowe, S. Poetsch, & M. Walsh (Eds.), *Re-awakening languages: Theory and practice in the revitalisation of Australia's Indigenous languages* (pp. 56–66). Sydney, Australia: Sydney University Press.

Arviso, M., & Holm, W. (2001). Tséhootsooídí Olta'gi Diné bizaad bíhoo'aah: A Navajo immersion program at Fort Defiance, AZ. In L. Hinton & K. Hale (Eds.), *The green book of language revitalization in practice* (pp. 203–215). San Diego, CA: Academic Press.

Austin, P. K. (Ed.). (2003). *Language description and documentation, vol. 1.* London, England: School of Oriental and African Studies.

Austin, P. K., & Sallabank, J. (Eds.). (2011). *The Cambridge handbook of endangered languages.* Cambridge, England: Cambridge University Press.

Cantoni, G. (Ed.). (1996). *Stabilizing Indigenous languages.* Flagstaff: Northern Arizona University. Retrieved May 12, 2013 from http://jan.ucc.nau.edu/~jar/SIL/

Conathan, L. (2011). Archiving and language documentation. In P. K. Austin & J. Sallabank (Eds.), *The Cambridge handbook of endangered languages* (pp. 235–254). Cambridge, England: Cambridge University Press.

Coronel-Molina, S. M., & McCarty, T. L. (2011). Language curriculum design and evaluation for endangered languages. In P. K. Austin & J. Sallabank (Eds.), *The Cambridge handbook of endangered languages* (pp. 354–370). Cambridge, England: Cambridge University Press.

Dorian, N. C. (1973). Grammatical change in a dying dialect. *Language, 49,* 413–438.

Dorian, N. C. (1981). *Language death: The life cycle of a Scottish Gaelic dialect.* Philadelphia: University of Pennsylvania Press.

Dorian, N. C. (Ed.) (1989). *Investigating obsolescence: Studies in language contraction and death.* Cambridge, England: Cambridge University Press.

Dwyer, A. M. (2006). Ethics and practicalities of cooperative fieldwork and analysis. In J. Hobson, K. Lowe, S. Poetsch, & M. Walsh (Eds.), *Re-awakening languages: Theory and practice in the revitalisation of Australia's Indigenous languages* (pp. 31–66). Sydney, Australia: Sydney University Press.

Fishman, J. A. (1991). *Reversing language shift: Theoretical and empirical foundations of assistance to threatened languages.* Clevedon, England: Multilingual Matters.

Fishman, J. A. (Ed.). (2001). *Can threatened languages be saved? Reversing language shift, revisited: A 21st century perspective.* Clevedon, England: Multilingual Matters.

Flores Farfán, J. A., & Ramallo, F. F. (2010). *New perspectives on endangered languages: Bridging gaps between sociolinguistics, documentation and language revitalization.* Amsterdam, The Netherlands: John Benjamins.

Gippert, J., Nikolaus, P., Himmelmann, N. P., & Mosel, U. (Eds.). (2006). *Essentials of language documentation.* The Hague, Netherlands: Mouton de Gruyter.

Goodfellow, A. M. (2009a). A community-based Gut'sala language program. In A. Goodfellow (Ed.), *Speaking of endangered languages: Issues in revitalization* (pp. 266–286). Newcastle upon Tyne, England: Cambridge Scholars Publishing.

Goodfellow, A. M. (Ed.) (2009b). *Speaking of endangered languages: Issues in revitalization.* Newcastle upon Tyne, England: Cambridge Scholars Publishing.

Grenoble, L. A., & Whaley, L. J. (2006). *Saving languages: An introduction to language revitalization.* New York, NY: Cambridge University Press.

Hale, K., Krauss, M., Watahomigie, L. J., Yamamoto, A. Y., Craig, C., Jeanne, L., & England, N. C. (1992). Endangered languages. *Language, 68*(1), 1–42.

Harrison, K. D. (2007). *When languages die: The extinction of the world's languages and the erosion of human knowledge.* Oxford, England: Oxford University Press.

Hill, J. H. (2006). The ethnography of language and language documentation. In J. Gippert, P. Nikolaus, N. P. Himmelmann, & U. Mosel (Eds), *Essentials of language documentation* (pp. 113–128). The Hague, The Netherlands: Mouton de Gruyter.

Himmelmann, N. P. (2006). Language documentation: What is it and what is it good for? In J.

Gippert, P. Nikolaus, N .P. Himmelmann, & U. Mosel (Eds.), *Essentials of language documentation* (pp. 1–30). The Hague, The Netherlands: Mouton de Gruyter.

Hinton, L. (2000). Language revitalization and language change. In M. Morúa Leyva & C. López Cruz (Eds.), *Quinto encuentro de lingüistica del Noroeste. Tomo II* [Fifth linguistics of the Northeast meeting. Volume II] (pp. 233–246). Hermosillo, Sonora, Mexico: Editorial UniSon.

Hinton, L. (Ed.). (2013). *Bringing our languages home: Language revitalization for families.* Berkeley, CA: Heyday Books.

Hinton, L., & Hale, K. (Eds.). (2001). *The green book of language revitalization in practice.* San Diego, CA: Academic Press.

Hinton, L., Vera, M., Steele, N., & Advocates for Indigenous California Language Survival (2002). *How to keep your language alive: A commonsense approach to one-on-one language learning.* Berkeley, CA: Heyday Books.

Hobson, J., Lowe, K., Poetsch, S., & Walsh, M. (Eds.). (2010). *Re-awakening languages: Theory and practice in the revitalization of Australia's Indigenous languages.* Sydney, Australia: Sydney University Press.

Holm, W. (2006). The "goodness" of bilingual education for Native American children. In T. L. McCarty & O. Zepeda (Eds.), *One voice, many voices — Recreating Indigenous language communities* (pp. 3–46). Tempe: Arizona State University Center for Indian Education.

Holton, G. (2009). Relearning Athabascan languages in Alaska: Creating sustainable language communities through creolization. In A. M. Goodfellow (Ed.), *Speaking of endangered languages: Issues in revitalization* (pp. 238–265). Newcastle upon Tyne, England: Cambridge Scholars Publishing.

Mato Nunpa, C. (2006). The Dakota–English dictionary project: A Minnesota collaborative effort. In T. L. McCarty & O. Zepeda (Eds.), *One voice, many voices — Recreating Indigenous language communities* (pp. 205–217). Tempe: Arizona State University Center for Indian Education.

McCarty, T. L., & Zepeda, O. (Eds.). (2006). *One voice, many voice — Recreating Indigenous language communities.* Tempe: Arizona State University Center for Indian Education.

McNaboe, D., & Poetsch, S. (2010). Language revitalisation: Community and school programs working together. In J. Hobson, K. Lowe, S. Poetsch, & M. Walsh (Eds.), *Re-awakening languages: Theory and practice in the revitalization of Australia's Indigenous languages* (pp. 216–224). Sydney, Australia: Sydney University Press.

Meek, B. A. (2010). *We are our language: An ethnography of language revitalization in a Northern Athabaskan community.* Tucson: University of Arizona Press.

Mosel, U. (2006). Fieldwork and community language work. In J. Gippert, P. Nikolaus, N. P. Himmelmann, & U. Mosel (Eds.), *Essentials of language documentation* (pp. 67–86). The Hague, The Netherlands: Mouton de Gruyter.

Nathan, D. (2006). Thick interfaces: Mobilizing language documentation with multimedia. In J. Gippert, P. Nikolaus, N. P. Himmelmann, & U. Mosel (Eds.), *Essentials of language documentation* (pp. 363–379). The Hague, The Netherlands: Mouton de Gruyter.

Nettle, D., & Romaine, S. (2000). *Vanishing voices: The extinction of the world's languages.* Oxford, England: Oxford University Press.

Olawsky, K. J. (2010). Going public with language: Involving the wider community in language revitalization. In J. Hobson, K. Lowe, S. Poetsch, & M. Walsh (Eds.), *Re-awakening languages: Theory and practice in the revitalization of Australia's Indigenous languages* (pp. 75–84). Sydney, Australia: Sydney University Press.

Platero, P. R. (2001). Navajo Head Start Language Study. In L. Hinton & K. Hale (Eds.), *The green book of language revitalization in practice* (pp. 87–97). San Diego, CA: Academic Press.

Poetsch, S., & Lowe, K. (2010). Introduction: Language in education. In J. Hobson, K. Lowe, S. Poetsch, & M. Walsh (Eds.), *Re-awakening languages: Theory and practice in the revitalization of Australia's indigenous languages* (pp. 157–161). Sydney, Australia: Sydney University Press.

Reid, N. (2010). English influence on the pronunciation of re-awakened Aboriginal languages. In J. Hobson, K. Lowe, S. Poetsch, & M. Walsh (Eds.), *Re-awakening languages: Theory and practice in the revitalization of Australia's Indigenous languages* (pp. 293–306). Sydney, Australia: Sydney University Press.

Reyhner, J. (Ed.). (1997). *Teaching Indigenous languages.* Flagstaff: Northern Arizona University Center for Excellence in Education. Retrieved May 12, 2013 from http://jan.ucc.nau.edu/~jar/TIL_Contents.html

Sallabank, J. (2011). Language policy for endangered languages. In P. K. Austin & J. Sallabank (Eds.), *The Cambridge handbook of endangered languages* (pp. 277–290). Cambridge, England: Cambridge University Press.

Schieffelin, B., Woolard, K., & Kroskrity, P. V. (Eds.). (1998). *Language ideologies: Practice and theory.* Oxford, England: Oxford University Press.

Skutnabb-Kangas, T. (2008). Human rights and language policy in education. In S. May & N.H. Hornberger (Eds.), *Encyclopedia of language and education vol. 1: Language policy and political issues in education* (pp. 107–119). New York, NY: Springer.

Skutnabb-Kangas, T., Phillipson, R., & Rannut, M. (1994). *Linguistic human rights: Overcoming linguistic discrimination.* Berlin, Germany: Mouton de Gruyter.

Supahan, T., & Supahan, S. E. (2001). Teaching well, learning quickly: Communication-based language instruction. In L. Hinton & K. Hale (Eds.), *The green book of language revitalization in practice* (pp. 195–197). San Diego, CA: Academic Press.

Trilsbeek, P., & Wittenburg, P. (2006). Archiving challenges. In J. Gippert, N. P. Himmelmann, & U. Mosel (Eds.), *Essentials of language documentation* (p. 311). The Hague, The Netherlands: Mouton de Gruyter.

Tsunoda, T. (2006). *Language endangerment and language revitalization: An introduction.* Berlin, Germany: Mouton de Gruyter.

Williams, T. M. K. (2006). Using Oneida language: Conscious speaking. In T. L. McCarty & O. Zepeda (Eds.), *One voice, many voices — Recreating Indigenous language communities* (pp. 49–57). Tempe: Arizona State University Center for Indian Education.

Wilson, W. H., & Kamanā, K. (2001). "Mai loko mai o a 'i'ini: Proceeding from a Dream": The 'Aha Pūnana Leo connection in Hawaiian language revitalization. In L. Hinton & K. Hale (Eds.), *The green book of language revitalization in practice* (pp. 147–176). San Diego, CA: Academic Press.

Woodbury, A. C. (2003). Defining documentary linguistics. In P. K. Austin (Ed.), *Language description and documentation* (pp. 35–51). London, England: School of Oriental and African Studies.

Woodbury, A. C. (2011). Language documentation. In P. K. Austin & J. Sallabank (Eds.), *The Cambridge handbook of endangered languages* (pp. 159–186). Cambridge, England: Cambridge University Press.

Yunkaporta, T. K. (2010). Our ways of learning in aboriginal languages. In J. Hobson, K. Lowe, S. Poetsch, & M. Walsh (Eds.), *Re-awakening languages: Theory and practice in the revitalization of Australia's Indigenous languages* (pp. 37–50). Sydney, Australia: Sydney University Press.

PREFACE

This volume was germinated over the winter of 2008–2009 in a series of conference panels that ultimately evolved into a theme issue of the *Journal of Language, Identity, and Education,* published in 2009 (McCarty & Wyman, 2009). In that issue we explored new directions in research on Indigenous youth language ideologies and practices, looking specifically at Native American communities undergoing rapid shift from the Indigenous language to the dominant/colonial language. In this volume we build on that earlier research, expanding its geographic breadth and scope, and articulating points of intersection between research on immigrant youth's bi/multilingualism and Indigenous language learners in settings of language endangerment. As readers will see in the chapters that follow, we position this research as explicitly counter-hegemonic, humanizing, and praxis-oriented, allying it with Indigenous efforts to maintain and revitalize their ancestral mother tongues.

The statistics regarding worldwide language endangerment are well known, with expert predictions of the imminent demise of as many as 90% of the 7,000-some languages currently spoken on the planet. Of these "disappeared" languages, most will be Indigenous mother tongues (UNESCO Ad Hoc Expert Group, 2003). Young people are arguably *the* central stakeholders in their communities' linguistic and cultural futures. Yet their voices and perspectives have been noticeably absent from the scholarly literature and often from the language planning process itself. Our goal in this book is to give voice to youth experiences and perspectives on the dynamic sociolinguistic environments in which they are growing up. To do this, the volume contributors train their gaze squarely on Indigenous youth bi/multilingualism in the "here and now" (Bucholtz, 2002) of their everyday lives, using critical ethnography as an orienting epistemological and methodological approach. This research contributes to a growing body of youth language scholarship in the fields of sociolinguistics, Indigenous studies, and educational and linguistic anthropology. Equally, however, our goal is to draw out lessons to inform Indigenous community-driven language reclamation initiatives and projects.

We begin with an introduction that lays the historical, theoretical, methodological, and praxis foundations of the volume, highlighting recent research on youth language practices and ideologies, and relating this to recent scholarship on Indigenous youth language and the ethnography of language policy. Understanding youth language ideologies is central to each of the chapters, and we spend time developing a theoretical framework for that understanding. We also discuss the ways in which the volume contributes to humanizing and decolonizing research with youth and Indigenous peoples (cf. Matua & Swadener, 2004; Paris, 2011; Paris & Winn, 2013; Smith, 2012), and to praxis—the transformative potential of this research.

Chapters 2 through 5 bring into focus the complex communicative repertoires and identity performances of Indigenous youth; some of these chapters also explore the potential for youth and young adults to take up new positions as language activists. In Chapter 2, Teresa McCarty, Mary Eunice Romero-Little, Larisa Warhol, and Ofelia Zepeda introduce a long-term, multisited ethnographic study of language shift and retention among American Indian youth in the southwestern United States. This study reveals the contexts for language socialization in American Indian communities to be much more complex than a unidirectional notion of "shift" suggests—complexities that these authors argue can and should be re-envisioned as resources for language recovery given appropriate levels of community and institutional support. Engaging Ortiz's (1992, p. 9) notion of continuance—something more than "remembrance" or a "romanticized future" of Indigenous languages—the authors ask, How can we use knowledge gained from youth language research to support youth and their communities in reclaiming endangered mother tongues?

In Chapter 3, Brendan O'Connor and Gilbert Brown also examine young people's communicative repertoires and identity negotiations, in this case through the emic perspectives and practices of Navajo hip hop artist, Jay. Tracing Jay's language socialization from his early home life to his current status as an established member of an underground hip hop community, the chapter explores how Jay employs "an impressive set of semiotic resources to problematize other people's views of how he ought to act, both as a Navajo/Indian and as a hip hop artist." Jay's innovative language practices reappropriate notions of Navajo/Indigenous identity, highlighting "the contradictory spaces many Native people inhabit" and the ways in which their participation in "translocal style communities" opens new pathways for linguistic and cultural expression. This chapter offers a nuanced portrait of the ways youth use gesture and new cultural forms to remake themselves, claiming deep connections to, yet rejecting essentialisms associated with Indigenous identities. At the same time, the chapter—like Jay himself—leaves open questions of whether and how these new cultural forms intersect with youth's expressed desire to support Indigenous language learning and teaching efforts.

In Chapter 4, Sheilah Nicholas explores Hopi youth language ideologies, detailing the processes through which primarily English-speaking Hopi youth construct a distinctly Hopi identity. Despite having been immersed in the Hopi culture throughout their lives, many Hopi youth do not understand or speak their heritage language. Focusing on the cultural and linguistic experiences of three Hopi youth, this chapter introduces the notion of "affective enculturation"—the development of an emotional commitment to Hopi ideals—cultivated through myriad practices that comprise Hopi oral tradition. Nicholas's study documents how, even without a strong origin in the language, youth learn to act, think, and feel Hopi through their active participation in the Hopi world. The chapter also reveals contradictory language ideologies as youth contend that the Hopi language is fundamental to fully participate in the Hopi way of life—a finding that, Nicholas asserts, offers hope for their (re)acquisition of the Hopi language.

Chapter 5, by Leisy Wyman, draws on a longitudinal study of youth in Piniq (pseudonym), a Yup'ik village in southwestern Alaska undergoing rapid language shift, to highlight what she calls linguistic survivance (building on Vizenor, 1994, 2008)—the use of communicative practices to creatively connect to community knowledge, exercise self-determination and/or express Indigenous identities and worldviews while confronting challenging situations like language endangerment stemming from deep societal inequities. The chapter demonstrates how adults' and young people's emerging ideologies of language endangerment may obscure vibrant bilingual community language practices as well as the impact of schooling and migration on heritage language maintenance. By comparing young men's stories of personal language loss with their collaborative storytelling about a highly significant cultural practice—seal hunting—the chapter further highlights the linguistic survivance of youth who expressed linguistic insecurities yet nevertheless found ways to translanguage and forge connections with adults, peers, a unique sub-Arctic setting, and an Indigenous knowledge system across potential linguistic boundaries. While illuminating multilayered challenges of language shift, the chapter demonstrates possibilities for bilingualism that exist within youth practice and innovation.

Chapters 6 through 9 further illuminate the potential for youth to take up new positions of activism vis-à-vis their ancestral language. Chapter 6, by Jacqueline Messing, draws upon reflective interviews with Nahuatl (Mexicano) language teachers ("former youth"), showing how youth who feel ambivalent toward their heritage language today may become language educators and activists in the future. Youth in historically Mexicano-speaking communities in Tlaxcala, Mexico manifest multiple ideologies. During young adulthood ideological positions on Indigenous language and identity can be in flux, with important consequences for language shift and revitalization. Data show how youth and young adults are caught up in a nexus of multiple ideologies of Indigeneity and modernity influenced by globalizing forces and racialized societal discourses. To the outside observer, ambivalence is at the center of youth ideologies of language and identity, yet the chapter shows how ideologies governing language shift can change over time. Reflective teacher narratives evidence these changing ideologies and offer hope for language revitalization.

In Chapter 7 Tiffany Lee addresses youth language attitudes and practices based on data from two action research projects with Navajo and Pueblo youth. In these studies, interviews and reflective writing by Navajo and Pueblo youth constituted counter-narratives that expressed youth's concerns, values, frustrations, celebrations, and dilemmas with regard to their heritage language and identity. Lee's studies affirm that language plays a central and complex role in contemporary youth identity, and that their Indigenous consciousness is not diminished by limited fluency in their heritage language—an important finding for inspiring a commitment to language revitalization. In Lee's research, youth become critically aware and involved in community efforts to disrupt ongoing language shift in school, home, and community contexts.

Chapter 8, by Shelley Tulloch, describes a unique international effort on the part of Inuit youth language activists from Russia, Alaska, Canada, and Greenland to "ignite a language movement" across the Circumpolar region. This chapter shows Inuit youth's active involvement in language planning as a collaborative, consensus-building process within a sociolinguistic context in which Inuit youth have become deliberate agents of Inuit language preservation. Tulloch discusses how youth are engaging at an organizational level by hosting two Inuit Circumpolar Youth Symposia on the Inuit language, participating in international forums, and advocating to local, regional, national, and international bodies for language policies and programs which reflect their needs and priorities. These initiatives exemplify Indigenous voice, choice, and agency, Tulloch states—necessary qualities for language recovery.

In Chapter 9, Kuunux Teerit Kroupa takes us to the Fort Berthold Indian reservation in North Dakota, relating a powerful effort by young adult language activists to foster revitalization of the critically endangered Arikara language community. Kroupa and a group of Arikara young adults are creating a society "of hope and dedication to language recovery." The chapter details how these young adults have rearranged their lives, individually and collectively, to recover the Arikara language and cultural traditions by pursuing university degrees, organizing immersion courses, reclaiming ceremonial spaces, and restoring Arikara societies. Youth, Kroupa states, are becoming "Ree-volutionaries" (building upon the 18th and 19th century term "Arikarees") through a range of activities focused on Arikara language awakening and revitalization, cultural preservation, and engaging in contemporary linguistic forms such as texting and code-switching with new vocabulary.

The volume concludes with three commentaries by leading scholars in Indigenous language and bi/multilingual education. The first commentary comes from William H. Wilson and Kauanoe Kamanā, well-known Hawaiian activists-educators, who reflect on the chapters and draw parallels to observations of youth from their 30 years of work with the Hawaiian language movement. Wilson and Kamanā observe that transitions to adulthood are marked as a time of great linguistic flux. They also highlight the critical role that schools play in moving away from damaging "two-world stereotypes" about Indigeneity, and toward a "one-world" philosophy that allows today's Indigenous youth to gain membership in international youth cultures while remaining Indigenous. The authors argue that this is achieved through "actualizing linguistic sovereignty"—changing the discourse around the "official use" of Indigenous languages accorded by federal legislation. They describe the processes they have used to do this by establishing academic programs that integrate new knowledge and activities into a vibrant learning community defined by use of the Hawaiian language.

In the second commentary, Walkie Charles, a Yup'ik language professor and leading Alaska Native language activist in the Far North, reflects on the historical roots of language endangerment. Drawing parallels with the chapters, Charles takes us back in time to consider the intergenerational disruption that occurred when Yup'ik youth were sent away to receive submersive English instruction in boarding schools, and later, as youth stayed home after the establishment of local village high schools. Portraying a unique moment in Yup'ik history, Charles vividly describes the ensuing confusion as generations of adults and new local teachers tried to connect to youth after their experiences of being displaced from local settings for decades. Sharing observations from his work as an instructor of Yup'ik language classes at the University of Alaska, Charles also discusses how the chapters reveal young people's current desires to learn their heritage languages in a very different historical moment. He calls on us to honor these desires with our support.

The third commentary comes from Ofelia García, a leading scholar of language shift, bi/multilingualism, and bilingual education with ties to work with Latino/a youth in the United States and Indigenous youth in Latin America. In her commentary, García applauds the chapter authors for sidestepping the monoglossic ideologies that can be imposed on Indigenous youth from both outside and inside Indigenous communities, pointing out how these keep Indigenous community members from benefiting from youths' desires to connect with their Indigenous lifeways. Noting young people's natural tendency toward linguistic innovation, García describes how the chapters highlight two forms of such innovation: *recursive bilingualism*, "where speakers take pieces of past language practices to reconstitute new practices that will serve them well in a bilingual future," and *dynamic bilingualism* in which speakers are "ever adjusting to the multilingual multimodal terrain of the communicative act." Arguing that both forms of bilingualism are key for Indigenous communities in the 21st century, García comments that youth innovation and translanguaging may ultimately sow the seeds of *language sustainability*—"the capacity [of languaging] to endure, but always in interaction with the social context in which it operates" in complex worlds (García, 2011, p. 7).

Taken together, the research-based chapters and commentaries raise challenging questions about the ways in which young people's language choices, hybridities, linguistic strategies, and yearnings for their heritage languages shape and are shaped by unique sociolinguistic contexts and Indigenous identities. Today's language learners do not want to hold their ancestral languages "at arm's length" for mere admiration (Moore, 2006, p. 299). Instead, the work here provides powerful testimony that contemporary language learners want to use their ancestral languages for reasons "deeply rooted within local relationships, practices, knowledge systems, and geographical places" (Wyman, 2009, p. 346). This research positions youth as part of broader communities of practice situated historically within processes of marginalization and counter-movements. As Lee's work demonstrates, when young people's "critical Indigenous consciousness" becomes raised over language issues, they may be eager to move into positions of agency in reversing language shift.

The studies also show how young people can activate and strategically deploy "unfinished" linguistic competences to make claims to local and ethnic belonging as they move away from dominant-language schooling and enter new situations, spaces, and social networks (Wyman, 2012). The authors consciously interpret young people's linguistic practices as evidence of natural tendencies of bilingual youth (and adults) to *language* and *translanguage* (García, 2009; Shohamy, 2006), or use varying communicative repertoires (Martin-Jones & Jones, 2000) to accomplish situated goals. Further, the authors show the fallacy of deficit assumptions about language and youth, documenting the sociolinguistic strengths of heritage language learners in settings of language endangerment.

It is nevertheless the case that Indigenous youth continuously negotiate everyday language uses against the privileged position of dominant languages. Youth may also serve as the focal point for societal anxieties about the loss of community languages. In many cases Indigenous youth are growing up keenly aware that their languages are on the brink of disappearing. Alternately, along with their families, they may be in denial about language endangerment. In some settings, youth may express justifiable anger or resistance when, on linguistic grounds, outsiders or state agents challenge their identity claims or deny them access to cultural, economic, or political resources. Youth are also the potential beneficiaries of movements to reclaim languages as educational assets.

As a whole, the studies here peel back the layers of heteroglossia and hybridity that characterize contemporary Indigenous youth language practices (Deloria, 2011). As editors, we argue that this work underscores innovative linguistic forms and practices that can and should be "recalibrated" (Meek, 2011), not as liabilities or hindrances, but as powerful—and necessary—*resources* in language reclamation. Rather than creating artificial binaries between "traditional" and "innovative" youth language forms and practices, or between "speaker" and "non-speaker," "fluent" and "nonfluent," the researchers here detail the complex linguistic repertoires, creative languaging and translanguaging, and practices of linguistic survivance and continuance that Indigenous youth activate in their everyday lives. Rejecting arguments for ossified, clinging-to-the-past language practices, the research presented here shows the ways in which youth are employing new language forms and uses for contemporary purposes, often positioning themselves in relation to enduring community practices and struggles.

As Lee notes in her chapter, "defining a Native identity for youth and young adults is not a simple, uncomplicated process, and ... youth's Native identity now encompasses multiple levels of cultural access, participation, and knowledge with or even without the Native language." By highlighting this complexity, this volume seeks to remedy the ways these new forms and uses are often "misrecognized" (Kroskrity, 2011) by community adults as well as scholars. The work also takes us beyond the flawed logic of binaries, providing an intricately nuanced view of Indigenous young people's languaging "on the ground." In the pages that follow, we invite readers into that contentious, ambiguous, yet hopeful sociocultural and sociolinguistic terrain.

References

Bucholtz, M. (2002). Youth and cultural practice. *Annual Review of Anthropology, 31*, 525–552.

Deloria, P. (2011). On leaking languages and categorical imperatives. *American Indian Culture and Research Journal, 35*(2), 173–181.

García, O. (2009). *Bilingual education in the 21st century: A global perspective.* West Sussex, England: Wiley-Blackwell.

García, O. (2011). From language garden to sustainable languaging: Bilingual education in a global world. *Perspective. A publication of the National Association for Bilingual Education*, Sept./Oct. 5–10, 5–9.

Kroskrity, P. V. (2011). All intimate grammars leak: Reflections on "Indian languages in unexpected places." *American Indian Culture and Research Journal, 35*(2), 161–172.

Martin-Jones, M., & Jones, K. (2000). Introduction: Multilingual literacies. In M. Martin-Jones & K. Jones (Eds.), *Multilingual literacies: reading and writing in different worlds* (pp. 1–15). Amsterdam, The Netherlands: John Benjamins.

Matua, K., & Swadener, B. B. (Eds.). (2004). *Decolonizing research in cross-cultural contexts: Critical personal narratives.* Albany: State University of New York Press.

McCarty, T. L., & Wyman, L. T. (Guest Eds.). (2009). Indigenous youth and bilingualism [Special issue]. *Journal of Language, Identity, and Education, 8*(5).

Meek, B. (2011). Failing American Indian languages. *American Indian Culture and Research Journal, 35*(2), 43–60.

Moore, R. (2006). Disappearing, Inc.: Glimpsing the sublime in the politics of access to endangered languages. *Language and Communication, 26*(3/4), 296–315.

Ortiz, S. J. (1992). *Woven stone.* Tucson: University of Arizona Press.

Paris, D. (2011). "A friend who understand fully": Notes on humanizing research in a multiethnic youth community. *International Journal of Qualitative Studies in Education, 24*(2), 137–149.

Paris, D., & Winn, M. (Eds.). (2013). *Humanizing research: Decolonizing qualitative research with youth and their communities.* Thousand Oaks, CA: Sage.

Shohamy, E. (2006). *Language policy: Hidden agendas and new approaches.* London, England: Routledge.

Smith, L. T. (2012). *Decolonizing methodologies: Research and Indigenous peoples* (2nd ed.). London, England:: Zed Books.

UNESCO Ad Hoc Expert Group on Endangered Languages. (2003). *Language vitality and endangerment.* Paris, France: UNESCO Intangible Cultural Heritage Unit. Retrieved December 12, 2012, from http://www.unesco.org/endangeredlanguages

Vizenor, G. (1994). *Manifest manners: PostIndian warriors of survivance.* Hanover, NH: Wesleyan UP of New England.

Vizenor, G. (2008). *Survivance: Narratives of Native Presence.* Lincoln: University of Nebraska Press.

Wyman, L. T. (2009). Youth, linguistic ecology, and language endangerment: A Yup'ik example. *Journal of Language, Identity, and Education, 8*(5), 335–349.

Wyman, L. T. (2012). *Youth culture, language endangerment and linguistic survivance.* Bristol, England: Multilingual Matters.

ACKNOWLEDGMENTS

We wish to thank, first and foremost, the authors who contributed to this volume. It is these colleagues' principled and leading-edge scholarship—and their commitment to the diverse Indigenous youth and communities with whom they work—that inspired us to propose a book on this topic. We also thank the editors of the *Journal of Language, Identity and Education,* Thomas Ricento and Terrence Wiley, who encouraged the theme issue upon which the book is based. We thank the four anonymous reviewers of our book proposal and extend special thanks to Elisabeth Soep for additional feedback on an earlier version of the book's introduction, and to reviewers of related pieces of this work over the years, including Martha Crago, Beth Dementi-Leonard, Norma González, Donna Patrick, Jen Roth-Gordon, Tarajean Yazzie-Mintz, and Shelley Tulloch, among others. We extend our deep appreciation to Naomi Silverman and the editorial staff at Routledge for their enthusiasm and support throughout this book project, and to Naomi, especially, for ever-sage editorial advice and a generous extension of time.

Individually and collectively we have benefited from the wisdom and support of many close colleagues: Bryan McKinley Jones Brayboy, Les Field, Joshua and Gella Fishman, Perry Gilmore, Norma González, Shirley Brice Heath, K. Tsianina Lomawaima, Mica Pollock, Bernard Spolsky, Guadalupe Valdés, Doris Warriner, Terrence Wiley, and Ana Celia Zentella. We also thank our close colleague (and co-author) Ofelia Zepeda for inviting us to host an intergenerational dialogue around youth and language as part of the American Indian Language Development Institute's 30th anniversary celebration, which gave us the unique opportunity, along with Kuunux Teerit Kroupa, another author within the volume, to put our scholarship to work with Indigenous teachers and youth in Tucson, Arizona while this volume was underway.

As for our individual work on this volume, Leisy thanks the youth, parents, elders, teachers, and colleagues she has known in "Piniq" over the past 20 years for the continuing inspiration to work on issues of Indigenous youth language learning and education. She also thanks the Spencer Education Foundation, the National Science Foundation's Arctic Social Science and Linguistic Programs, as well as Dean Ron Marx of the College of Education at the University of Arizona for funding her research, and the Lower Kuskokwim School District and the "Piniq" Traditional Council for additional support. She is grateful to the many friends who have helped her family during periods of travel to Alaska. For enlightening discussions, she also especially thanks Alaskan colleagues Fannie Andrew, Oscar and Sophie Alexie, Ray Barnhardt, Elena Dock, Alice Fredson, Chase Hensel, Grant Kashatok, Mary Jane Mann, Patrick Marlow, Gayle Miller, Phyllis Morrow, Rachel Nicholai, Paul Ongtooguk, Nita Rearden, and Beverly Williams, and the faculty and graduate students she has had the pleasure to work with in the Language, Reading and Culture program and the American Indian Language Development Institute at the University of Arizona, including Maxine Sam and Danny Lopez, whose insights she still remembers and treasures in their absence.

Sheilah thanks Teresa McCarty and Leisy Wyman for the invitation to collaborate on this project. She also thanks Bruce Johnson, Head of the Department of Teaching, Learning, and Sociocultural Studies at the University of Arizona, for approving the lead time from teaching to work on the book. She also expresses appreciation to Hopi language teachers Bernita Duwahoyeoma, Ada Curtis, Marilyn Parra, the Hopi Tribe, Leigh Kuwanwisiwma and Dawa Taylor of the Hopilavayi Program, as well as Principal Dr. John Thomas, Hopi Day School. Special thanks to Gladys Onsae and Arvis Myron. Each of these individuals provided critical insights into the challenges and rewards of heritage language teaching, as they confirmed their own commitment to the vitality of the Hopi language and culture and expressed the yearnings of Hopi youth working to learn their language.

Teresa thanks Alice Wiley Snell and Richard Snell for their generous support of her work over more than 8 years. Her contributions to this book were also aided by a sabbatical leave from Arizona State University (ASU) and a National Endowment for the Humanities Residential Fellowship at the School for Advanced Research (SAR) in Santa Fe, New Mexico. For support of that work, she thanks ASU School of Social Transformation Director Mary Margaret Fonow and former Social Sciences Dean Linda Lederman; and SAR President James Brooks, Vice President John Kantner, Director of Scholar Programs Nicole Taylor, and fellow SAR scholars Margaret Bruchac, Kitty Corbett, Aimee Garza, Craig Janes, Nancy Owen Lewis, Jennifer McCarty, Nancy Mithlo, Kelsey Potdevin, Woosen Argaw Tegegn, and Julie Weise.

We reserve our final expression of gratitude for the youth and communities with whom we have been privileged to work over the years, and for our families who have encouraged and stayed with us through our various research and writing journeys: Michael, Jules and Evy Wyman, and John and Julia Thornton; Joseph, Sarah, Seth, and Rachel LaMantia, the late Laura Nasetoynewa and Emory Sekaquaptewa; and John Martin, Jennifer and Stuart Martin, Valerie Mussi, Julie McCarty, Mildred McCarty, and the late Virginia Heckert Doulin and James Lawrence McCarty.

To our readers and to all who have supported this work, we say a multilingual Yup'ik-Hopi-Navajo "Thank you":

Quyanaqvaa!
Askwali!
Ahéhee'!

1

BEYOND ENDANGERMENT

Indigenous Youth and Multilingualism

Leisy T. Wyman, Teresa L. McCarty, and Sheilah E. Nicholas

Throughout the world Indigenous communities are vigorously engaged in efforts to reclaim and revitalize their languages. Many revitalization efforts are being carried out in schools—highly charged environments, as schools have been primary sites for Indigenous linguistic and cultural repression. Equally, however, language reclamation takes place in the context of families and communities. While the circumstances and approaches to these language reclamation efforts differ, all share the goal of ensuring that present and future generations have access to language practices that have transported distinct knowledge systems and connections to place and peoplehood through time. Youth are prime stakeholders in these efforts, and it is to Indigenous youth in endangered-language settings that this volume is devoted.

Our geographic focus is North America, where a shift to dominant colonial languages has in some cases occurred within the space of only 5 to 10 years. Within this dynamic sociolinguistic landscape, we forefront the work of Indigenous and non-Indigenous scholars with longstanding ties to language planning efforts in diverse Indigenous communities, including Navajo, Hopi, O'odham, Yup'ik, and Arikara communities in the United States, circumpolar Inuit communities in the Far North, and Mexicano (Nahuatl) communities in Mexico. Together, the chapters highlight the complex positioning of Native American youth in communities experiencing rapid cultural and sociolinguistic change. The chapters also bring into high relief youth agency and sociolinguistic innovation. Commentaries by scholars who work with Indigenous language revitalization movements and Latino/a bilingual education further illuminate how youth negotiate crosscutting themes of language ideologies, intergenerational dynamics, and linguistic human rights.

Our goals in the book are threefold. First, we chart new ground in Indigenous language research by critically examining youth language ideologies, practices, and agency. The introductory chapter title—"Beyond Endangerment"—hints at this new ground, as we go beyond commonplace rhetorics of endangerment that tend to invisibilize youth perspectives, concerns, and practices within language reclamation efforts. Historically, most Indigenous-language research has overlooked youth altogether or made passing observations of youth culture. Youth's purported disinterest in traditionally rooted cultural forms and practices, and adult and youth's related feelings of alienation in rapidly changing societies have also been seen as major causal factors in emerging dynamics of language endangerment.

More recently, however, Indigenous youth language scholars in the fields of linguistic and educational anthropology, applied linguistics, and Indigenous studies have shown the complex ways that young people participate in a dynamic, interconnected world, crisscrossing multiple symbolic, discursive, and physical borders and transforming local and global communities of practice. This growing body of work bridges the divide between research focused on young people's emic perspectives and youth linguistic creativity, and research oriented toward adult-determined developmental and educational goals (cf. Rymes, 2011). This research also brings a much-needed youth perspective to the field of language planning and policy (LPP).

Second, the volume exemplifies new work in the ethnography of language policy (Hornberger & Johnson, 2011; Johnson, 2009; McCarty, 2011a). From this perspective, policy is viewed not as a "disembodied thing, but rather [as] a situated sociocultural process: the complex of practices, ideologies, attitudes, and formal and informal mechanisms that influence people's language choices in profound and pervasive everyday ways" (McCarty, 2011b, p. xii). Within this framework language policy is examined as de facto and de jure, implicit and explicit, bottom-up and top-down (McCarty, 2011c, p. 2; see also Hornberger & McCarty, 2012; Shohamy, 2006). In the chapters that follow, carefully situated, critical ethnographic research offers insights into the ways that implicit and explicit language policies reflect and refract language identities and ideologies, generational and cultural learning opportunities, as well as conflict and linguistic human rights. By taking a close, nuanced look at Indigenous youth bi/multilingualism across diverse cultural and linguistic settings, the authors here go beyond endangerment in another sense, illuminating youth language hybridities, heteroglossia, and innovation in diverse sociolinguistic contexts, and arguing for these as resources rather than liabilities in heritage-language reclamation.

Finally, we position this work as explicitly humanizing, counter-hegemonic, and praxis-driven. As Paris (2011) writes, humanizing youth research entails "a certain stance and methodology, working with [youth] in contexts of oppression and marginalization" (p. 137; see also Paris & Winn, 2014). All chapter authors have long histories of experience with the communities with which they work. Some identify as cultural insiders, and all embrace an ethic of respect, responsibility, relationality, and reciprocity—qualities that character-ize what Brayboy, Gough, Leonard, Roehl, and Solyom (2012) call a "critical Indigenous research methodology," and what Smith (2012) and others describe as decolonizing research (see also Kovach, 2009; Matua & Swadener, 2004). From this perspective we go beyond endangerment in yet another way, outlin-ing the praxis potential of youth-centered LPP research to support community-driven language reclamation and youth empowerment.

In the remainder of this chapter, we review relevant research on Indigenous youth language, connecting the contributions of the present volume to current youth studies and bi/multilingualism research, laying out key considerations and identifying crosscutting themes. We then discuss the humanizing, decolo-nizing, and praxis-oriented stance the chapters and the book exemplify.

Research on Native American Youth Language Practices and Ideologies

Situating Indigenous Youth Language Research

In many Native American communities, elders are viewed as knowledge keep-ers with crucial roles in sharing historically rooted Indigenous knowledge sys-tems. Indigenous youth, in comparison, have historically been studied from the perspectives of Western socialization models in pre-existing community ways of speaking, and movement along adult-organized developmental trajectories with predictable transitions and rites of passage. In efforts to conceptualize tensions around language and cultural difference, contact and conflict in Indig-enous communities, early researchers typically positioned youth as passive, troubled victims of these tensions, or romanticized youth as modern agents wishing to be free of the "backward" cultural beliefs and constraints espoused by older community members.

From a language planning perspective, youth have often been viewed as problems to be fixed en route to school achievement, or as the last line of defense in Indigenous-language maintenance. Passing comments about Indig-enous young people's connections to new media, in particular, assumed Indig-enous young people's engagement with circulating forms of youth culture straightforwardly indicated their disconnection from their elders, families, and communities. Leading scholars described youth as gullible imbibers of "cul-tural nerve gas" (i.e., electronic media [Krauss, 1980]), or as "cultural beings in need of reprogramming" (discussed in Reynolds, 2009, p. 234).

Recent language and youth culture research has moved toward a serious engagement with youth as interpreters and shapers of society, with an emphasis on youth agency and identity (Bucholtz, 2002; Bucholtz & Hall, 2005), stylistic performance (Eckert, 1989, 2000; Mendoza-Denton, 2008), language crossing and sharing (Paris, 2011; Rampton, 1995, 2006), global circulation and ongoing localization of popular cultural forms such as hip hop (Alim, Pennycook, & Ibrahim, 2009; Deyhle, 1998; Morgan, 2009), ethnography of communication (Alim, 2007; Heath, 1998), media learning, use, and production (Horst, Antin, & Finn, 2010; Hull, 2003; Ito, Knobel, & Lankshear, 2011; Lam, 2006; Soep & Chávez, 2010), and language rights and activism (Paris & Winn, 2014; Scott, Straker, & Katz, 2009).

Current youth language researchers highlight the role of larger social, economic, and political systems in structuring inequities, focusing on youth culture to illuminate "the production of cultural centers or margins" and which bodies and discourses "are privileged, condemned, or overlooked" (Maira & Soep, 2005, p. xix). This research explicitly recognizes that, like adults, youth "act as agents, resignifying and articulating the different and conflicting messages" they receive (Szulc, 2009, p. 144). Like adults, youth "make sense of inequality and difference in their local situations," interpreting them across a range of gender, social class, regional, and generational relationships (Rampton, 2006, p. 19). Studying young people's emic views, language ideologies, and identities can provide insights into how social and political processes are lived and constructed through language use.

As we see in this volume, many youth researchers also see the potential for engaging youth in addressing educational and social inequities. At the same time, the field continues to wrestle with the tensions between analyzing youth as agentive actors offering critical insights and positive innovations in the face of untenable situations (Bucholtz, 2002), and analyzing how youth are deeply impacted and constrained by the inequities that lead to such situations (Roth-Gordon & Woronov, 2009).

Indigenous youth language scholars similarly show how young people contest and grapple with racialized societal inequities, and how youth responses to these inequities are shaped by their experiences, relationships, and subjectivities in particular times and locales. Importantly, Indigenous youth language scholars are also deeply engaged in understanding the ways in which access to particular relationships, learning opportunities, and linguistic resources lay the groundwork from which young people negotiate a range of challenges that include the looming specter of language endangerment, education inequities, and a wider range of threats to community, family, and personal well-being.

Engaging with complex system theories, scholars have documented how the sociolinguistic settings in which many Indigenous and immigrant youth are growing up are far more complex than the word "bilingual" or even "multilingual" implies (Hornberger, 2002; Makoni, Brutt-Griffler, & Mashir, 2007; McCarty, Romero-Little, Warhol, & Zepeda 2009). In recent years, scholars have also noted how the communicative repertoires of heritage language learners[1] vary dramatically within communities, peer groups, and families, depending on the ways that youth move along individualized and shared language learning trajectories (Kagan, 2005; King, 2013; McCarty et al., 2009, 2013; Nicholas, 2011; Valdés, 2005; Wyman, 2012). Scholars have additionally recorded how young people's everyday interactions in multileveled, multidirectional language socialization processes shape possibilities for language learning and expression, as well as larger dynamics of language shift and bi/multilingualism (Garrett & Baquedano-Lopez, 2002; Wyman, 2012; Zentella, 1997).

As we see in this volume, contemporary Indigenous youth commonly contend with lack of access to key language learning resources and learning environments. Their accumulating language learning opportunities, or lack thereof, also shape their communicative repertoires and language ideologies in complex ways. At the same time, youth show tremendous agency, innovation, and adaptation as they use their communicative repertoires, and "language" and "translanguage" (García, 2009, this volume; Shohamy, 2006), performing identities and positioning themselves in emerging interactional moments in classrooms, family homes, and other out-of-school spaces (Jørgensen, 1998; McKay & Wong, 1996; Mendoza-Denton, 2008; Wyman, 2012; Zentella, 1997).

In this regard the experiences of youth from Indigenous and immigrant communities in North America share certain similarities. Increasing numbers of Indigenous youth from Latin America are migrating north with their families; many Indigenous groups in North America have migrated in the history of their peoples, and many contemporary Indigenous youth are flowing with their families among urban and rural spaces, so the very categories of "immigrant" and "Indigenous" contain important areas of overlap (Collins, 2012; Fox & Rivera-Salgado, 2004; King & Haboud, 2011; McCarty et al., this volume). Both Indigenous and immigrant youth language research shows how youth cloak or uncloak language competencies as they engage with, contest, and co-construct language ideologies, language learning opportunities, and the fluid interactional dynamics around them (Mendoza-Denton, 2008). Indigenous communities, like immigrant communities, commonly negotiate tensions related to heritage language loss, given hopes for maintaining unique funds of knowledge and fostering strong intergenerational relationships of trust in and out of school (González, Moll, & Amanti, 2005; Wong-Fillmore, 1991). Even in Indigenous settings that are seemingly homogenous and remote, the dynamics of language shift, schooling, migration, and peer cultures can mirror those found within immigrant social networks in diverse urban areas in important ways (Wyman, 2012, 2013).

When discussing Indigenous youth language, however, scholars often are at least indirectly referencing young people's relationships to endangered languages. As such, approaches to the study of Indigenous youth language demand additional consideration and sensitivity, as families, communities, and youth struggle with the realization that their languages may disappear from the earth altogether with the death of elders, the keepers of these linguistic systems and related accumulated oral bodies of Indigenous knowledge. If Turkish youth in Denmark, or Spanish or Chinese heritage language speakers in California gain only minimal skills in their heritage languages, those languages exist elsewhere. The same is not true for speakers of endangered Indigenous languages.

Youth language research is documenting how, in contrast to early erroneous assumptions, many youth share adult allegiances to and interest in maintaining Indigenous languages as part of Indigenous knowledge systems and ways of being, and express deep concerns about language endangerment and desires to change the reverberating effects of oppressive histories of colonization. At the same time, youth inhabit challenging positions within ongoing dynamics of language endangerment that are important to understand. Since these youth are often at the forefront of linguistic innovation and change, their language practices are likely to be cast as problematic (McCarty et al., Tulloch, and Wyman, this volume). Youth are also often charged with the daunting task of carrying endangered Indigenous languages into the future. In many ways, changing language ideologies and the rapid, wholesale erosion of Indigenous language learning opportunities set up the conditions of language endangerment long before youth appear on the scene, and youth can experience understandable insecurities, embarrassment, guilt, and resentment when they are blamed for language endangerment circumstances out of their control. Commonplace rhetorics such as counting the dwindling numbers of fluent Indigenous-language speakers place youth who are dealing with linguistic insecurities and minimal Indigenous-language learning opportunities in tremendously difficult positions. Due to the ways that languages syncretize during language shift (Hill & Hill, 1986), youth are not only the least likely to speak heritage languages but the least likely to know the unique linguistic features of their languages, even if they claim "speakerhood in some form" (Hill, 2002). Scholarly arguments that Indigenous languages need to be preserved because they represent our collective knowledge of the human capacity for organizing the world in different ways may fall short of motivating youth to take up sustained Indigenous language learning, and potentially devalue young people's existing linguistic competencies.

There is nonetheless growing evidence that many Indigenous youth express "great yearning" (Wilson & Kamanā, 2009) to speak and support Indigenous languages as part of valued Indigenous knowledge systems (Lee, this volume). In taking up the concerns of language endangerment, youth language activists often engage in sophisticated language learning that extends far beyond what they are typically offered in school, as they involve themselves in intergenerational "planful thinking" (Heath, 1998) and envision how they can contribute to their communities' linguistic survivance and continuance.

Building on Vizenor's (1994, 2008) notion of survivance, Wyman (2012) considers linguistic survivance as the use of language to creatively express, adapt, maintain, and defend Indigenous identities and knowledge systems under difficult or hostile circumstances. As Wyman has detailed in her work with Yup'ik adults and youth, linguistic survivance can range from direct attempts to pass on Indigenous language and knowledge, to translanguaging between English "legalese" and genres of elders' socializing talk in the negotiation of sovereignty rights, to forms of Indigenous humor, commentary, and learning that draw upon wide-ranging symbolic resources. Gilmore and Wyman (2013) further discuss how Alaska Native youth and young adults have historically demonstrated linguistic survivance in appropriating new language and literacy practices and forms of activism while interacting with hostile, inequitable academic environments. Ortiz's (1992) notion of cultural continuance also "pushes us to think beyond 'saving' Indigenous languages, to (re)value the hybridity of youth communicative repertoires, and to build language regenesis efforts around that hybridity rather than deny or negate it" (McCarty et al., this volume). It is from this position—taking seriously the concerns of language endangerment while placing these concerns within an expanded view of linguistic survivance and continuance—that we explore in this chapter existing research on young people's language ideologies, learning opportunities and trajectories, everyday performances of identities, and new forms of language activism.

The Critical Intersection of Indigenous Youth Language Ideologies, Learning Opportunities, and Activism

The authors within this volume investigate the challenges that prohibit and the opportunities that foster Indigenous youth connections to ancestral languages, and broader intergenerational learning and positive social change. A growing body of work documents ideological contrast between the "declared youth attitudes, experiences and expectations and adults' taken-for-granted assumptions of their experiences in other Indigenous contexts" (Tulloch, this volume). Many scholars note the intergenerational tensions that can arise in endangered-language communities when adults assume that youth are rejecting Indigenous identities and languages by speaking a dominant language. Such discrepancies "highlight the need to listen to youth voices when planning for the future of Indigenous languages" (Tulloch, this volume).

A great fallacy about youth in endangered-language communities is that they simply choose to speak dominant languages as a way to be modern. Yet the choice to abandon or reclaim a language involves social assessments about the possibilities and purposes of multilingualism, as well as value judgments about the role of the heritage language in maintaining community. Language ideologies—power-laden, seemingly commonsense assumptions about languages related to communities' sociohistorical circumstances—lay the groundwork for language shift (Dorian, 1989; Gal, 1979) and also play an important role in shaping when and how Indigenous community members, including youth, participate in language renewal efforts (Field & Kroskrity, 2009). Language ideologies "underpin not only linguistic form and use but also the very notion of the person and the social group" (Woolard, 1998, p. 3); as such, they shape the subtle workings of discourses about particular kinds of people in the lives of marginalized youth. Ethnographic work continues to teach us, for instance, about the complicated ways that youth perceive and respond to racialized discourses ranging from those framing Muslim youth as threatening since 9/11 (Abu El-Haj, 2006), to discourses of citizenship, illegality, and anti-bilingual education surrounding Latino/a immigrant youth (González & Arnott-Hopffer, 2002; Mendoza-Denton, 2008; O'Connor, 2012), to "model minority" stereotypes impacting Asian American and other minority youth (Lee, 2009; Ng, Lee, & Pak, 2007).

Scholars have also begun to explore how Indigenous young people make sense of, enact, and reshape language ideologies through interpretive and interactive processes, and how young people's language ideologies intersect with processes of language learning, shift, and reclamation (Kulick, 1992; Meek, 2007; Wyman, 2012). In approaching this topic, researchers must first recognize the ideological multiplicity within and across Indigenous communities (Field & Kroskrity, 2009), the ways that varying language ideologies have been introduced into Native American communities through dominant institutions such as schools, and how language ideologies proliferate as community members gain awareness of language endangerment or engage with language reclamation (Hill, 2006; Kroskrity, 2011).

Research also points to common, troubling ways that Indigenous youth are positioned within contradictory language ideologies emanating from the broader society and their communities. Examining these ideologies, and looking deeply into young people's discourses about language, we can begin to understand the challenging positions of youth in settings of language endangerment. As we see in this volume, discourses of Indigenous language use have been plagued by the binary assumptions that originated in classification schemes used to justify histories of colonization, starting with distinctions between "savage" versus "civilized" peoples, and "small-scale" versus "complex" societies. Even today, "Indigenous peoples are often portrayed as either heroic or tragic, as traditional or modern" as "orient[ing] towards local or global practices, Indigenous languages or English, subsistence versus cash economies, or traditional versus modern worlds" (Wyman, this volume) or as producing "authentically localized" or "non-authentic" forms of global youth culture (O'Connor & Brown, this volume). Similarly, Indigenous youth have commonly been classified as "speakers" or "non-speakers" of Indigenous languages, a binary distinction that scholars are increasingly viewing as problematic (McCarty et al., this volume; Meek, 2011; Wyman, 2012). Meek's (2011) work further documents how an ideology of dysfluency permeates assumptions about Indigenous language learners, casting forms of Indigenous language learning and use as failure.

At the same time, we must use caution making claims about the ways in which language ideologies intersect with on-the-ground processes of language learning and sociolinguistic change, since individual, family, and community practices are also shaped by the availability of specific linguistic resources at particular times, in particular places. To continue situating young people's emic perspectives, experiences, and practices within broader dynamics of Indigenous language loss and reclamation, we next consider how ideologies, everyday policymaking, and language learning opportunities come together in schools as particularly important but contested spaces of linguistic survivance and continuance.

Language Ideologies, Resources, and Policymaking in Schools

Historically, in many places around the world language education policies have labeled Indigenous languages as linguistically and morally deficient and in need of eradication. Youth are receivers of these unerasable histories of linguistic and cultural genocide, and, like adults, continue to live with the "linguistic wrongs" of a history of past policies (Skutnabb-Kangas, 2000; see also Charles, this volume). This commonly manifests generationally in parents' choices to socialize their children in dominant languages to spare children the abuse their parents faced in school for speaking their mother tongue, and the emerging effects of children's linguistic choices. Youth can also be painfully aware of the ways such historically oppressive language policies influenced their parents' language choices (McCarty et al., this volume).

To understand the myriad ways that language ideologies are linked to and constitutive of positions of power (Irvine & Gal, 2000; Woolard, 1998), and shape language endangerment and reclamation, we must also carefully consider how other contemporary forms of everyday policymaking—both formal and informal—help drive language shift and endangerment. While schools may no longer ban Indigenous languages, schools and society evidence a deep "ideology of contempt" for Indigenous languages based on "ignorance of the complexity and expressivity of indigenous languages, ... and ... belief in the onerousness of bi- or multilingualism" (Dorian, 1998, p. 123). Messing's chapter in this volume, for example, highlights how Mexicano youth and young adults encounter this contempt in schools and society. Lee (this volume) similarly notes that Native languages are often "relegated to a position in the past, as static and vanishing." Common everyday school practices frame Indigenous languages as inherently incapable of adapting to contemporary purposes. A related ideology is that Indigenous languages hold youth back from academic and life success (Wyman et al., 2010; Lee, this volume), and that youth must

speak English or other dominant languages to get ahead, *salir adelante*, in a globalized world (Messing, this volume).

Many Native American communities have experienced decades of language
shift alongside decades of efforts to teach Indigenous languages in school. In the
United States, culturally and linguistically responsive educational approaches
have been effective for Indigenous students (Castagno & Brayboy, 2008; Demmert & Towner, 2003). The 1990/1992 Native American Languages Act also
established the right of Native Americans to teach their languages in schools.
Nevertheless, "significant incongruities" exist "between the Federal protective
statuses regarding language and culture" and the implementational realities of
other federal and state laws and assessment practices that privilege dominant
languages and ideologies of linguistic development (Beaulieu, 2006, p. 60). By
the time Indigenous youth leave K-12 systems, they have typically spent thou-
sands more hours focused on learning English than Indigenous languages (Hinton, 2001). Lee's and Kroupa's chapters highlight how Native youth perceive
and critique such school-based imbalances. Other studies have documented
how high-stakes testing serves as a de facto language policy (Menken, 2008),
destabilizing earlier bilingual education programs and outcomes (Romero-
Little, McCarty, Warhol, & Zepeda, 2007; Wyman et al., 2010).

Currently there is a great need to understand how teachers, principals,
school board members, parents, and youth are negotiating the dual pressures of
Indigenous language shift and high-stakes testing in schools serving Indigenous
students. An important additional question is how Indigenous youth interpret
and experience such policy disjunctures. Several chapters in this volume show
how youth may critique the ways that racialized imbalances in teaching staff
and curriculum undercut schools' stated goals of valuing Indigenous languages
and cultures. As Lee notes (this volume), youth may also condemn schools "for
neglect[ing] to make education relevant to their present-day lives" and for providing "hostile environments toward their cultural backgrounds."

Uncaring or distrustful relations between teachers and students can further
impact when, whether and how youth feel safe bringing out their Indigenous
languages in school. Kroupa's chapter suggests that Indigenous students' language use in schools can be interpreted within racialized dynamics of distrust as
White teachers display "linguistic paranoia" (Haviland, 2003). Lack of personal
involvement with Indigenous teachers, as well, can negatively impact young
people's feelings of linguistic security (Lee, this volume; McCarty et al., this
volume).

Yet, as Lee notes, in contemporary communities experiencing rapid language shift, "youth often have no choice but to utilize the school for learning
their Native languages." Lee's research informs us of the ways Indigenous youth
show tremendous agency as they "locate and create safe spaces with particular
teachers or courses" to access resources for learning the Indigenous language
and fostering an Indigenous identity and how some "develop a critical language
awareness" through this process. Wyman's (2012) research as well documents

how youth who expressed insecurities speaking Yup'ik translanguaged between Yup'ik and English to help one another and benefit from connections to Indigenous teachers, and how they used token Yup'ik as an in-group boundary-marker in a school characterized by racialized dynamics of distrust.

Ideological Crosscurrents and Youth Authenticity

Indigenous educators and their non-Indigenous allies have, in some cases, worked within this tangled ideological milieu described above to bring local language practices and knowledge systems into school spaces (for examples in this volume, see chapters by Kroupa, Lee, Messing, and Wilson & Kamana, see also Lipka et al. 1998). Language ideologies have also migrated out of schools into Indigenous communities over time, with the results that many parents now consider their home language choices in light of multiple sets of school-based assumptions about bilingualism and language learning rooted in differing periods in the educational histories of Native American communities. The boundaries between school, family, community, and larger societal language ideologies are porous and complex.

Nevertheless, researchers have documented the tremendous staying power of the ideologies through which many Native American communities value Indigenous languages as part of community identities and knowledge systems, and how such ideologies contain assumptions about showing respect for elders as knowledge-keepers. Like immigrant language ideologies, these Indigenous-language ideologies "push against the exclusions and hierarchies" of racial-ized indexical orders (Dick, 2011, p. 234). Related discourses can also work as potent alternate hegemonies that are sustained through patterned language use in ceremonial spaces, traditional councils, on ancestral lands, and through practices of storytelling (Kroskrity, 1998, 2012). Meek's (2007) work with Kaska youth, Wyman's (2012) work with Yup'ik youth, Nicholas's (2009) work with Hopi youth, and Lee's (2009), Romero's (2003), and McCarty et al.'s (2009) work with Indigenous youth in the U.S. Southwest all documented how even Indigenous youth who do not speak their heritage languages may continue to orient strongly toward locally specific language ideologies valuing Indigenous languages, local land-use practices, and elderly speakers of Indigenous languages.

In these same contexts, however, youth may find themselves confronted by community beliefs that posit Indigenous-language monolingualism as an authentic marker of ethnic identity. Hill (1998) has shown how this can manifest in a "discourse of nostalgia" in which imagined "pure" and "traditional" uses of language are valued over what may be more vibrant practices in everyday life (see also King, 2001; Meek, 2007; Messing, this volume; Wilson & Kamanā, this volume). Similarly, youth can be disenfranchised by scholarly research that overtly values traditional Indigenous practices while neglecting contemporary ones and privileging elderly speakers who grew up using only one language as idealized "native speakers" (Cruikshank, 1998; Kramsch, 1997; see also Bucholtz, 2003). As Māori scholar Linda Tuhiwai Smith writes, "The belief in an authentic self ... has been politicized by the colonized world in ways which invoke simultaneous meanings" (2012, p. 73). Indigenous community adults and language activists may further "grapple with authenticity ... not only as a linguistic issue but also as a cultural and educational one" as they "negotiate new and old identities" and "difficult decisions as to what to teach that can best represent an earlier ancestral culture or indeed a present day one" (Henze & Davis, 1999, pp. 14–15).

Much current research shows how competing, contradictory discourses produce powerful "ideological crosscurrents" as youth seek to understand their language learning and practice in relation to language endangerment (McCarty, Romero, & Zepeda, 2006). Based on a survey and interview study of 215 Navajo high school students, Lee (2007) noted the respect with which Navajo youth hold their heritage language, even as they contend with demeaning stereotypes that associate speaking Navajo with "backwardness" and traditionalism. In subsequent research, Lee (2009; this volume) documents youth agency and intervention as they developed a "critical Indigenous consciousness" about language shift. Similarly, in ethnographic research with Native youth in seven southwestern U.S. school-community sites, McCarty et al. (2009) and McCarty, Romero-Little, Warhol, and Zepeda (2011) examined the conflicting language ideologies that position Indigenous languages as highly valued by youth and simultaneously as "just the past" (2011, pp. 41–42).

Looking at Hopi youth, Nicholas (2009, 2011) investigated the family, community, and school dynamics in which ideologies of Indigenous language and culture valuation are nurtured and expressed. Although Hopi youth indicated a desire to learn the Hopi language, they often expressed fear of being ridiculed for linguistic errors. Nicholas posited that Hopi oral tradition constitutes a powerful language transmission mechanism that gives rise to an emotional commitment to the ideals of the communal Hopi society.

Muehlmann (2008) documented how a national policy shift valorizing Indigenous-language use called into question Cucapá youth's identity claims in northern Mexico. Cucupá youth strategically deployed Cucapá swearwords in the presence of outsiders to "negotiate claims to indigeneity" (p. 43) and to counter a long history of racial and economic injustice.

Further complicating this picture, a growing body of research shows how youth encounter ideological crosscurrents and negotiate new kinds of Indigeneity in their use of globally circulating forms of youth culture. Deyhle's early research on Navajo youth break dancing (1998) showed what many ethnographic studies have since shown: that Indigenous youth often glocalize popular forms of youth culture originating outside their communities, embedding them in locally-specific practices and beliefs (see discussion and related citations in O'Connor and Brown, this volume; Alim et al., 2009). More recent studies, including O'Connor and Brown's chapter in this volume, show how ideologies of authenticity can accompany these forms, imposing further demands that Indigenous youth "keep it real" by representing certain local practices and identities over others, even as they seek to establish themselves as Native artists developing widely circulating forms of multimodal expertise and performance.

These are just a few examples of the ways in which recent Indigenous youth language research complicates the "two world" binary (Henze & Vanett, 1993) often associated with Indigenous peoples, helping us better understand when and how appeals to linguistic authenticity benefit or marginalize Indigenous youth. The growing literature on Indigenous youth language also shows how dangerous it can be when youth are judged as authentic or inauthentic community members based on Indigenous-language competency alone.

Youth, Ideological Emergence, and Communities of Practice

Recent research has increasingly emphasized the emergent nature of language ideologies and their contentiousness within and across communities (Field, 2009). In contemporary linguistic ecologies, young people play key roles in ideological emergence, as well as the reshaping of language learning opportunities. First, youth can generate new ideological choices in language shift settings. Second, youth are often seen as icons of community members' doubts and hopes, with implications for intergenerational language socialization.

Multiple studies show how youth "make" language policy in their everyday social practice, "sometimes in resistance to wider English-only policy discourses, and sometimes in ways that are likely to yield further language shift" (McCarty et al., this volume). Ethnographic studies of Indigenous family-level language shift provide striking evidence of how even very young children generate new regimes of language use, engaging in everyday policymaking in ways that shape sociolinguistic settings as they make seemingly conscious choices not to speak their heritage languages to their parents (Kulick, 1992; Meek, 2007; Parsons-Yazzie, 1996/1997; Wyman, 2012, 2013). Research further shows how children and youth in communities undergoing language shift can, within a very short timeframe, evidence emerging sociolinguistic constraints, expressing feelings of embarrassment and hesitation about speaking endangered languages. Heritage language learners commonly feel tongue-tied, especially if they have been teased, criticized, or stigmatized for their language use (Messing, this volume; Santa Ana, 2004). Many Indigenous youth feel acute embarrassment over unfinished Indigenous-language competencies (Lee, this volume). Such insecurities play a leading role in seemingly agentive choices to speak dominant languages or token everyday words and phrases, and influence when, whether and how youth use their existing Indigenous language competencies with others. Linguistic insecurities are always ideological in that they show speakers' orientations toward particular societal assumptions about what counts as linguistic competency (Woolard, 1998). In her commentary in this volume, García notes how such insecurities can reflect the monoglossic standards that are imposed from within as well as outside Indigenous communities—standards that rarely map easily onto young people's translanguaging, modalities, and relationships.

Given ongoing forms of policymaking in and out of schools, new types of movement across rural and urban spaces, multilayered processes of language maintenance/shift, and related complexities of ideological emergence in contemporary linguistic ecologies, youth do not necessarily share language ideologies or linguistic competencies. Instead, young people's varying language ideologies and competencies develop in relation to language learning opportunities within schools, families, and sibling and peer groups, as language learning assumptions and opportunities change hand in hand (Mendoza-Denton, 2008; Schecter & Bayley, 2002; Wyman, 2012, this volume; Zentella, 1997, 2005). When heritage language learners have not had sufficient opportunities to hear, practice, and use their ancestral language, they may position themselves as listeners versus speakers (Valdés, 2005).

No matter how quickly these speakers and their sociolinguistic settings trend toward language shift, however, we still often see young people who, "growing up within earshot" of their Indigenous languages (Pye, 1992), continue to develop understandings of the ideological and sociolinguistic dimensions of who speaks what to whom under what circumstances (McCarty et al., 2009; Meek, 2007; Paugh, 2005). Importantly, many of these youth also evidence "emergent bilingualism" (Reyes, 2006), and use their incipient bilingual skills and varying linguistic repertoires in interaction with others. As we see in the chapters that follow, positive shifts in these young people's language learning can foster feelings of confidence and momentum, inspiring youth to "keep expanding" (O'Connor & Brown; Kroupa) their multilingualism.

Chapters by Lee, McCarty et al., and Messing and commentaries by Charles and Wilson and Kamanā highlight the potential for youth to take up new positions vis-á-vis their Indigenous languages as they join new postsecondary communities of practice and develop "common knowledge and beliefs, ways of relating to each other, [and] ways of talking" in the course of mutual endeavors (Eckert & McConnell-Ginet, 2003, p. 57). Youth may decide, with a fervor, to take up traditional Indigenous language and cultural practices and declare that these are key for maintaining collective identities. When youth voice even token amounts of Indigenous languages that haven't been spoken by children for decades, their language use can be an especially powerful symbol of decolonization for community members. In their commentary, Wilson and Kamanā note how forms of youth activism have played a major role in the Hawaiian language revitalization movement. Even small groups of families can make a difference in young people's agentive decisions to use Indigenous languages;

individual friendships can also help young people activate receptive skills as they move into young adult life.

Such moves on the part of enthusiastic youth and young adults may make parents uncomfortable with their own previous choices to speak dominant languages in the face of racist pressures (St. Denis, 2003). Young adult activists may also experience discomfort within their personal relationships if they are seen to be taking up new roles as "language police" (Lee, this volume). Yet youth and young adults show how they actively negotiate myriad sets of tensions as they "recreate themselves while maintaining claims to indigeneity" (McCarty & Wyman, 2009, p. 285; see also Kroupa, this volume; O'Connor & Brown, this volume).

One powerful new trend in this vein documents how Indigenous youth and young adults use new media to strategically widen possibilities for sharing Indigenous languages laterally and intergenerationally (Harrison, 2012). On the Fort Mojave reservation in California, for example, a group of Mojave teens and adults is using high-quality audio-visual equipment to document Mojave bird songs, considered a core expression of Mojave identity and traditionally, not a cultural form subject to recording (McCarty et al., this volume). The language documentation process has opened new language learning opportunities as youth interact with elder speakers and adult language learners. Writing of similar efforts for an Aboriginal youth media movement in Australia, Kral (2011) explains that youth "take on the role of 'expert'" (p. 6), constructing identities not simply as learners, but as "knowledgeable, capable citizens of mobile local, national, and global communities" (p. 11).

A common use of new media for supporting Indigenous youth language learning and self-expression is digital storytelling, whereby youth "control the images and structures through self-representations that challenge the taken-for-granted ... representations along with the misrepresentations of indigenous peoples in dominant society" (Iseke & Moore, 2011, p. 21). This and related types of collaborative Indigenous youth media production are "as much about the process of community relationships as they are about the development of digital products and research outcomes" (Iseke & Moore, 2011, p. 1). Through self-publishing in media arenas like YouTube, youth speak back to commonplace assumptions that they are indifferent to their heritage languages and cultures, as in the case of *When It's Gone, It's Gone*, a Google video shot and posted by American Indian students in Oklahoma that widely circulated the message that "young Indigenous people care about their heritage language" (discussed by Huaman, 2011). Youth and young adults bring their energy to exploring the malleability and potential of these media, creating impressive digital language-learning tools and resources, even as their efforts result in the broader development of Indigenous young people's capabilities (Huaman, 2011). Rarely do such projects set the goals of producing fluent Indigenous language speakers. Still, young people's engagement in new media in support of endangered languages can offer "the ability … to gain exposure to a variety of language possibilities within revitalization, protection, preservation and maintenance—including specific ideas around leadership, policy development and advocacy, fellowship and acknowledgement and celebration of successes" (Huaman, 2011, para. 33; Iseke & Moore, 2011).

While these youth-inspired efforts create new "ideological and implementational spaces" (Hornberger, 2006) for Indigenous-language learning, they are not without accompanying tensions. Many Indigenous communities exist on the wrong side of the digital divide of access to technology, broadband connections, and mentors knowledgeable in digital literacies (Hull, 2003; Knobel & Lankshear, 2011; Warschauer, & Matuchniak, 2010). Further, youth working in new media production often "challenge the designation of certain languages and vernaculars as broadcast ready and others deemed as inappropriate and offensive" (Soep & Chávez, 2010, p. 14). On the one hand, this makes their work powerful and important, since youth "defy the tendency to homogenize whole communities of people, erasing their internal complexities … contradictions" (Soep & Chávez, 2010, p. 14), and varied strengths. On the other hand, when Indigenous youth and young adults produce new media in Indigenous languages—whether that be YouTube videos of slam poetry, Indigenous language-learning apps for Ipods (Tulloch), text messages (Kroupa), or Websites—their efforts may be rejected by community adults and even other youth if the resulting products are seen as "crossing the line" in terms of deference to the ways languages have been conceived, used, and represented in times past (Nevins, 2004). As youth embed Indigenous knowledge into new spaces, community members may also have strong concerns about the potential for misunderstanding and appropriation by outsiders. This raises important questions about how youth and young adults might contribute to language efforts in new media yet do so in ways that respect tribal protocols and wishes.

Nevertheless, as we see in this volume, youth and young adults' related forms of language activism can creatively support Indigenous language learning as a means of strengthening peer and intergenerational bonds, as Indigenous youth around the world find ways to move Indigenous languages into new cultural spaces. Young people's efforts can also be inspirational to the adults around them, who often interpret the use of Indigenous languages and young Indigenous voices on new media platforms as a sign that Indigenous peoples, as well as Indigenous languages, have vibrant future possibilities. Multiple chapters in this volume show how collaborative work in and around Indigenous languages, especially when it is supported by key adult or peer mentors in organized collectives with resources, can profoundly alter the language ideologies and development trajectories of youth and young adults in positive ways. Tulloch's chapter in this volume, for example, highlights an ongoing international youth-led language planning effort, and how Inuit elders and youth have learned to work together, generating a powerful discourse of caring and solidarity.

This research and activism takes us beyond endangerment, showing how negative language ideologies and intergenerational tensions can be disrupted, and how young people who express insecurities, embarrassment and/or ambivalence around speaking Indigenous languages can develop bi/multilingualism under different circumstances, and use their new competences to "make powerful claims to belonging, even if they may never reach upper levels of fluency" (Wyman, 2013, p. 80; see also discussions in Kroupa, Lee, McCarty et al., Messing, Nicholas, Tulloch, this volume). Serious engagement with Indigenous youth language research can open reflexive dialogues between and among youth, elders, and other community adults, helping to disrupt damaging societal discourses and simplistic assumptions about language learning, and bridging intergenerational divides.

Toward Humanizing, Decolonizing, and Praxis-Driven Youth Language Research

Going beyond endangerment in Indigenous youth language research requires us to go beyond bleak statistics of massive language loss to examine the politics of language in youth's everyday lives. Ethnography, the quintessential humanistic and democratizing science (Blommaert, 2010b; Hymes, 1980), is ideally suited for this purpose. Critical ethnographic inquiry into young people's experiences can both problematize and clarify theoretical debates about language, culture, globalization, and society (Maira & Soep, 2005). In endangered-language settings, ethnography also provides a means of analyzing youth language practices and ideologies as they emerge within sociolinguistic ecologies, revealing, and re-presenting "grounded, insider perspectives on linguistic needs and aspirations" while also showing "local realizations" of tacit and official language policies and practices (Canagarajah, 2006, p. 164).

Within this critical ethnographic paradigm, we privilege youth counternarratives, characterized by a critique of official texts and taken-for-granted assumptions and by a concern with the social and political as well as the personal (Gilmore & Smith, 2005; Peters & Lankshear, 1996). Throughout the volume the authors also emphasize young people's "own acts of cultural critique and cultural production in the face of often untenable situations" (Bucholtz, 2002, p. 535). By examining the ways in which youth shape both the linguistic here and now and the futures of their peer groups, families, and communities, the studies frame their analyses within multigenerational Indigenous experiences and provide new insights into the ways in which youth act as "the youngest policy makers" in rapidly changing linguistic ecologies (McCarty et al., 2009).

This work is in keeping with what Brayboy et al. (2012) call a critical Indigenous research methodology, which "forefronts the self-determination and inherent sovereignty of Indigenous peoples ... and is driven explicitly by community interests" (p. 424). As insiders and "allied others" (Kaomea, 2004) who are simultaneously involved with Indigenous LPP, the chapter authors interpret young people's discursive practices and their tacit and explicit policymaking in light of historical and intergenerational struggles to maintain Indigenous languages and knowledge systems in communities under pressure. This work also shows ways of developing research in conversation with Indigenous community members (Smith, 2012) and of maintaining a necessary "triple vision" in Indigenous youth research "that recognizes and forwards academic, youth, and broader community projects" (McCarty, Wyman, & Nicholas, 2013, p. 99). By developing this triple vision, we show how youth researchers can use their work to support and foster humanized, intergenerational relationships within the communities with whom they work.

Ultimately, as the authors here demonstrate, Indigenous youth language research can help us understand how youth are part of broader communities situated historically within processes of marginalization and counter movements. Sidestepping simplistic celebratory stances toward global youth culture, youth agency, and hybridity—even as we position these as resources for learning and positive social change—the chapters here detail how Indigenous language issues are embedded in contemporary inequities and ongoing struggles over the long-term maintenance of distinctive knowledge systems and identities. Desanitizing, reclaiming, and creatively employing these histories remain central to fostering Indigenous linguistic and educational self-determination.

Indigenous youth language research is also breaking new ground in fostering activist research and a commitment to praxis—"the place where theory and practice come together in noticeable and important ways" (Brayboy et al., 2012, p. 429). Our hope is that this research will both re-present and inspire action by and for youth on behalf of their communities' goals for cultural persistence, continuance, and survivance. We recognize, however, that youth cannot be expected to act alone; they require the support of a larger nexus of authorizing agents—their families, elders, educators, tribal leaders, and the schools in which they spend much of their lives. In this volume Wyman identifies transformative possibilities for asserting linguistic rights in the Far North, pointing out how community members and educators must attend to school practices and youth language to realize those possibilities. Lee suggests that educators become more proactive in heritage language reclamation by promoting dialogic opportunities among youth around the historical causes of heritage language stigmatization, and by linking heritage languages to young people's everyday lives. McCarty et al. suggest strategies through which educators can "invite youth into" school- and community-based language planning. García's commentary urges us to envision schools that engage with all that youth have to offer while providing healthy opportunities for youth to develop their bilingualism. Tulloch shows how NGOs serve as important spaces where youth can organize grassroots language movements across contexts, generations, and nation-states. Kroupa's chapter demonstrates how small groups of young adults can strategically use higher education to create communities of practice with the potential to reclaim academic resources and ancestral spaces even as they extend language learning opportunities into afterschool organizations such as Boys and Girls Clubs. Wilson and Kamanā detail how leaders of the Hawaiian language revitalization movement have strategically positioned the relearning of an ancestral language as the basis for building multilingualism and academic achievement among Indigenous youth who were previously underserved in the state school system. Together, these chapters show how youth and young adults can provide "striking narrative[s] of adaptation, learning ... and re-grouping" (Kroupa, this volume) of Indigenous identities, and the ways in which innovative youth practice may complement, intersect with, and shape adult language activism. We also see how youth's and young adults' interest in Indigenous languages can form the basis for new "ideological and implementational spaces" (Hornberger, 2006) for language learning and reclamation.

In her influential work with language reclamation with adults from critically endangered language communities in California, Leanne Hinton (2009) discusses the unique situation and potential of what she calls the "missing generation"—the first generation of Indigenous community members to grow up not comfortably speaking but hearing an Indigenous language spoken around them. As Hinton shows, individuals from this generation often have strong desires to speak their ancestral languages. They are also increasingly the ones who are taking up the work of language revitalization, strategically considering how to learn endangered languages and sometimes demonstrating intense commitments to creating new Indigenous language learning opportunities across generations (Hinton, 2009).

By looking closely and ethnographically at rapid intra- and intergenerational changes within diverse Native American contexts and highlighting Indigenous youth language ideologies, communicative repertoires, and activism, we gain new insight into what youth are missing from adults and others around them in terms of understanding and language learning opportunities in dynamic situations of language shift. We also begin to see how we can learn from youth, so we don't miss important opportunities for bringing Indigenous languages into the future.

Many of the studies described here show how young people navigate multiplex language ideologies in relation to individualized language socialization trajectories (Wortham, 2006), and how careful tracking of young people's multilingualism and educational experiences over time and space can lead to a more critical, praxis-oriented "anthropolitical" linguistics (Zentella, 1997). While the complexity of issues shows how language reclamation requires constant negotiation and hard work, this work is, in García's words (this volume), a means of securing the future of Indigenous lifeways. In the chapters that follow, we invite readers to join us in envisioning those possibilities in Indigenous communities across Native America—beyond endangerment to sustainable linguistic self-determination.

Note

1 Discussions of Indigenous-language learning do not fit neatly within conventional scholarly discourses of heritage language learning. Some scholars and activists object to the use of the term "heritage" with regard to Indigenous languages as it seems to connote immigrant status; others believe that a heritage language is one in which children have some degree of first-language abilities. Our position is that, even though many Indigenous languages are no longer acquired by children as first languages, they are nonetheless languages of heritage, affinity, and identity (cf. McCarty, 2008, 2013, p. xxiv).

References

Abu El-Haj, T. R. (2006). *Elusive justice: Wrestling with difference and educational equity in everyday practice*. New York, NY: Routledge.

Alim, H. S. (2007). Critical hip-hop pedagogies: Combat, consciousness, and the cultural politics of communication. *Journal of Language, Identity, and Education, 6*(2), 161–176.

Alim, H. S., Pennycook, A., & Ibrahim, A. (2009). *Global linguistic flows: Hip hop cultures, youth identities, and the politics of language*. New York, NY: Routledge.

Beaulieu, D. (2006). A survey and assessment of culturally based education programs for Native American students in the United States. *Journal of American Indian Education, 45*(2), 50–61.

Blommaert, J. (2010a). *The sociolinguistics of globalization*. Cambridge, England: Cambridge University Press.

Blommaert, J. (2010b). *Ethnographic fieldwork: A beginner's guide*. Bristol, England: Multilingual Matters.

Brayboy, B. M. J., Gough, H. R., Leonard, B., Roehl, R.F. II, & Solyom, J.A. (2012). Reclaiming scholarship: Critical Indigenous research methodologies. In S. D. Lapan, M. T. Quartaroli, & F. J. Riemer (Eds.), *Qualitative research: An introduction to methods and designs* (pp. 423–450). San Francisco, CA: Jossey-Bass.

Bucholtz, M. (2002). Youth and cultural practice. *Annual Review of Anthropology, 31,* 525–552.

Bucholtz, M. (2003). Sociolinguistic nostalgia and the authentication of identity. *Journal of Sociolinguistics. 7*(3), 398–416.

Bucholtz, M., & Hall, K. (2005). Identity and interaction: A sociocultural linguistic approach. *Discourse Studies, 7*(4-5), 585–614.

Canagarajah, S. (2006). Ethnographic methods in language policy. In T. Ricento (Ed.), *An introduction to language policy: Theory and method* (pp. 153-169). Malden, MA: Blackwell.

Castagno, A., & Brayboy, B. M. J. (2008). Culturally responsive schooling for Indigenous youth: A review of the literature. *Review of Educational Research, 78*(4), 941–993.

Collins, J. (2012). Migration, sociolinguistic scale, and educational reproduction. *Anthropology and Education Quarterly, 43*(2), 192–213.

Cruikshank, J. (1998). *The social life of stories: Narrative and knowledge in the Yukon territory*. Lincoln: University of Nebraska Press.

Demmert, W. G., & Towner, J. (2003). *A review of the research literature on the influences of culturally-based education on the academic performance of Native American students*. Portland, OR: Northwest Regional Educational Lab.

Deyhle, D. (1998). From break dancing to heavy metal: Navajo youth, resistance and identity. *Youth and Society, 3*(3), 3–31.

Dick, H. P. (2011). Language and migration to the United States. *Annual Review of Anthropology, 40,* 227–240.

Dorian, N. C. (1989). *Investigating obsolescence: Studies in language contraction and death*. Cambridge, England: Cambridge University Press.

Dorian, N. C. (1998). Western language ideologies and small-scale prospects. In L. A. Grenoble & L. J. Whaley (Eds.), *Endangered languages: Language loss and community response* (pp. 3-21). Cambridge, England: Cambridge University Press.

Eckert, P. (1989). *Jocks and burnouts: Social identity in the high school.* New York, NY: Teachers College Press.

Eckert, P. (2000). *Linguistic variation as social practice: The linguistic construction of identity in Belton High.* Malden, MA: Blackwell.

Eckert, P., & McConnell-Ginet, S. (2003). *Language and gender.* Cambridge, England: Cambridge University Press.

Field, M. C. (2009). Changing Navajo language ideologies and changing language use. In P. V. Kroskrity & M. C. Field (Eds.), *Native American language ideologies: Beliefs, practices and struggles in Indian Country* (pp. 31–47). Tucson: University of Arizona Press.

Field, M. C., & Kroskrity, P.V. (2009). Introduction: Revealing Native American language ideologies. In P. V. Kroskrity & M. C. Field (Eds.), *Native American language ideologies: Beliefs, practices, and struggles in Indian Country* (pp. 3–28). Tucson: University of Arizona Press.

Fox, J., & Rivera-Salgado, G. (2004). *Indigenous Mexican migrants in the United States.* Boulder, CO: Lynne Rienner.

Gal, S. (1979). *Language shift: Social determinants of linguistic change in bilingual Austria.* New York, NY: Academic Press.

García, O. (2009). *Bilingual education in the 21st century: A global perspective.* Malden, MA: Wiley-Blackwell.

Garrett, P., & Baquedano-López, P. (2002). Language socialization: Reproduction and continuity, transformation and change. *Annual Review of Anthropology, 31,* 339–361.

Gilmore, P., & Smith, D. M. (2005). Seizing academic power: Indigenous subaltern voices, metaliteracy, and counternarratives in higher education. In T. L. McCarty (Ed.), *Language, literacy, and power in schooling* (pp. 67–88). Mahwah, NJ: Erlbaum.

Gilmore, P., & Wyman, L. (2013). An ethnographic long look: Language and literacy over time and space in Alaska Native Communities. In K. Hall, T. Cremin, B. Comber, & L. Moll (Eds.), *International handbook of research on children's literacy, learning, and culture* (pp. 121–138). Malden, MA: Wiley-Blackwell.

González, N., & Arnott-Hopffer, E. (2002). Voices of the children: Language and literacy ideologies in a dual language program. In S. Wortham & B. Rymes (Eds.), *Linguistic anthropology of education* (pp. 213–243). Westport, CT: Praeger.

González, N., Moll, L. C., & Amanti, C. (Eds.). (2005). *Funds of knowledge: Theorizing practices in households, communities, and classrooms.* Mahwah, NJ: Erlbaum.

Harrison, K. D. (2012). Global trends. Retrieved December 16, 2012, from http://www.swarthmore.edu/SocSci/langhotspots/globaltrends.html/

Haviland, J. (2003). Ideologies of language: Some reflections on language and U.S. law. *American Anthropologist, 105*(4), 764–774.

Heath, S. B. (1998). Working through language. In S. M. Hoyle & C. T. Ager (Eds.), *Kids talk: Strategic language use in later childhood* (pp. 217–240). Oxford, England: Oxford University Press.

Henze, R., & Davis, K. A. (1999). Authenticity and identity: Lessons from Indigenous language education. *Anthropology and Education Quarterly, 30*(1), 3–21.

Henze, R. C., & Vanett, L. (1993). To walk in two worlds — or more? Challenging a common metaphor of Native education. *Anthropology and Education Quarterly, 24*(2), 116–134.

Hill, J. (1998). Don Francisco Márquez survives: A meditation on monolingualism. *International Journal of the Sociology of Language, 132,* 167–182.

Hill, J. (2002). "Expert rhetorics" in advocacy for endangered languages: Who is listening, and what do they hear? *Journal of Linguistic Anthropology, 12*(2), 119–133.

Hill, J. (2006). The ethnography of language and language documentation. In J. Gippert, N. Himmelmann, & U. Mosel (Eds.), *Essentials of language documentation* (pp. 113–128). Berlin, Germany: Mouton de Gruyter.

Hill, J., & Hill, K. (1986). *Speaking Mexicano: Dynamics of syncretic language change in central Mexico.* Tucson: University of Arizona Press.

Hinton, L. (2001). New writing systems. In L. Hinton & K. Hale (Eds.), *The green book of language revitalization in practice* (pp. 239–250). San Diego, CA: Academic Press.

Hinton, L. (2009, June). The Breath of Life-Silent No More Institute. Keynote address, American Indian Language Development Institute 30th Anniversary Symposium and Celebration, University of Arizona, Tucson.

Hornberger, N. H. (2002). Multilingual policies and the continua of biliteracy: An ecological approach. *Language Policy, 1*(1), 27–51.

Hornberger, N. H. (2006). *Nichols to NCLB*: Local and global perspectives on US language education policy. In O. García, T. Skutnabb-Kangas, & M.E. Torres-Guzmán (Eds.), *Imagining multilingual schools: Languages in education and glocalization* (pp. 223–237). Clevedon, England: Multilingual Matters.

Hornberger, N. H., & Johnson, D. C. (2011). The ethnography of language policy. In T. L. McCarty (Ed.), *Ethnography and language policy* (pp. 273–289). New York, NY: Routledge.

Hornberger, N. H., & McCarty, T. L. (Guest Eds.). (2012). Globalization from the bottom up: Indigenous language planning across time, space, and place [Special issue]. *International Multilingual Research Journal, 6*(1).

Huaman, I. (2011). Indigenous language revitalization and new media: Postsecondary students as innovators. *Global Media Journal, 11*(18), Article No. 3. Retrieved December 16, 2012, from http://lass.purduecal.edu/cca/gmj/sp11/gmj-sp11-article3.htm Global Media Journal/

Hull, G. (2003). At last: Youth culture and digital media: New literacies for new times. *Research in the Teaching of English, 38*(2), 229-233.

Hymes, D. (1980). *Language in education: Ethnolinguistic essays.* Washington, DC: Center for Applied Linguistics.

Irvine, J., & Gal, S. (2000). Language ideology and linguistic differentiation. In P. V. Kroskrity (Ed.), *Regimes of language: Ideologies, polities, and identities* (pp. 35-83). Santa Fe, NM: School of American Research Press.

Iseke, J. & Moore, S. (2011). Community-based Indigenous digital storytelling with elders and youth. *American Indian Culture and Research Journal, 35*(4), 19–38.

Ito, M., Horst, H., Antin, J., & Finn, M. (2010). *Hanging out, messing around and geeking out: Kids living and learning with new media.* Boston, MA: MIT Press.

Johnson, D. C. (2009). Ethnography of language policy. *Language Policy, 8*(2), 139–159.

Jørgensen, J. (1998). Children's acquisition of code-switching for power-wielding. In P. Auer (Ed.), *Code-switching in conversation: Language, interaction and identity* (pp. 237-261). London, England: Routledge.

Kagan, O. (2005). In support of a proficiency-based definition of heritage language learners: The case of Russian. *International Journal of Bilingual Education and Bilingualism, 8*(2/3), 213–221.

Kaomea, J. (2004). Dilemmas of an Indigenous academic: A Native Hawaiian story. In K. Mutua & B. B. Swadener (Eds.), *Decolonizing research in cross-cultural contexts: Critical personal narratives* (pp. 27–44). Albany: State University of New York Press.

King, K. A. (2001). *Language revitalization processes and prospects: Quichua in the Ecuadorian Andes.* Clevedon, England: Multilingual Matters.

King, K. A. (2013). A tale of three sisters: Language ideologies, identities, and negotiations in a bilingual, transnational family. *International Multilingual Research Journal, 7*(1), 49-65.

King, K. A., & Haboud, M. (2011). International migration and Quichua language shift in the Ecuadorian Andes. In T. L. McCarty (Ed.), *Ethnography and language policy* (pp. 139–159). New York, NY: Routledge.

Knobel, M., & Lankshear, (2011). *DIY media: Creating, sharing and learning with new technologies.* New York, NY: Peter Lang.

Kovach, M. (2009). *Indigenous methodologies: Characteristics, conversations, and contexts.* Toronto, Canada: University of Toronto Press.

Kral, I. (2012). *Talk, text and technology: Literacy and social practice in a remote Indigenous community.* Bristol, England: Multilingual Matters.

Kramsch, C. (1997). Guest column: The privilege of the nonnative speaker. *Publications of the Modern Language Association of America (PMLA), 112*(3), 359–369.

Kroskrity, P. V. (1998). Arizona Tewa kiva speech as a manifestation of a dominant language ideology. In B. Schieffelin, K. Woolard, & P. V. Kroskrity (Eds.), *Language ideologies: Practice and theory* (pp. 103–122). Oxford, England: Oxford University Press.

Kroskrity, P. V. (2011). All intimate grammars leak: Reflections on "Indian languages in unexpected places." *American Indian Culture and Research Journal, 35*(2), 161–172.

Kroskrity, P. V. (Ed.). (2012). *Telling stories in the face of danger: Language renewal in Native American communities.* Norman: University of Oklahoma Press.

Kulick, D. (1992). *Language shift and cultural reproduction: Socialization, self, and syncretism in a Papua New Guinean village.* Cambridge, England: Cambridge University Press.

Lam, W. S. E. (2006). Re-envisioning language, literacy, and the immigrant subject in new mediascapes. *Pedagogies: An International Journal, 1*(3), 171–195.

Lee, S. J. (2009). *Unraveling the "model minority" stereotype: Listening to Asian American youth* (2nd ed.) New York, NY: Teachers College Press.

Lee, T. S. (2007). "If they want Navajo to be learned, then they should require it in all schools": Navajo teenagers' experiences, choices, and demands regarding Navajo language. *Wicazo Sa Review,* (Spring), 7–33.

Lipka, G., with Mohatt, G. & the Ciulistet Group. (1998). *Changing the culture of schooling: Yup'ik Eskimo examples.* Mahwah, NJ: Erlbaum.

Maira, S., & Soep, E. (Eds.). (2005). *Youthscapes: The popular, the national and the global.* Philadelphia: University of Pennsylvania Press.

Makoni, S., Brutt-Griffler, J., & Mashir, P. (2007). The use of "indigenous" and urban vernaculars in Zimbabwe. *Language in Society, 3*(1), 25–49.

Matua, K., & Swadener, B. B. (Eds.). (2004). *Decolonizing research in cross-cultural contexts: Critical personal narratives.* Albany: State University of New York Press.

McCarty, T. L. (2008). Native American languages as heritage mother tongues. *Language, Culture and Curriculum, 21*(3), 201–225.

McCarty, T. L. (Ed.). (2011a). *Ethnography and language policy.* New York, NY: Routledge.

McCarty, T. L. (2011b). Preface. In T. L. McCarty (Ed.), *Ethnography and language policy* (pp. xii–xiii). New York, NY: Routledge.

McCarty, T.L. (2011c). Introducing ethnography and language policy. In T. L. McCarty (Ed.), *Ethnography and language policy* (pp. 1–28). New York: Routledge.

McCarty, T. L. (2013). *Language planning and policy in Native America — History, theory, praxis.* Bristol, England: Multilingual Matters.

McCarty, T. L., Romero, M. E., & Zepeda, O. (2006). Native American youth discourses on language shift and retention: Ideological cross-currents and their implications for language planning. *International Journal of Bilingual Education and Bilingualism, 9*(5), 659–677.

McCarty, T. L., Romero-Little, M. E., Warhol, L., & Zepeda, O. (2009). Indigenous youth as language policy makers. *Journal of Language, Identity, and Education, 8*(5), 291–306.

McCarty, T. L., Romero-Little, M. E., Warhol, L., & Zepeda, O. (2011). Critical ethnography and Indigenous language survival: Some new directions in language policy research and praxis. In T. L. McCarty (Ed.), *Ethnography and language policy* (pp. 31-51). New York, NY: Routledge.

McCarty, T. L., Wyman, L. T., & Nicholas, S. E. (2013). Activist ethnography with Indigenous youth: Lessons from humanizing research on language and education. In D. Paris & M. T. Winn (Eds.), *Humanizing research: Decolonizing qualitative inquiry with youth and communities* (pp. 81–104). Thousand Oaks: Sage.

McKay, S. L., & Wong, S. C. (1996). Multiple discourses, multiple identities: Investment and agency in second-language learning among Chinese adolescent immigrant students. *Harvard Educational Review, 66*(3), 577–608.

Meek, B. (2007). Respecting the language of elders: Ideological shift and linguistic discontinuity in a Northern Athapascan community. *Journal of Linguistic Anthropology, 17*(1), 23–43.

Meek, B. (2011). Failing American Indian languages. *American Indian Culture and Research Journal, 35*(2), 43–60.

Mendoza-Denton, N. (2008). *Homegirls: Language and cultural practice among Latina youth*. Malden, MA: Blackwell.

Menken, K. (2008). *English learners left behind: Standardized testing as language policy*. Clevedon, England: Multilingual Matters.

Morgan, M. (2009). *The real hiphop: Battling for knowledge, power, and respect in the LA underground* (pp. 47–84). Durham, NC: Duke University Press.

Muehlmann, S. (2008). "Spread your ass cheeks": And other things that should not be said in indigenous languages. *American Ethnologist, 35*(1), 34–48.

Nevins, M. E. (2004). Learning to listen: Confronting two meanings of language loss in the contemporary White Mountain speech community. *Journal of Linguistic Anthropology, 14*(2), 269–288.

Ng, J., Lee, S., & Pak, Y. (2007). Contesting the model minority and perpetual foreigner stereotypes: A critical review of literature on Asian Americans in education. *Review of Research in Education, 31*, 95–130.

Nicholas, S. E. (2009). "I live Hopi, I just don't speak it" — The critical intersection of language, culture, and identity in the lives of contemporary Hopi youth. *Journal of Language, Identity, and Education, 8*(5), 321–334.

Nicholas, S. E. (2011). "How are you Hopi if you can't speak it?" An ethnographic study of language as cultural practice among contemporary Hopi youth. In T. L. McCarty (Ed.), *Ethnography and language policy* (pp. 53–75). New York, NY: Routledge.

O'Connor, B. (2012). Racial identification, knowledge, and the politics of everyday life in an Arizona science classroom: A linguistic ethnography. (Unpublished doctoral dissertation), University of Arizona, Tucson.

Ortiz, S. J. (1992). *Woven stone*. Tucson: University of Arizona Press.

Paris, D. (2011). "A friend who understand fully": Notes on humanizing research in a multiethnic youth community. *International Journal of Qualitative Studies in Education, 24*(2), 137–149.

Paris, D., & Winn, M. (Eds.). (2014). *Humanizing research: Decolonizing qualitative inquiry with youth and communities*. Thousand Oaks, CA: Sage.

Parsons-Yazzie, E. (1996/1997). Niha'ałchíní dayistł'ǫ́ nahalin. *Journal of Navajo Education, 14*(1/2), 60–67.

Paugh, A. (2005). Multilingual play: Children's code-switching, role play, and agency in Dominica, West Indies. *Language in Society, 34*(1), 63–86.

Peters, M., & Lankshear, C. (1996). Postmodern counternarratives. In H. A. Giroux, C. Lankshear, P. McLaren, & M. Peters (Eds.), *Counternarratives: Cultural studies and critical pedagogy in postmodern spaces* (pp. 1–40). New York, NY: Routledge.

Pye, C. (1992). Language loss among the Chilcotin. *International Journal of the Sociology of Language, 93*, 75–86.

Rampton, B. (1995). *Crossing: Language and ethnicity among adolescents*. London, England: Longman.

Rampton, B. (2006). *Language in late modernity: Interaction in an urban school*. Cambridge, England: Cambridge University Press.

Reyes, I. (2006). Exploring connections between emergent bilingualism and biliteracy. *Journal of Childhood Literacy, 6*(3), 267–292.

Reynolds, J. (2009). Shaming the shift generation: Intersecting ideologies of family and linguistic revitalization in Guatemala. In P. V. Kroskrity & M. C. Field (Eds.), *Native American language ideologies: Beliefs, practices and struggles in Indian Country* (pp. 213–237). Tucson: University of Arizona Press.

Romero, M. E. (2003). Perpetuating the Cochiti way of life: A study of child socialization and language shift in a Pueblo community (Unpublished doctoral dissertation). University of California, Berkeley.

Romero-Little, M. E., McCarty, T. L., Warhol, L., & Zepeda, O. (2007). Language policies in practice: Preliminary findings from a large-scale study of Native American language shift. *TESOL Quarterly, 41*(3), 607–618.

Roth-Gordon, J., & Woronov, T. (2009). Youthful concerns: Movement, belonging and modernity. In M. Bucholtz & E. Chun (Guest Eds.), Youth language at the intersection [Special issue]. *Pragmatics, 9*(1), 129–143.

Rymes, B. (2011). Deference, denial and beyond: A repertoire approach to mass media and schooling. *Review of Research in Education, 35,* 208–238.

Santa Ana, O. (Ed.). (2004). *Tongue-tied: The lives of multilingual children in public education.* Lanham, MD: Rowman and Littlefield.

Schecter, S. R., & Bayley, R. (2002). *Language as cultural practice: Mexicanos en el Norte.* Mahwah, NJ: Erlbaum.

Scott, J. C., Straker, D. Y., & Katz, L. (2009). *Affirming students' right to their own language: Bridging language policies and pedagogical practices.* New York, NY and Urbana, IL: Routledge and National Council of Teachers of English.

Shohamy, E. (2006). *Language policy: Hidden agendas and new approaches.* London, England: Routledge.

Skutnabb-Kangas, T. (2000). *Linguistic genocide in education— Or worldwide diversity and human rights?* Mahwah, NJ: Erlbaum.

Smith, L. T. (2012). *Decolonizing methodologies: Research and Indigenous peoples* (2nd ed.). London, England: Zed Books.

Soep, E., & Chávez, V. (2010). *Drop that knowledge: Youth Radio stories.* Berkeley: University of California Press.

St. Denis, V. (2003). Real Indians: Cultural revitalization and fundamentalism in Aboriginal education. In C. Schick, J. Jaffe, & A. Watkinson (Eds.), *Contesting fundamentalisms* (pp. 35–47). Halifax, Canada: Fernwood.

Szulc, A. (2009). Becoming Neuquino in Mapuugun: Teaching Mapuche language and culture in the province of Neuquén, Argentina. *Anthropology and Education Quarterly, 40*(2), 129–149.

Valdés, G. (2005). Bilingualism, heritage language learners, and SLA research: Opportunities lost or seized? *Modern Language Journal, 89*(3), 410–426.

Vizenor, G. (1994). *Manifest manners: PostIndian warriors of survivance.* Hanover, NH: Wesleyan University Press of New England.

Vizenor, G. (2008). Aesthetics of survivance: Literary theory and practice. In G. Vizenor (Ed.), *Survivance: Narratives of Native presence* (pp. 1–23). Lincoln: University of Nebraska Press.

Warschauer, M., & Matuchniak, T. (2010). New technology and digital worlds: Analyzing evidence of equity in access, use and outcomes. *Review of Research in Education, 34*(1), 179–225.

Wilson, W. H., & Kamanā, K. (2009). Indigenous youth bilingualism from a Hawaiian activist perspective. *Journal of Language, Identity, and Education, 8*(5), 369–375.

Wong-Fillmore, L. (1991). When learning a second language means losing the first. *Early Childhood Research Quarterly, 6,* 323–346.

Woolard, K. A. (1998). Introduction: Language ideology as a field of inquiry. In B. B. Schieffelin, K. A. Woolard, & P. V. Kroskrity (Eds.), *Language ideologies: Practice and theory* (pp. 3–47). New York, NY: Oxford University Press.

Wortham, S. (2006). *Learning identity: The joint emergence of identification and academic learning.* Cambridge, UK: Cambridge University Press.

Wyman, L. T. (2009). Youth, linguistic ecologies and language endangerment: A Yup'ik example. *Journal of Language, Identity, and Education, 8*(5), 335–349.

Wyman, L. T. (2012). *Youth culture, language endangerment, and linguistic survivance.* Bristol, England: Multilingual Matters.

Wyman, L. T. (2013). Indigenous youth migration and language contact. *International Multilingual Research Journal, 7*(1), 66–82.

Wyman, L., Marlow, P., Andrew, C. F., Miller, G., Nicholai, C. R., & Rearden, Y. N. (2010). High stakes testing, bilingual education and language endangerment: A Yup'ik example. *International Journal of Bilingual Education and Bilingualism, 13,* 701–721.

Zentella, A. C. (1997). *Growing up bilingual: Puerto Rican children in New York.* Oxford, England: Blackwell.

Zentella, A. C. (2005). *Building on strengths: Language and literacy in Latino families and communities.* New York, NY: Teachers College Press.

2

GENEALOGIES OF LANGUAGE LOSS AND RECOVERY

Native Youth Language Practices and Cultural Continuance[1]

Teresa L. McCarty, Mary Eunice Romero-Little, Larisa Warhol, and Ofelia Zepeda

Analysis of comparative ethnographic data on Native American youth language practices reveals those practices to be much more nuanced, rich, and varied than standard school-based assessments suggest, and to be rooted in complex histories of official and unofficial language policies. This chapter takes a close look at the ways in which explicit and implicit policies about language are constructed intergenerationally in contexts of linguistic and cultural oppression and shift, and how those policies take shape in Indigenous young people's lives. Finally, the chapter asks, how can we use knowledge gained from youth language research to support youth and their communities in reclaiming endangered mother tongues?

> My mother grew up and saw the bad things that were done … over at the school …, punishing [students] for speaking their own language…. She didn't want us to go through that…. She spoke to us in English.
>
> *(parent interview, 2006)*

> I just want to learn [my Native language] real bad … because I think it is a big important part of my life if I am going to be a Native.
>
> *(Damen, youth interview, 2004)*

The statements above—the first by a Native American parent and the second by a 14-year-old Native youth—illuminate intergenerational dynamics of language shift and reclamation, situating those processes within the legacy of colonial schooling. The excerpts also suggest young people's desires to be full participants in their cultural communities—desires they link to learning their heritage mother tongue.

In this chapter we examine the language practices, repertoires, and ideologies of Native American youth, arguably the most crucial stakeholders in

Indigenous language futures. How are young people responding to dynamic situations of language shift? How is language use situated in the here and now (Bucholtz, 2002) of their everyday lives? What is the nature of youth's communicative repertoires? What ideologies about language do youth hold, and how do those ideologies influence their language practices? What can we learn from a closer look at youth language practices to inform community-driven language reclamation?

We begin by discussing findings from a 5-year (2001–2006) study undertaken at seven American Indian school-community sites in the southwestern United States. Within that discussion, we present narrative portraits crafted from in-depth interviews with youth that illuminate facets of the questions above. The portraits counter stereotypes of youth as disinterested in their heritage languages, even as they foreground the ideologically fraught sociolinguistic environments in which youth are growing up. The youth accounts lead us to consider another group of stakeholders—young adults—many of whom are young parents beginning to establish family language policies of their own. In the final part of the chapter, we relate the youth and young adult accounts to Simon Ortiz's (1992, 1994) notion of *cultural continuance*, a notion that pushes us to think beyond "saving" Indigenous languages, to (re)value the hybridity of youth communicative repertoires, and to build language regenesis efforts around that hybridity rather than deny or negate it, thereby fostering youth self-empowerment and enhanced possibilities for language revitalization.

Youth Language Practices, Ideologies, and Desires

About the Study

In the spring of 2001, with funding from the U.S. Department of Education, we embarked on a multi-year study of the impact of Native language shift and retention on American Indian students' language learning, identity formation and academic achievement.[2] Given the limited research on Indigenous youth language attitudes, ideologies, and practices, our goal was to investigate how language loss and revitalization are experienced on the ground by Native youth—and with what consequences for their language practices, identities, and school achievement.

We did not recruit research participants in the conventional sense, but instead worked with Indigenous communities with whom we had longstanding relationships through our years of work in Indigenous education. Seven school-community sites participated in the study, representing linguistic ecologies (Hornberger, 2003) in which intergenerational transmission of the Native language was still taking place (albeit at a diminishing rate), to those in which nearly all Indigenous-language speakers were beyond childbearing age, to cases in which only a few elderly Native-language speakers remained.

Reservation, urban-periphery, and urban-center settings were represented among the schools serving these communities, which together enrolled over 2,000 Native students in grades pre-K–12.

Over half the families in the study were living below federal poverty levels, and unemployment was extremely high—as much as 80% at some project sites. These economic disparities mirrored profound educational disparities. The high school completion rate among community members at project sites ranged from 33% to 51%—half the national average. All but two of the seven schools faced some form of corrective action under the federal No Child Left Behind (NCLB) Act of 2001.

Central to our research approach were principles of respect, reciprocity, responsibility, and relationship building discussed by Brayboy, Gough, Leonard, Roehl, and Solyom (2012) as fundamental to critical Indigenous research methodologies. We were especially concerned that the research serve "the needs of the [local] people … as well as … advance intellectual inquiries" (Brayboy et al., 2012, p. 435). Thus, at each site we worked closely with teams of Indigenous educators identified as community research collaborators (CRCs). The CRCs were both self-nominated and nominated by our primary site contacts (teachers, school administrators, parents). Altogether, 21 CRCs participated in the project. The CRCs facilitated entrée and access, co-constructed research protocols, and assisted with data collection. In ongoing dialogue sessions, they advised us on participant recruitment (including identifying the youth interviewees profiled here) and provided invaluable contextual information that guided data analysis and interpretation. In addition, the CRCs explicitly positioned themselves as change agents; their leadership guided local applications of the study's findings once the study ended.

We employed an ethnographic case study approach, making 80 site visits over 5 years to collect data, debrief and plan with the CRCs, and report back to tribal councils, school boards, and other stakeholders. Our data included demographic records, 1- to 3-hour audiotaped interviews with 168 adults and 62 children and youth in grades 3–12, sociolinguistic questionnaires (500) designed to elicit participants' language practices and attitudes, observation of language use and teaching, documents (lesson plans, school mission statements, etc.), and student achievement data. The qualitative data produced over 3,300 pages of single-spaced text. Of those data, the ethnographic interviews constitute the largest corpus, and this is the database examined here.

In structuring interviews, we adapted Seidman's (2006) three-interview sequence, condensing his tripartite format into single 60- to 120-minute interviews that included:

1. A focused life history, concentrating on participants' home-, school-, and community-based language learning experiences.

2. Details of the ways in which participants employed their communicative repertoires and their observations of others' language practices at home, in school, and within the community.

3. Participants' normative assessments of the role of families, community members, tribal governments, and local schools in language education planning.

Individually and in meetings of the university-based research team, we coded and organized the qualitative data using NVivo 7, a software tool for organizing, retrieving, and interpreting text data. (For more on the analysis procedures, see McCarty, Romero-Little, Warhol, & Zepeda, 2013, p. 163.) In site-based debriefing sessions, the CRCs provided feedback on the evolving study findings, which in turn informed the crafting of qualitative case studies for each site. Within each case study, the narrative profiles of youth language practices, competencies and beliefs or ideologies about language became focal points of the analysis.

As we have reported elsewhere (McCarty, Romero-Little, Warhol, & Zepeda, 2009), a core finding from this study was a pronounced difference between the perspectives on youth's language abilities, practices and beliefs held by adults, and those expressed and manifested by the youth themselves. Figure 2.1 compares educators' and youth's characterizations of students' home-community language environments. With the exception of Site 3, in which there were a significant number of child speakers of the Indigenous language, most educators reported that very few (0%–20%) of their students were likely to hear the Indigenous language spoken at home or in their communities. In contrast, many youth (47%–90%) reported hearing the Indigenous language spoken at home, at tribal events, and in various other contexts within their communities. Similarly, when we asked adults and youth to characterize youth's linguistic abilities, most educators reported that very few (0%–20%) of their students spoke an Indigenous language fluently, while youth described more hybrid, variegated language abilities (see Figure 2.2).

Similar differences were reflected in the interview data, with educators characterizing local Indigenous languages as largely absent from young people's lives and youth as often indifferent to learning their heritage language. At the same time, students were likely to be labeled as "limited English proficient" or "language delayed" because they spoke a variety of English influenced by the local Indigenous language, and because of their performance on English standardized tests. These labeling practices found their way into school curricula, where their certification in print often served to cement the notion that students' language practices constituted what Meek (2011) calls a logic of linguistic "dysfluency." The state-prescribed remediation was to intensify scripted English reading instruction, leading to the reduction or elimination of Indigenous language and culture instruction at several school sites. As one

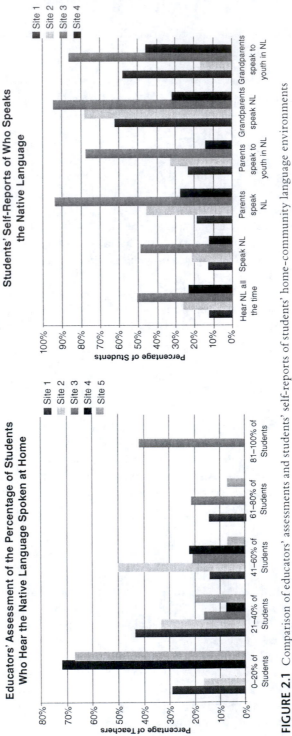

FIGURE 2.1 Comparison of educators' assessments and students' self-reports of students' home–community language environments (NL = Native American language).

CRC remarked, "All the [bilingual–bicultural] curriculum we developed went out the door" (field notes, February 17, 2004).

Yet, even as their language practices and communicative repertoires were often constructed as limited and a hindrance to school-defined success, the youth described dynamic sociolinguistic environments in which multiple linguistic varieties—one or more Indigenous language(s) and varieties of English and Spanish—were present but distributed unevenly among members of different age groups and households. As Figure 2.2 shows, most youth reported feeling most comfortable speaking English, but they also described being overhearers of some variety/ies of an Indigenous language—at home, at cultural events, and, in some cases, on local radio broadcasts. Some youth had entered school as primary speakers of an Indigenous language and/or Spanish, and some were learning to read and write a local Indigenous language as well. Most youth also expressed deep yearnings for the opportunity to become more capable users of their heritage mother tongue.

These sociolinguistic environments, then, were more accurately characterized as multilingual rather than bilingual, as youth were differentially exposed to multiple Indigenous languages, multiple Englishes, and in some cases multiple Spanishes. As we will discuss, these experiences of multilingualism complicate our understanding of language shift trajectories and the possibilities for Indigenous-language recovery.

The divergent youth and adult responses raise questions about the reasons underlying the differences. Were the adults simply unaware of what was occurring with regard to language in youth's lives (even though many adults were community members)? Were youth closeting their Indigenous-language abilities and desires—and if so, why? What was happening in these social contexts to influence young people's language practices and the perceptions of those practices by adults? Answering these questions, we believed, could shed new light on ways to enhance language education and Indigenous-language revitalization. With these goals in mind, we now present a sample of the youth narrative profiles. Although space prohibits a full exposition of our database, each profile illuminates facets of a larger case. We go first to the pseudonymous Black Foothills Unified School District.

Language Use at Black Foothills Community and School

The Black Foothills School District (all names are pseudonyms) is one of the largest urban public school districts in the United States. Within this school district one of our sites was Cactus High. Located in a working-class largely Latino and Native American neighborhood in a large metropolitan area, Cactus High enrolled over 1,600 students, of whom 11% (168) were identified as Native American, 67% (1,131) as Latino, 4% (69), as African American, and 17%

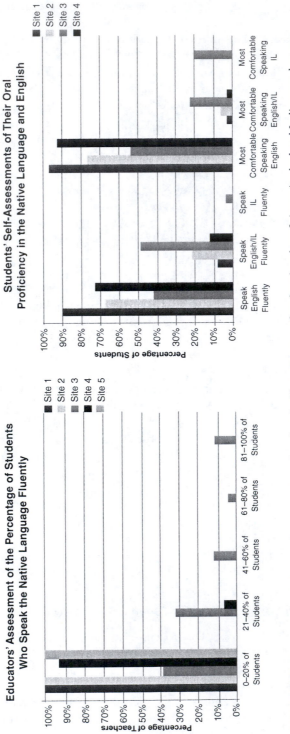

FIGURE 2.2 Comparison of educators' assessments and students' self-assessments of students' oral proficiency in the local Indigenous language (IL = Indigenous langage).

(287) as White. At Cactus High we heard from educators (who were mostly non-Native) that

> English is [students'] first language and everyone speaks English in the home ... there is just no [Indigenous language] in the family.
>
> *(interview, May 10, 2004)*

> [W]hen I have spoken to the families they have never mentioned that [the Indigenous language] is their native language ... so I don't believe that the kids ... are very familiar with or influenced by ... [the Indigenous language]—mostly ... English.
>
> *(interview, May 10, 2004)*

Introducing Nora.   Nora Valenzuela was an 18-year-old senior and softball star at Cactus High when we interviewed her in 2004. Nora's grandparents were survivors of the diaspora of Indigenous people who had fled northern Mexico in the wake of a scorched earth campaign that preceded the Mexican Revolution. (At the request of the tribe and to protect its privacy, we do not use the tribe's name or the name of its language.) Nora's grandparents' family had settled near an emerging urban area in the U.S. Southwest. Nora grew up hearing the stories of hardship endured in the diaspora, and through tribal summer programs she had visited the original towns in Mexico where many of her relatives still lived.

Nora's father worked for the tribe as a landscaper; her mother taught at the tribal preschool. As Nora was growing up, her mother "spoke [the Indigenous language] to us ... almost all the time, everyday," she said. Her father grew up with Spanish as a primary language and "just spoke to us in Spanish," Nora added. However, having been married to Nora's mother for many years, "he's starting to understand the [Indigenous] language."

Nora entered elementary school bilingual in the Indigenous language and Spanish, and understanding some English, "but I couldn't speak it well. So I had to go to some kind of tutoring ... It was ... difficult for me." Meanwhile, she related, "I started forgetting how to speak [the Indigenous language]..."

At home, at school, and in her cultural community, Nora moved fluidly between multiple linguistic systems; she was an adept "translanguager" (García, 2009). This interview excerpt illustrates Nora's interfamilial and intergenerational linguistic border crossing:

> To my brothers I use Spanish [but] my youngest [brother], he doesn't really understand Spanish, so I speak English with him, and with my mom and grandmother, it would be [the Indigenous language].
>
> *(interview, May 11, 2004)*

Moreover, Nora articulated a clear understanding of the language pragmatics of her household and community, as this response to our interview question illustrates:

Interviewer: Your parents—when they visit with people their own age, do you notice if they have a preference [for the languages they use]?

Nora: My dad speaks English when he is working landscaping ..., and my mom speaks both languages, English and [the Indigenous language], 'cause her co-workers ... all speak the [Indigenous] language. But if they were to go outside [the community], like to conferences, they would speak English.

(interview, May 11, 2004)

Introducing Vaida.   Vaida King was Nora's close friend, a member of the same cultural community and a trumpeter in a well-known mariachi band. The two girls had gone to school together since elementary school. Vaida's father also worked in landscaping; her mother worked at home, caring for her grandchildren.

Vaida reported that her "first language is Spanish and ... that was the main language spoken around the house ... except for English when we would use it from time to time...." Her maternal grandmother and her father's family spoke the Indigenous language but "overall," Vaida reiterated, "I've never really heard it [at home]" (interview, May 11, 2004).

Vaida entered elementary school bilingual in Spanish and English; English "was not difficult for me," she said, "because I pretty much really knew it." With her peers she spoke Spanish, although, as she said, "English or Spanish, no difference." Like Nora, Vaida articulated a clear understanding of the tacit language policies within her community: "Yeah, ... some people, they will communicate in Spanish, but if they have to go somewhere, say for an interview or to meet someone, they would speak English" (interview, May 11, 2004).

Prior to the implementation of NCLB, the feeder schools for Cactus High offered instructional programs in the Indigenous language taught by teaching assistants from the Native American community. Vaida and Nora had participated in these programs, and both expressed disappointment that the classes had been canceled when their language teachers were determined to lack the NCLB "highly qualified" credentials—an associate's degree or equivalent. Although they were esteemed elders in their community—a revered group of multilingual culture-bearers—they did not possess the NCLB-required certification and were therefore dismissed from the school district or reassigned to low-level clerical positions.

Asked whether schools with significant Native American enrollments should offer Native language and culture instruction, Vaida insisted that "It is something of our own that we should know." Recalling the hardships of the diaspora, she added: "Our ancestors had to sacrifice to get us here ... [This is] our entire history and culture … we appreciate what our people had to deal with" (interview, May 11, 2004).

Both Vaida and Nora worried that their heritage language was in danger of falling silent; according to census data, a little over 100 individuals within their cultural community reported speaking the Indigenous language at home, and most were beyond child-bearing age. "[There are] only certain people who know the language," Vaida pointed out:

> What would happen if those people become deceased? I think [the Indigenous language] is a very precious thing, and that they [tribal citizens] should know—I should know.
>
> *(interview, May 11, 2004)*

Vaida and Nora were not alone in expressing a yearning for their heritage language, or in the sociolinguistic dexterity they evidenced. We go now to another school community in our study, which we call Ak Wijid.

Language Use at Ak Wijid Community and School

The K–8 Ak Wijid School is located just outside another major metropolitan area, within a Native American nation that includes multiple Indigenous-language groups. Flanked by mountains, the community is bisected by an expansive floodplain. Once a primary source of livelihood for the Native peoples of the region, the river was diverted for irrigation by White farmers in the early 20th century. This had life-altering ramifications for Native families, as they were forced to relocate near irrigable land or to seek off-reservation wage labor. As individuals were pulled into a cash economy, traditional village structures were dissolved, setting the stage for the breakdown of intergenerational language transmission. These historical experiences and the imposition of English-only mission schools a century earlier served to "tip" (Dorian, 1981) community language use toward English.

Introducing Damen.   Damen Johns was a 14-year-old eighth grader attending Ak Wijid Middle School. A class president and star three-point basketball shooter, he had recently been named Most Valuable Player of his school's basketball team. Damen aspired to go to the nearby public university and one day to play for the National Basketball Association.

Damen was from a family of well-known Indigenous artisans, and his grandparents were among a handful of Indigenous-language speakers. Damen's mother had grown up hearing her parents' language but, in light of their experience as mission school survivors, they had socialized their children in English. As a consequence, Damen's mother rarely used the Indigenous language with her children at home. "I really don't hear her [speak the language]," Damen said, adding that his mother was nevertheless appreciative of his and his sisters' efforts to learn the Indigenous language at school: "[S]he will listen to us ... or I will go home and tell her what I learned and she will ask me what certain words mean, ... and I tell her" (interview, June 1, 2004).

Damen's mother was raising Damen and his two sisters as a single parent, and because she worked full-time outside the home, Damen had spent his early years going "back and forth," in his words, between his mother's and his maternal grandparents' households. There, he was exposed to his heritage language.

Damen was growing up in an environment that included his maternal grandparents' native language as well as a linguistically unrelated Indigenous language that was the heritage language of his father. The community's agricultural base had drawn farmworkers from Mexico, and northern Mexican Spanish was part of Damen's sociolinguistic environment. In addition, because the community bordered a sprawling metropolitan area and had been the object of extended missionization, English had a prominent if conflicted role in the community's sociolinguistic ecology as well.

Damen's primary language was English, but he was growing up within earshot (Pye, 1992) of multiple languages and language varieties. Although his Indigenous-language abilities were admittedly weak, he emphasized repeatedly that

> I want to learn it real bad ... I just want to learn my language because I think it is a big important part of my life if I am going to be a Native.
> *(interview, June 1, 2004)*

Damen, Nora, and Vaida were raised in Indigenous communities situated near or within large urban areas. In the next ethnographic vignette, we go to a different setting—a community we call Beautiful Mountain.

Language Use at Beautiful Mountain Community and School

The pre-K–12 Beautiful Mountain Community School is situated on a high plateau within the southwestern United States. A two-lane highway leads into the community, cutting through sage- and juniper-covered foothills that abut the pseudonymous Beautiful Mountain. On a typical weekday morning the road to Beautiful Mountain is busy with school buses, pick-up trucks, and cars on their way to work and school. At the time of the study, the community included 89 families and 113 households. Near the school lies a complex of school facilities and dormitories, clusters of modern housing, a store, and a church.

According to census data gathered at the time of our study, a majority of Beautiful Mountain community members spoke Navajo at home. However, according to the adults we interviewed, most speakers were older adults and elders. As one educator described students' linguistic repertoires: "I would say about half of my [students] understand [Navajo] but are not able to speak it" (interview, September 19, 2002).

Introducing Jonathan. At Beautiful Mountain we met Jonathan Nez, a 16-year-old ninth grader when we interviewed him in the spring of 2004. Jonathan had grown up with Navajo as his first language and he entered school having little exposure to English.

Interviewer: So you were saying that your early school experiences with a Native-speaking teacher didn't instill in you a good feeling about your language—

Jonathan: No they didn't ... That [teacher] didn't know how to ... bring out that kind of—I don't know, that kind of pride and the continuation of the language in a positive sense ... And she was mainly forcing us to learn English ... it was a real confusing time, I guess.

(interview, May 6, 2004)

Jonathan related these early language-learning experiences to "what I like to call the Long Walk Syndrome," a reference to the Navajo people's forced relocation (the Long Walk) to a federal concentration camp at Fort Sumner, New Mexico, in the winter of 1863–64. Jonathan spoke of the "inherited trauma" of that historic time, which "goes from generation to generation," leading some contemporary youth to deny their Indigeneity. "You forsake who you are to accommodate the mainstream life," Jonathan declared (interview, May 6, 2004).

Not long after the Navajos' release from federal imprisonment, a different kind of Long Walk ensued, as children were forcibly removed from their families and taken to distant boarding schools. "They [government officials] took the children away from their families at a young age," Jonathan reflected, "and they instilled this image that is still alive—this image of self-hate" (interview, May 6, 2004).

Jonathan's account brings into sharp focus the rebounding impacts of oppressive language policies within contemporary youth language practices and trajectories. "It's being told that [the Indigenous language] is stupid," Jonathan said, "to speak Indian is the way of the devil." At the same time, Jonathan expressed a strong attachment to his native language: "[H]aving [Navajo] as my first language ... helps not lose the identity of who I am, of where I come from..." (interview, May 6, 2004).

Lessons about Language from Native American Youth

There is much in these youth accounts to help us understand youth's language ideologies and practices, and the sociolinguistic environments they negotiate each day. Certainly the accounts counter popular notions of youth as disinterested or as simply abandoning their heritage languages and cultures in favor of "powerful" English (cf. McCarty & Wyman, 2009). The accounts also challenge the binaries that continue to populate the scholarly and popular discourse on language loss and revitalization:

- Speaker versus non-speaker—what constitutes speakerhood in these settings?
- Fluent versus non-fluent—what does it mean to say an individual speaks a language fluently, and how do perceptions of fluency influence efforts at language recovery in endangered-language communities?
- Extinct versus living with reference to languages—when is an allegedly dying or extinct language really only sleeping (Leonard, 2011), and what can be done to awaken sleeping languages among younger generations?

The youth accounts also provide a nuanced understanding of the often closeted communicative repertoires of youth, and the on-the-ground, minute-by-minute pressures influencing their language choices. Most importantly, the data attest to significant, if latent, resources for language reclamation—resources that may go undetected, unappreciated, and even stigmatized by the schools in which youth spend so much of their lives.

In all the youth accounts, there are implicit and explicit identity connections across a web of extended kin networks, including older siblings and out-of-school young adults. While we had designed our research protocols to tap into language practices and ideologies across multiple generations, we did not, initially, fully appreciate the significance of the families' language policies (King, Fogle, & Logan-Terry, 2008) that the interview data would reveal. It was well into the data analysis that we realized that, in order to understand language in the lives of the school-age youth whom we interviewed, we needed to look more closely at their accounts in light of those of older siblings and family members—that is, those who self-identified and whom their communities recognized as young adults. The next section considers those data.

Young Adults "in the Middle"

There are 33 interviews with Native American young adults in our database. In terms of chronological age, these individuals, at the time of the research, were in their 20s and early 30s. Although in some cases they were only a few years older than the school-age youth we interviewed, these young people held adult status in their communities by virtue of their increasing social and economic independence within community social networks. Some held staff positions in the schools attended by the adolescents we interviewed. Some were attending college, and many were young parents beginning to raise families of their own. Like the adolescents, the language profiles of these young adults reflect the histories and circumstances of their respective communities. However, across all young adult accounts there were two readily discernible themes: an expressed feeling of (1) being "in the middle," between generations of older language users and adolescents with less Native-language exposure and ability; and (2) responsibility for helping to secure the linguistic and cultural futures of their communities. As one 32-year-old educator and mother-to-be put it:

> I see our language as ... our bridge to our history ... I want to encourage my community [and] all [Native] families to perpetuate that ... I want to do all that I can so that [youth] at least have something and can identify themselves as [Native].
>
> *(interview, September 19, 2002)*

Four Young Adult Vignettes

Introducing Darrell.   Darrell Tsosie was 25 and a fourth-grade teacher assistant at Beautiful Mountain when we interviewed him in 2002. Darrell grew up in what he described as a traditional family, "herding sheep and taking care of animals [livestock]" and being "taught by my grandparents [in] a hooghan [a traditional Navajo dwelling] we all lived in." Darrell described his early language socialization:

Interviewer: And you were raised in [the] Navajo language?
Darrell: Yes, I was raised in Navajo language.... I had a lot of cousins and my grandma ... and we all used to communicate in Navajo.... I'm still speaking Navajo.

> *(interview, October 17, 2002)*

Exposed to English for the first time when he entered kindergarten, Darrell nonetheless remembered it being "easy" to learn: "I think it was easy for me to learn both languages, English and Navajo," he said.

Darrell had two young sons, the oldest of whom attended Beautiful Mountain preschool. "I'm going to teach him the way I was taught to speak Navajo," Darrell told us. "I'm not ashamed to speak my language," he insisted; "I love my language" (interview, October 17, 2002).

Yet, Darrell admitted to struggling with "which way to go" in working out a family language policy at home. "[R]ight now I'm just ... right in the middle—right in the middle," he reiterated:

> And I don't know which way to go ... So I'm just like caught in the middle.... Because ... what if my son just learns nothing but Navajo? And if they gave him a paper like this [holding up a worksheet], he's not going to [be able to] read it ... So I hate to say it, but ... like I said, it's just really confusing to me. I mean I'm just right in the middle.
>
> *(interview, October 17, 2002)*

Asked to project the future of his mother tongue, Darrell worried that "it's gradually fading away"—an expression echoed throughout the young adult interviews. At the same time, he implied that the responsibility for language continuity "is upon us"—his generation, he said.

Introducing Naysa.   Naysa Begay was Darrell's contemporary, 28 years old, and the mother of two young girls when we interviewed her in 2003. Naysa, who worked as a program assistant at Beautiful Mountain School, came from a prominent family of bilingual educators. Her grandparents on both sides were esteemed community elders and strong Navajo speakers. Naysa had been raised in a largely English-speaking household, though, as her stepfather did not speak the language and "we just got used to not speaking Navajo at home" (interview, December 12, 2003). Fortunately, Naysa had the opportunity to study Navajo in her school's bilingual education program and was surrounded by the language within her larger community. At 28, she considered herself a proficient speaker, reader, and writer of the language.

Naysa recognized that many of her students hid their Native-speaking ability for the very reasons that Jonathan had suggested, noting that as a young adult her high school-age students had been "really surprised to hear me talk Navajo." She used her position to encourage students to "open up" in Navajo, telling them to "be proud that you speak Navajo!" (interview, December 12, 2003).

In contrast to Darrell, Naysa felt "caught in the middle" in a different way; she worried that her own daughters "are not knowing as much [Navajo] and I'm afraid that it's just ... going down with each generation.... That kind of scares me." She was determined to establish a "mostly Navajo" language policy at home:

> I always talk to [my daughters] in Navajo ... because I just don't want to *not* do anything at all.... I'm going to make sure my kids pick it up.
>
> *(interview, December 12, 2003)*

However, Naysa admitted, it was an uphill battle: "I always tell my girls that when they get about my age, ... they're going to wish they knew Navajo" (interview, December 12, 2003).

Introducing Sabrina.   Sabrina López was 25 when we interviewed her in 2003. A member of Nora's and Vaida's cultural community, Sabrina lived an hour's drive from that community, working as a teacher at Damen's school. Sabrina's first language was Spanish. She recalled feeling "caught between the two—English, all English, or bilingual and ESL—as a child growing up." Entering kindergarten, "it was either swim or drown inside the classroom" (interview, May 14, 2003).

Sabrina's parents were teachers, as were her aunts. Her father spoke the Indigenous language and her mother "knows a little bit, not as much as my dad," but "for some reason they [her parents and grandparents] never taught us," she said.

> I know they talked amongst each other and the elders in our home … in our Native language, but never to us. My parents and my grandparents, within their school, were hit if they spoke any other language besides English. So I have cousins and uncles who never taught their kids even Spanish because of what happened to them in school.
>
> *(interview, May 14, 2003)*

Sabrina was an active participant in her Indigenous nation's cultural and religious ceremonies, which she believed required knowledge of the Indigenous language.

> I think, what are all of these young people—including my children and even my peers—what are they understanding of the ceremony if they don't understand the language we're talking or the prayers we're saying? … [W]hat are they comprehending?
>
> *(interview, May 14, 2003)*

To be a "full participant" in her cultural community, Sabrina had "gone back to school to learn my [Indigenous] language." Her own family language policy was to use Spanish and the Indigenous language at home:

> I'm very confident that my kids will all learn English in school, and I don't have to worry about that part. My daughter's first language was Spanish, and when she went to school she did not know a word of English. Not one word…. But by the end of that school year, she didn't speak [Spanish] any more…. She'd answer me in English. So I force my kids to respond to me in Spanish, or to speak it, or to ask for something in Spanish or [the Indigenous language] before they get what they want.
>
> *(interview, May 14, 2003)*

With her grandparents, she added, "It's hard for them … just to speak to us in Spanish, and … I have to remind them to talk to me in [the Indigenous language] because we need that practice."

Introducing Gabriela.   The final profile we will present is of Gabriela Ramírez, aged 30 when we interviewed her in 2003. Like Sabrina, Gabriela was a member of Nora's and Vaida's cultural community but was teaching at Damen's school. Her maternal grandmother had been part of the diaspora; her father had relocated voluntarily and more recently from Sonora, Mexico.

As a child, Gabriela had begun to learn the Indigenous language from her maternal grandmother, who passed away when Gabriela was 10. "And there's just a few words that I remember," Gabriela said, "but after my *nana* died, there was nobody around [to teach the language]." Her parents, she explained, "speak a little,... but they can't hold a conversation or anything." Gabriela's first language was Spanish: "[I]n the home we always spoke Spanish, ... and when we were out with friends or playing outside ... what we always spoke was Spanish ... I don't remember hearing [the Indigenous language] when I was a kid, other than my *nana*" (interview, May 28, 2003).

At the time of our interview, Gabriela had three children, aged three, four, and nine. What she desired for her children, as well as her Native students "is for them not to lose their culture and ... help them, ... value it, keep it, never want to lose it." For that to happen, she admitted, "we [young adults] also need to be taught." Gabriela felt "caught in the middle" in yet another way; she desperately longed for the support of elder speakers so that she and her contemporaries could fulfill what she perceived as their responsibility to future generations. "We haven't really been taught," Gabriela reiterated. She closed her interview with this reflection on her position in a larger cultural community:

> Our elders [are the primary speakers of the Indigenous language]. And we have ... a growing [age group]—well, I'm 30—that are interested now in learning the language.... I'm thinking of us that went to school around the same time and have kids ... we have an interest and we now have our kids [to teach]. I think our language would flourish again, you know, because I see the interest coming, being here again.
>
> *(interview, May 28, 2003)*

Toward Linguistic and Cultural Continuance

We began this study with a central question: What can we learn about language loss and reclamation by attending closely to the experiences and perspectives of Indigenous youth? We believed it was important to focus on youth—and, as the research process evolved, on young adults—because their voices have been noticeably absent from scholarly inquiry into language loss and revitalization, and often from the language planning process itself. This inquiry into young people's lives led inescapably to their and their communities' linguistic genealogies. The stories underlying these genealogies are not easy, as they interweave with rebounding legacies of colonization, genocide, and racial and linguistic discrimination.

In some cases—notably Nora's, Vaida's, Sabrina's, and Gabriela's—young people struggle to sustain multiple heritage languages which have been stigmatized in their own and their elders' schooling. Consider, for example, Sabrina's experience in which family members who had been exposed to both the Indigenous language and Spanish "never taught their kids even Spanish because of what happened to them in school." In these multilingual families it may seem easier to focus on the heritage language with greater social currency—Spanish in this case—yet it is important to note that Sabrina resisted this kind of linguistic triage. At the time of the study she was taking courses in her Indigenous heritage language and urging elders "to talk to me in [the Indigenous language]" so that she could "participate fully" in her multilingual community.

Finding ways to confront a barrage of false binaries and mixed messages (Lee, 2009) about the value of Indigenous languages is a theme that percolates throughout these young people's accounts. Consider Darrell, for instance, who stated that he "loved" his native language and that learning English as a second language came easily for him in school. Darrell nevertheless worried that his own children faced an either-or choice: Learn English and succeed according to Western standards, or learn Navajo and be left behind. On a daily basis, virtually every societal message these young people receive, "from the language privileged in their print environment, in the media, and via technology to overt and covert schooling practices … conveys the supremacy of English" (McCarty et al., 2009, p. 303). As we see in these accounts, young people take up these messages in different ways—resisting, accommodating, and sometimes, as Jonathan poignantly described, feeling compelled to "forsake who they are."

In our attempts to come to grips with these conflicting language ideologies and what they might mean for language recovery, we have been inspired by Simon Ortiz's notion of *continuance*. As he writes in his book, *Woven Stone*—a reference to his father's craft as a stone mason but also a metaphor for the crisscrossing connections between generations within Indigenous communities—continuance is "something more than memory or remembering" and also more than an abstract or "romanticized future that is impractical": "We must not forsake the present reality of our continuing lives," Ortiz says (1992, pp. 9, 32; see also Dunsmore, 2009).

Applied to the project of language reclamation, continuance pushes beyond the false binaries of Indigenous-language-versus-English, speaker-versus-nonspeaker, fluent-versus-nonfluent, reminding us that reclaiming a language is not about bringing it back to some rarified, purified state, but rather moving it forward into ever-evolving sociolinguistic domains (Hornberger & King, 1996). The data reported here strongly indicate that this needs to be a whole-community effort that acknowledges the dysjuncts as well as the bonds across and within generations, the sources of the dysjuncts within colonizing histories, and the present reality and continuing lives of all community members—including youth and young adults. This means acknowledging the hybridity of young people's communicative repertoires, the heteroglossia of their sociolinguistic environments (Deloria, 2011; García, 2009), and the pressures and mixed messages (Lee, 2009) they encounter as they negotiate their self-identifications and family language policies. The mixed messages, we believe, can be reframed and even erased when hybridity and heteroglossia are constructed as *resources* for language reclamation, rather than as markers of limitation and shame.

These ideological and pedagogic transformations are being effected by the CRCs at some of our school-community study sites, where Native-language immersion and family language classes are being vigorously implemented. These efforts recognize, as Lee (2007) points out, that language regenesis activities must connect directly with the contemporary lives of Native American youth. Such transformations are also represented by a larger youth movement for linguistic and cultural continuance. We close with a few illustrations of that movement.

For more than a decade, 800 Native American students from several states have gathered each summer for a 2-day Native American Youth Language Fair at the University of Oklahoma (UO). The fair provides a public forum for youth to use their Native languages. According to Mary Linn, curator of Native American languages at UO, the fair gives an incentive "for the students to work toward through the year as they learn their languages," encouraging them and their teachers as they have the opportunity "to interact with so many others who are learning their Native languages":

> They can see how important it is to Native people all across the country and how many people are working together to help prevent languages from being lost.
>
> *(Linn, cited in* Indian Country Today, *2011, para. 4)*

Each summer since 2009, 10 Shoshone/Goshute high school students from Idaho, Utah, and Nevada—the self-described "future guardians" of the mutually intelligible Shoshone and Goshute dialects—have participated in a 6-week residential internship with Shoshone master teachers and elders at the University of Utah's Center for American Indian Languages (Brunden, 2009, para. 1). The Shoshone effort is noteworthy because youth and elder speakers are undertaking language documentation to create new language learning materials, including books, films, and a Shoshone/Goshute talking dictionary. They then "share these materials with elementary-aged learners of the language when they return home" (Center for American Indian Languages, 2011, para. 5).

On the Fort Mojave reservation in California and Arizona, Mojave teens are working with adult language learners and a core group of elders to document Mojave bird songs—social songs that are integral to Mojave orature and that are traditionally sung by males and accompanied by female singers or *hapuk*. The single fluent male Mojave bird song singer, Hubert McCord, is 84 years old. "[W]hat we are fighting to preserve and revitalize [is] our Mojave identity," says Natalie Diaz, director of the Mojave Language Recovery Program (cited in Zrioka, 2012, para. 22). In addition to documenting the bird songs, summer camps and after-school activities aim to provide youth with basic conversational abilities in the language. "We want to let young people … write it, … text in it,… Facebook in it," says Diaz, who is a young-adult Mojave language learner and teacher herself (cited in Zrioka, 2012, para. 20).

In Santa Fe, New Mexico, a group known as the "young ancestors"—Pueblo high school students attending Santa Fe Preparatory School—is working on a project co-sponsored by their school and the Santa Fe-based Indigenous Language Institute to "integrate the way we live with the way we talk and think" (Camino Vérité Films, 2012). Using a self-taught course for which they (ironically) receive foreign language credit, these Native students and their mentor, reading teacher Laura Jogles, have "established a little community where it [is] safe to learn the language" (Camino Vérité Films, 2012). "This isn't something where we dress up for a day or two ... and play Indian for a day," states Jeremy Montoya, a senior in the class of 2012; "we're serious about it" (Camino Vérité Films, 2012).

All of these are significant acts of youth self-empowerment aimed at repatriating languages of heritage in their lives, their families and their communities. These acts of language reclamation, while important locally, are also part of a global movement in which youth "are transforming their visibility by engaging in new forms of cultural production" (Kral, 2011, p. 5). Writing of these efforts for an Aboriginal youth media movement in Australia, Kral notes that youth "take on the role of 'expert,'" constructing identities not simply as learners, but as knowledgeable, capable citizens of mobile local, national, and global communities (2011, pp. 6, 11).

The research examined here, along with that of many others, shows Indigenous youth and young adults to be informed, thoughtful, critically conscious, and vested stakeholders in Native-language futures. Moreover, they are making language policy in their everyday social practice—sometimes in resistance to wider English-only discourses, and sometimes in ways that are likely to yield further language shift. We argue, then, that youth should be at the center of our LPP research, and, even more importantly, at the heart of the activism informed by that research. "I want to share my language with little kids," a high school senior told us, because "[t]heir family probably [doesn't speak the Native language] to them, and it would be best for them to know how to speak it" (interview, May 5, 2004).

To fulfill these goals, we believe that it is necessary to "recalibrate" expectations for youth language practices and competencies (Meek, 2011, p. 56), making room for a wide range of varieties and fluencies. It is also important for youth and young adults, including young parents, to have the support of more powerful authorizing agents—their elders, especially—as well as their Indigenous nations, communities, and schools. This positions youth to build on their total communicative repertoires and to construct linguistic identities in terms of success and accomplishment rather than limits and attrition. Such an approach also positions youth as both language learners and language planners—a forward-looking orientation that bodes well for the prospect of cultural continuance.

Acknowledgments

We express sincere gratitude to the CRCs and the young people who partici-pated in this research. We hope we have faithfully represented your experi-ences, your concerns, and your hopes for your community's and your own linguistic and cultural futures. We also thank Julie Weise of California State University Long Beach for raising important questions on the work that caused us to expand our analysis and its implications for language renewal. Thanks to Inée Slaughter of the Indigenous Language Institute and Rebecca Allahyari of the School for Advanced Research, both in Santa Fe, New Mexico, for call-ing the Young Ancestors project to our attention. Finally, many thanks to our colleague and co-editor Leisy Wyman, for extensive insightful feedback on an earlier draft of this chapter. Any remaining errors and limitations are our own.

Notes

1 This chapter is slightly modified from McCarty, Romero-Little, Warhol, and Zepeda (2013); used with permission of Multilingual Matters.
2 At the request of the Internal Review Board (IRB) that sanctioned the Native Language Shift and Retention Study from 2005 to 2007, we include this disclaimer: All data, state-ments, opinions or implications in this discussion of the study solely reflect the view of the authors and research participants, and do not necessarily reflect the views of the funding agency, tribes or their tribal councils, the Arizona Board of Regents or Arizona State University (ASU), under whose auspices the project operated. This information is pre-sented in the pursuit of academic research and is published in this volume solely for educa-tional and research purposes. Pursuant to our agreement with ASU's IRB, this chapter may not be reproduced in any medium, transmitted or distributed, in whole or in part, without the authors' prior written consent.

References

Bucholtz, M. (2002). Youth and cultural practice. *Annual Review of Anthropology, 31*, 525–552.

Brayboy, B. M. J., Gough, H. R., Leonard, B., Roehl, R. F. II, & Solyom, J. A. (2012). Reclaim-ing scholarship: Critical Indigenous research methodologies. In S. D. Lapan, M. T. Quar-taroli, & F. J. Riemer (Eds.), *Qualitative research: An introduction to methods and designs* (pp. 423–450). San Francisco, CA: Jossey-Bass.

Brunden, J. (2009, July 19). Ten teens study to guard their native language. National Public Radio *Weekend Edition*. Retrieved June 12, 2012, from http://www.npr.org/templates/story/story.php?storyid=106783656

Camino Vérité Films. (2012). *The young ancestors*. Retrieved June 26, 2012, from http://www.theyoungancestors.com/TheYoungAncestors/Home.html

Center for American Indian Languages. (2011). Shoshone/Goshute Youth Language Appren-ticeship Program. SYLAP 2011. Retrieved May 30, 2012, from http://www.cail.utah.edu/?pageid=5750

Deloria, P. J. (2011). On leaking languages and categorical imperatives. *American Indian Culture and Research Journal, 35*(2), 173–181.

Dorian, N. C. (1981). *Language death: The life cycle of a Scottish Gaelic dialect*. Philadelphia: Univer-sity of Pennsylvania Press.

Dunsmore, R. (2009). Simon Ortiz and the lyricism of continuance: "For the sake of the people, for the sake of the land." In S. B. Brill de Ramírez & E. Zuni Lucero (Eds.), *Simon J. Ortiz: A poetic legacy of Indigenous continuance* (pp. 205–212). Albuquerque: University of New Mexico Press.

García, O. (2009). *Bilingual education in the 21st century: A global perspective.* Malden, MA: Wiley-Blackwell.

Hornberger, N. H. (Ed.). (2003). *Continua of biliteracy: An ecological framework for educational policy, research, and practice in multilingual settings.* Clevedon, England: Multilingual Matters.

Hornberger, N. H., & King, K. A. (1996). Bringing the language forward: School-based initiatives for Quechua language revitalization in Ecuador and Bolivia. In N. H. Hornberger (Ed.), *Indigenous literacies in the Americas: Language planning from the bottom up* (pp. 299–319). Berlin, Germany: Mouton de Gruyter.

Indian Country Today. (2011, June 22). Native American students helping preserve language. Retrieved May 10, 2012 from http://Indiancountrytodaymedianetwork.com/2011/06/22/native-american-students-helping-preserve-language-39595

King, K. A., Fogle, L., & Logan-Terry, (2008). Family language policy. *Language and Linguistics Compass, 2*(5), 907–922.

Kral, I. (2011). Youth media as cultural practice: Remote Indigenous youth speaking out loud. *Australian Aboriginal Studies. Journal of the Australian Institute of Aboriginal and Torres Strait Islander Studies, 1,* 4–16.

Lee, T. S. (2007). "If they want Navajo to be learned, then they should require it in all schools": Navajo teenagers' experiences, choices, and demands regarding Navajo language. *Wicazo Sa Review,* Spring, 7–33.

Lee, T. S. (2009). Language, identity, and power: Navajo and Pueblo young adults' perspectives and experiences with competing language ideologies. *Journal of Language, Identity, and Education, 8*(5), 307–320.

Leonard, W. Y. (2011). Challenging "extinction" through modern Miami language practices. *American Indian Culture and Research Journal, 35*(2), 135–160.

McCarty, T. L., Romero-Little, M. E., Warhol, L., & Zepeda, O. (2009). Indigenous youth as language policymakers. *Journal of Language, Identity, and Education, 8*(5), 291–306.

McCarty, T. L., Romero-Little, M.E., Warhol, L., & Zepeda, O. (2013). Language in the lives of Indigenous youth. In T. L. McCarty (Ed.), *Language planning and policy in Native America — History, theory, praxis* (pp. 156–181). Bristol, England: Multilingual Matters.

McCarty, T. L., & Wyman, L. T. (2009). Introduction: Indigenous youth and bilingualism — Theory, research, praxis. *Journal of Language, Identity, and Education, 8*(5), 279–290.

Meek, B. A. (2011). Failing American Indian languages. *American Indian Culture and Research Journal, 35*(2), 43–60.

Ortiz, S. J. (1992). *Woven stone.* Tucson: University of Arizona Press.

Ortiz, S. J. (1994). The language we know. In P. Riley (Ed.), *Growing up Native American: An anthology* (pp. 29–38). New York, NY: Morrow.

Pye, C. (1992). Language loss among the Chilcotin. *International Journal of the Sociology of Language, 93,* 75–86.

Seidman, I. E. (2006). *Interviewing as qualitative research* (3rd ed.). New York, NY: Teachers College Press.

Zrioka, P. (2012, April 10). Cultural conservation: Keeping Indigenous languages alive. *Cultural Survival Quarterly.* Retrieved June 11, 2012 from http://www.culturalsurvival.org/news/cultural-conservation-keeping-indigenous-languages-alive

3

JUST KEEP EXPANDING OUTWARDS

Embodied Space as Cultural Critique in the Life and Work of a Navajo Hip Hop Artist

Brendan H. O'Connor and Gilbert Brown

This case study of Jay, a Navajo hip hop artist, focuses on the back-and-forth movement between the local and the global that characterizes the identity performances of many Indigenous youth, and documents how youth bring global cultural and linguistic flows, like hip hop, to bear on their relationships to particular places and the people who inhabit them. Our multimodal analysis incorporates Jay's everyday spoken and gestural practice, along with elements of his hip hop performance and ethnographic detail about his involvement in hip hop. We use the concept of embodied space to capture how a particular young Diné man interacts with enduring realities of place that influence how others see and read his innovative stylistic practice. His example demonstrates that youth may see "dynamic" forms of bilingualism as culturally and ideologically compatible with "recursive" forms (García, this volume), even as they use dynamic practices to subvert others' expectations about their place-based identities.

Language activism is often tied to the persistence of Indigenous senses of place, the "geographies of social meaning and identity" (McCarty, Nicholas, & Wyman, 2012, p. 51) that ground individuals' lived experience in a people's cultural history, as manifested in particular localities, natural processes, land-use practices, and features of landscape (e.g., Basso, 1996). Recent work on Indigenous youth's linguistic practice has also emphasized the human-centered processes by which places come to be seen as meaningful, as well as the malleability of place-based meanings (Nicholas, 2009; Teves, 2011; Wyman, 2012). Along with community language and cultural resources, many Indigenous youth use globally-circulating forms of popular culture in locally specific ways to make sense of place, as they come to understand Indigenous identity in concert with transnational cultural flows and movements, like hip hop, that can be used to link local histories of racism and exploitation across national boundaries (Ballivían & Herrera, 2012; Pennycook & Mitchell, 2009).

In this chapter, we consider how Jay (Jamie Brown), an underground Navajo (Diné) MC (hip hop artist) and producer, interacts with enduring realities of place that influence how others interpret his innovative stylistic practice. Using the concept of embodied space, we analyze everyday speech and gesture alongside performance elements and ethnographic data, and demonstrate that youth may see dynamic forms of bilingualism, flexible and ever adjusting to 21st-century terrain, as culturally and ideologically compatible with recursive forms handed down from previous generations (García, this volume). We also show how youth acknowledge the places where they come of age as "culturally meaningful terrestrial ... region(s)" (Munn, 1996, p. 465) even as they use innovative practices to subvert others' expectations about their place-based identities. Reflecting deeply on Jay's music and conversations with Jay, we offer this chapter as a productive opportunity to explore the multiple and inter-semiotic ways that Native youth recruit global linguistic flows (Alim, 2009a) into their local and translocal projects of place-making.

Space, Place, and the Body

Theorizations of culturally specific senses of place have sometimes character-ized places as pauses in movement through space. Each pause, and the accom-panying opportunity to get intimately acquainted with a particular location, "makes it possible for location to be transformed into place" (Tuan, 1977, p. 6). Barnhardt and Kawagley (2005, pp. 11–12) give a detailed account of the natu-ral "regularities" and "unseen patterns of order" that have come to form (and inform) Indigenous worldviews and knowledge systems, due to long histories of Indigenous peoples' learning to "decipher and adapt" to the ever-changing world around them (see also Deloria, 2003). Indigenous knowledge systems are, in great part, "encoded in and expressed through local languages" developed as "ways of living and making a living within particular locales" (McCarty, Bor-goiakova, Gilmore, Lomawaima, & Romero, 2005, p. 2). This sense of place is important for upholding the value of traditional linguistic and cultural practices that, despite having endured through centuries of colonization and genocide, are even now "under assault" by hegemonic globalizing influences (McCarty, 2003, p. 147). Still, researchers who advocate this sense of place also recognize that "there are real relations with real content, economic, political, cultural, between any local place and the wider world in which it is set" (Massey, 1993, p. 67).

Our analysis focuses on the real relations between local places and the wider world, and on the back-and-forth movement between the local and the global that characterizes the identity performances of Native youth with "multiple lev-els of cultural access, participation, and knowledge" (Lee, 2009, p. 318). Thus, it is useful to conceive of place as "constructed out of particular interactions and mutual articulations of social relations, social processes, experiences, and understandings" (Massey, 1993, p. 67). Working with this sense of embodied space, we strive to keep people's interactions and activities at the center of our investigations of what space and place mean to them (Munn, 1996). Low (2009, p. 29, citing Pred, 1986) urges us to think about the relationship between culturally meaningful places and the human bodies that move through and orient to them—in particular, to consider how "[t]he person as a mobile spatial field ... creates space as a potentiality for social relations ... and ultimately through the patterning of everyday movements, produces place and landscape."

To speak of place as produced by individuals' embodied activity is not to say that individuals create senses of place from scratch. Rather, the concept of embodied space provides a starting point for uncovering how a particular person (Jay) *interacts,* in the moment, with enduring spatiotemporal realities (i.e., cultural-historical senses of place) that help to define the parameters of the kinds of linguistic and cultural practice that are framed as traditional, innovative, appropriate, and so on, for a young Navajo man.

Basso (1996, p. 6) comments,

> Building and sharing place-worlds ... is not only a means of reviving former times but also of *revising* them, a means of exploring not merely how things might have been but also how, just possibly, they might have been different from what others have supposed.

Just so, Jay's complementary ways of embodying space, in musical performance and in everyday linguistic and gestural practice, both recognize and seek to revise others' preconceptions of what sort of sense of place he ought to have, being who he is.

Relationships and Researcher Positionality

Gilbert is Jay's father; as such, Gilbert's contribution to this project is informed by his participation in, and unique perspective on, Jay's language socialization. While Jay was growing up, his mother spoke only English, and he heard English spoken most often at home, even though Gilbert speaks Diné (Navajo) fluently and tried to address Jay in both languages. Jay regularly heard Diné from his grandparents, and developed good receptive competence. Unfortunately, his productive abilities remained limited, due in large part to his immersion in English at home, with friends, and in school. At the time, Gilbert had not yet recognized language shift's impact on the Diné language. His awakening awareness of language loss has led him to his current path, as a language and culture teacher in his community and later as a student and scholar of language and culture revitalization.

Prior to Jay's engagement with hip hop, Gilbert had limited exposure to and very little knowledge of that music genre. Nevertheless, he found himself intrigued by possible connections between Native oral traditions and hip hop as a form of verbal performance. Also, as Gilbert sought to support his son during Jay's readjustment to civilian life, after his military service in Iraq, Gilbert saw parallels between the linguistic aspects of Jay and other Diné veterans' military experience. Gilbert's uncles entered the Marine Corps as non-English speakers, but learned English and Japanese during World War II, and returned to the Navajo Nation trilingual. Jay entered the Marines knowing English and some Navajo, and returned home well-versed in "Hip Hop Nation Language" (Alim, 2006) and somewhat familiar with Arabic, which he picked up doing informal interpretation work. Ultimately, deep engagement with Jay's hip hop practice gave Gilbert uncommon insight into his son's artistic journey, and an additional way to relate to the younger Native students he serves.

Brendan first met Jay in 2006, while collaborating with Gilbert (and others) on a short ethnographic film focused on Navajo youth and political life. Encouraged by Jay's eagerness to talk about his hip hop, the two authors determined to undertake an in-depth investigation of his work as an MC. The topic attracted Brendan, who is White, because of his own work with minoritized and Indigenous youth and teachers and his scholarly interest in youth practice. Gilbert felt that it was crucial for Brendan and Jay to get to know each other in a variety of settings—at home, at concerts, and not just in the context of data collection—in order for our research to be humanizing (cf. Paris, 2011).

Since commencing this project in 2006, we have collected further video-recorded interview data, attended Jay's performances throughout the Southwest, collected and analyzed data from his hip hop crew's Website, listened carefully and repeatedly to his recordings, and transcribed lyrics to selected tracks (songs). We have stayed in touch with Jay—Gilbert regularly; Brendan, less frequently—and have sought to make the most of our unusual long-term access to an emerging Navajo hip hop artist. Each of us brings different elements of insider- and outsider-ness (Brayboy & Deyhle, 2000) to the shared endeavor: Gilbert, though an insider as a family member and fellow Diné, comes from an older generation and was initially unfamiliar with hip hop music and culture; Brendan, who is a musician and much closer to Jay in age, and sometimes appeared insider-like in those respects, negotiates his profound outsider-ness as a White person engaged in research with a Native participant.

Linda Smith (2012, p. 151) includes "representing" in a list of "twenty-five indigenous projects," commenting that Indigenous *self*-representation is, in part, "about countering the dominant society's image of indigenous peoples" as well as "trying to capture the complexities of being indigenous." Our research will never do this as skillfully as Jay does in his music, nor would we dare to claim the right or responsibility to represent him in this way. We hope, however, to do him justice by representing him in the hip hop sense (cf. Pennycook, 2007, p. 112); that is to say, we intend our academic *representing* as a show of respect for his music and his perspective on the issues we discuss. In our meth-odological and analytical choices, we have tried, above all, to avoid *mis*repre-sentation by making space for Jay's voice in our analysis. Jay has reviewed our written work throughout this project, and has given his blessing to the chapter.

Glocalizing Hip Hop: Identity, Authenticity, Indigeneity

Jay's use of hip hop can be seen as a microcosm of how local artists around the world are said to be "indigenizing" and transforming popular forms of expres-sion disseminated through global media, such as hip hop. Participants in the "Global Hip Hop Nation" (Alim, 2009a) not only borrow and adapt globally-circulating elements of hip hop language, music, and style, but also transform hip hop on the ground by imbuing it with local concerns, musical traditions, and ways of speaking (cf. the contributors to Alim, Ibrahim, & Pennycook, 2009). While hip hop spread from its "culturo-historical[ly] specific" origins in the Bronx, New York (Alim, 2009a, p. 8, quoting Maxwell, 2003; Morgan, 2009) to various parts of the world, performers and consumers around the world have also recreated hip hop with the materials and experiences at hand, making it a truly glocal art form (Pennycook & Mitchell, 2009).

Often scholars' analyses of how Indigenous performers and groups are glo-calizing hip hop have focused on perceived continuity between hip hop pro-ductions and traditional cultural and linguistic practices (including the use of Indigenous languages), or on the consciousness-raising function of hip hop (see, e.g., Ballivián & Herrera, 2012, and Tarifa, 2012, on Bolivia; Mitchell, 2000, on Aotearoa/New Zealand; Stavrias, 2005, on Australia). Pennycook and Mitchell (2009) go further, arguing that modern-day Australian MCs *re*-appropriate already local older ways of speaking and performing from global-ized contexts and re-embed these in Indigenous societies.

Others, however, point to the outsize influence of mass-mediated com-mercial hip hop on its local incarnations, expressing skepticism about how local "local" hip hop cultures really are (Keeler, 2009), cautioning that young MCs' perspectives do not always map neatly onto liberatory political programs (Newman, 2007), and struggling with ideological contradictions in place-making Indigenous hip hop where "cultural resistance" co-exists with "violent misogyny" (Teves, 2011). There is a productive tension between work that celebrates the ways "Hip Hop Cultures" (Alim, 2009a, p. 3) can support local cultural forms and projects, and work that questions the scholarly tendency to view all hip hop in this light.

This conversation about cultural authenticity and "realness" permeates discussions of Indigenous identity and the moral universe of hip hop. Smith (1999, p. 73) outlines how the oppositional notion of authenticity that under-girds political demands for Indigenous rights can, in other contexts, entrap Indigenous individuals in ideas about culture as eternal and unchanging.

Related questions often arise in Indigenous communities pursuing language and cultural revitalization, where youth may exhibit considerable dexterity and innovation in enacting their identities, even as they assert the value of older linguistic, ceremonial, and land-use practices (Henze & Davis, 1999; McCarty & Wyman, 2009; Nicholas, 2009; Wyman, 2012).

Similarly, what Alim (2009a, p. 9) calls "the search for 'the real'" has a powerful effect on how contributions to the Global Hip Hop Nation are formulated and judged, locally and globally. The notion of "keeping it real," of staying true to oneself, *and* to the ideals, values, and styles enshrined in hip hop tradition—particularly for underground MCs, like Jay, who see themselves to some extent as "keepers of the flame" (cf. Morgan, 2009)—is omnipresent in hip hop discourse (cf. Cutler, 2003). But, for performers (again, like Jay) who do not hail from the traditional urban capitals of hip hop culture, "keeping it real" also translates into "a great deal of (often self-conscious) cultural work … in an effort to express local identities through engagement with the global" (Alim, 2009a, p. 9), or a quest for "glocal distinctiveness" (Alim, 2009b, p. 109). These performers balance awareness of "a cultural dictate to adhere to certain principles of what it means to be authentic" with the recognition that "staying true to oneself" is going to look, and sound, very different in different localities (Pennycook, 2007, p. 103). In the following section, we describe how Jay accomplishes this, in social and practical terms, as a young Navajo man from Farmington, New Mexico.

The Underground Route to the Global Hip Hop Nation

Upon returning from his second tour of duty in Iraq, about 6 years earlier than the date of this writing, Jay started becoming socialized into the local hip hop underground, forming a crew called iLL Methods with two friends and fellow performers. ("Underground" generally refers to smaller communities of practice within the Global Hip Hop Nation, associated with specific performance ideologies and a moral framework that prizes artistic integrity over commercial success; see Morgan, 2009, for discussion.) The social practices through which Jay and other iLL Methods crew members initially constructed their identities and eventually performed their membership in the broader underground community included listening to and interpreting hip hop tracks, "spittin" verses while performing, soliciting collaborations with other performers, working to create beats and produce tracks, and distributing their music on mixtape CDs and over the Internet. (For details of Jay's language socialization into hip hop, see O'Connor & Brown, 2008.)

As time went on, Jay's involvement in underground hip hop broadened geographically, as he honed his craft, began to gain recognition for his rhymes and beats, and collaborated with MCs and producers from other areas of the Southwest and the country. In keeping with hip hop tradition, he also acquired a wide number of performing names and aliases, some linked to specific styles or personae (very often associated with different crews or musical projects) that co-exist as part of his increasingly diverse artistic repertoire. (He now performs primarily as Angry Monk, in a crew called PinkyThink Music.)

Jay, like many emerging participants in the Global Hip Hop Nation, came of age far from Boston, Chicago, New York, Los Angeles, and other urban cultural centers of hip hop. In addition to developing the knowledge and skills mentioned above, he also had to negotiate his and his crew's entry to the broader world of hip hop beyond Farmington, New Mexico. Jay has embraced the challenges of trying to establish oneself on the periphery as a source of underdog pride. During our first interview, as Jay was showing us his apartment, he picked up a turquoise necklace, grinning, and remarked, "This is my bling—I call it 'Diné Bling.' I don't need that other stuff. I got the real thing, right here." This came off as a sly commentary on Jay's geographically and racially peripheral status vis-à-vis the wider underground world, as well as a tongue-in-cheek criticism of mainstream hip hop's materialism, in which ostentatious displays of wealth (bling) are *de rigueur*.

In a song about his home ("Play School," 2010c), Jay reminisces about his early days in the hip hop underground, when he and iLL Methods were less firmly established in the local scene and had to fight for respect in "the boons" of New Mexico:

> The truth, I kicked some ass with some old crews
> Crews that played in the boons
> Remember when I started I was booed …
> Cause I played fools without Pro Tools
> Like we back in Play School

"I played fools without Pro Tools" (a software program commonly used for music production) refers to Jay's status as a self-made performer who had to persevere when he was initially booed, even though he was already "kicking ass," as he remembers it. The sentence is ambiguous in terms of whether Jay, a sophisticated performer who used Pro Tools, showed up rival MCs in "the boons" who did not use it, or whether Jay, even without access to Pro Tools, bested the "fools" who opposed him in MC battles. Either way, the track evidences Jay's pride that he could use the resources at hand to develop his skills and distinguish himself in the underground world of "the boons."

Senses of Place and Self in Gesture and Discourse

Understanding Jay's hip hop performance requires moving beyond an "assumed isomorphism of space, place, and culture" that is especially untenable for youth, like Jay, who "inhabit the borderlands" (Gupta & Ferguson, 1992, p. 7). Literally speaking, Jay inhabits the border town of Farmington, New Mexico, just out-side his family's ancestral homeland on the Navajo Nation. Metaphorically speaking, as a young Navajo man, underground hip hop artist, and Iraq war veteran, he inhabits an exceedingly complex "borderland" of identity. Because of this, according to him, some of his activities and choices leave him open to criticism that he is acting in un-Indian ways. As we will show, he counters others' insinuations that he ought to embrace a certain, narrowly defined sense of place (and self) with a transformative spatial practice, in music and everyday communication, that expands the range of possibilities for self-expression for Native youth in the borderlands.

Our decision to analyze both Jay's spoken discourse and gestures, along-side song lyrics, so as to reveal his use of embodied space for cultural cri-tique in finer detail, may strike some readers as surprising or unorthodox. With Haviland (2004, p. 197), however, we assume that gesture, like language, is "a potential resource for interactants as they negotiate social worlds," and find that our analysis is enriched by attention to the ways gesture can complement speech, since "the four-dimensional, imagistic, embodied channel of gesture has communicative potential inherently different from that of the digital, lin-earized flow of words" (p. 198). More and more, linguistic anthropologists (e.g., Goodwin, 2000; Haviland, 2004) and cognitively-oriented researchers (e.g., Enfield, 2009; Kendon, 1997; McNeill et al., 2001) espouse a view of communicative action that finds "signs co-occurring with other signs, acquir-ing unified meaning through being interpreted as co-relevant parts of a single whole" (Enfield, 2009, p. 7). Many of these scholars use multimodal approaches to discourse analysis (O'Halloran, 2011) in order to bring forth "[t]he 'inter-semiotic' (or inter-modal) relations arising from the interaction of semiotic choices" (O'Halloran, 2011, p. 121), such as the interaction between language and gesture.

For our purposes, it is most important to recognize that both discourse orga-nization and gesture are integral to Jay's transformative spatial practice, as dis-cussed in the next two sections. Specifically, we focus on an aspect of gestural practice called *metaphorical spatialization* (Mendoza-Denton & Jannedy, 2011) as it coordinates with, or complements, a feature of discourse organization called *grammatical parallelism* (briefly, the repetition of structurally similar utterances in order to evaluate or comment on a topic under discussion; Tannen, 1989). In the first section, as Jay is speaking, he uses gesture to "place" himself and his crew—who aim to transcend local classification and participate in a translo-cal style community—in one metaphorical space, and places their imagined critics in another, contrasting space, which we might gloss loosely as "back home." In the second section, he uses metaphorical spatialization in concert with grammatical parallelism first to set up, and then to deconstruct, an opposi-tion between groups identified as "Indians" and "the army."

Embodied Space as Cultural Critique, Part 1: "We're not tryin to sound Native ... we're tryin to sound hip hop"

While hip hop is not a traditional Navajo art form, it cannot thereby be inferred that Jay sees his music as a break with the values or attitudes of older Navajo generations. In fact, certain of Jay's comments suggest that just the opposite is true. For example, in response to a question about his track "Battleground" (2007), he explains his choice of a sample (an audio clip, used as background for MCs' rhyming) for the song this way:

> [T]he sample dude was like, it was funny 'cause he's like, "I don't like to go up to town- and be like nobody I don't wanna be." He's like, "I'll stay here at home!" It just talks about those people on the reservation, like ... the older elders? and—y'know, [laughing] ... they're real, you know, they're- they're straight real, that's- that's what I heard. They're real like that. They don't go to town and act like they're y'know, anybody else. They live their life out on the [Navajo Nation] and they don't need that stuff in town, y'know.

In other words, Jay does not see his hip hop as incompatible with the values of the older elders; instead, he says, the sample expresses something he values and endorses in the elders' ethos: the fact that they're "straight real" and don't "act like they're ... anybody else." Interestingly, Jay contrasts "going up to town," as a comparatively inauthentic practice, with "staying here at home" on the Navajo Nation and, we are led to infer, being self-sufficient and secure in one's identity. His use of "straight real" might be read to draw both on Indigenous discourses of authenticity, as associated with elders and traditional lands, and on hip hop cultural notions of keeping it real.

Thus, Jay clearly acknowledges the place where he came of age as a hip hop artist as a "culturally meaningful terrestrial ... region" (Munn, 1996, p. 465). However, he bristles at the suggestion that he and his crew should limit themselves to local standards for hip hop. According to Jay, listeners have expressed surprise that the iLL Methods MCs are Native, because they don't sound like other Native MCs:

> "You guys are Native, too?" y'know, "You guys don't sound like any Natives!" and then like—y'know, we're not tryin to sound Native, we're not tryin to sound—anything ... We're tryin to sound hip hop, y'know?

When pressed to speculate as to why some people have reacted this way, Jay implies that expanding one's ability and influence in the world of underground hip hop—becoming "prominent to our universe/just keep expanding outwards," as he puts it in his song "Livin All Seasons" (2010b)—entails further development of one's knowledge and technique, and that not all members of the local underground can be expected to follow his expanding trajectory.

In the following interview excerpt, Jay uses repetition to emphasize a point about iLL Methods' glocal distinctiveness. His parallel grammatical structures give his account a sense of coherence for us, his listeners, and orient us, as outsiders, to the intra-underground tensions he describes. In particular, he frames his position as a series of oppositions between (a) what other Native/Navajo MCs are doing, (b) what he and his crew are trying to do, and (c) what they are *not* trying to do:

> **because back home like—**
> like Natives already set the standards for—for their way of hip hop. so
> **they all sound** the same. and
> **we're not—tryin** to sound like them. I mean,
> **we're not—**
> **we don't—**
> **we're not sayin**
> **we don't wanna** sound like them? that
> **we're shyin away** from them for a reason? it's because
> **we're not doin** that,
> **we're doin it** because
> **we wanna do** the way
> **we wanna do it.**
> it's not—**it's not cause**
> **we're like—**
> **we think** we're better than them.
> **They have** their style of hip hop, go, I mean, more power to 'em,
> **they can do** what they want with it, you know,
> **they already—**but
> **we're doin** our own thing,
> goin our own direction and
> it's not—**it's not**
> **we're like hatin** on them it's just
> **we're not—tryin** to be part of them or
> **we're just tryin** to do our own thing or be our own way

Jay painstakingly explains that iLL Methods is *not* trying to "shy away" from other Native MCs "for a reason" or show disrespect to them ("it's not we're like hatin on them") but that they are simply "doin [their] own thing" and trying to go in a different stylistic direction. Behind his words is a concern to "save face"; after all, showing disrespect is a serious offense in many hip hop communities, not to mention many Native American communities. Jay's parallel utterances, bolded above, coalesce into a poetic structure that contrasts what the crew is *not* doing, in his view, with what they *are* doing, in part to preempt judgment from those "back home" (as he says at the beginning of the excerpt) who might see his crew's actions as inauthentic or as a rejection of Native identity.

Once we bring gesture into the picture, what Jay is doing comes into even clearer focus. The screen shots in Figure 3.1 depict Jay's gestural *strokes,* the most recognizable and effortful part of each gesture (McNeill, 1992), for the same strip of interaction as the previous example. (Strokes tend to be aligned with pitch accents in spoken language, "local prosodic prominences ... usually associated with the stressed syllable of a word" [Mendoza-Denton & Jannedy, 2011, p. 270]. Together, the synchronized strokes and pitch accents highlight new or noteworthy information against the backdrop of Jay's unstressed words and syllables.) The numbered screen shots correspond to the bolded numbers in parentheses in the transcript: that is, when **(1)** appears in the transcript, Jay's stroke reached the apex shown in screen shot #1, corresponding with the following word (for #1, "sound").

Sequence 1: "We're just tryin to do our own thing ... or be our own way"

(J = Jay, B = Brendan O'Connor)

1	J	because back home like
2		like Natives already set the standards for — for their way of hip hop.
3	B	ok
4	J	So they all sound the same.
5	B	oh, really? ok
6	J	And we're not- tryin to **(1)** sound like them.
7		I mean, we're not—we don't —
8		we're not sayin we don't **(2)** wanna sound like them?
9		That we're shyin **(3)** away from them for a reason?
10		It's because we're not doin **(4)** that,
11		we're doin it because we wanna do the way we wanna do it.
12		It's not- It's not cause we're like-
13		we think we're **(5)** better than them.
14		They **(6)** have their style of hip hop,
15		go, I mean, more power to 'em,
16		they can do what they want with it, you know, they already ...
17		but we're **(7)** doin our own thing,
18		goin our own direction
19	B	right
20	J	and it's not — it's not we're like **(8)** hatin on them
21	B	yeah
22	J	it's just we're not — tryin to be part of them
23		or we're just tryin to do our **(9)** own thing
24	B	right
25	J	or be our own way

To summarize: For gesture (1), as Jay says "We're not tryin to sound like them," he brings his right arm, with his right palm perpendicular to the table, across his body, so that his right hand ends up pointing away from him, slightly

FIGURE 3.1 Gestural strokes in sequence 1.

to his left. A moment later, when he says, "We're not sayin we don't wanna sound like them?" (2), he raises both arms from the pre-stroke hold (their position before the beginning of the stroke) and, holding them parallel, makes a more exaggerated, semicircular, upward and outward-pointing motion in the same direction (i.e., to his left). In denying that the iLL Methods MCs are "shyin away" from other Native MCs "for a reason," Jay brings his right arm back across his body, with his palm in the same position, so that it is pointing away from him to his right.

This pattern continues throughout Sequence 1: Whenever Jay refers to what other Native MCs are doing (line 10, gesture 4), how they might mistakenly interpret his actions as arrogant or disrespectful (line 13, gesture 5; line 20, gesture 8), or the style of hip hop they practice (line 14, gesture 6), he places them in a metaphorical space away from him to his left. On the other hand, literally, when Jay refers to his crew's respectful disalignment from the other MCs (line 9, gesture 3), and how iLL Methods are "doin [their] own thing" instead (line 17, gesture 7; line 23, gesture 9), he places himself and his crew in a contrasting metaphorical space, away from him to his right. In this way, his gestures complement the point he makes so carefully with the parallelism in his spoken discourse. Through his gestural practice, he embodies the spatial opposition expressed in the poetic structure he achieves through repetition.

At one point, when we asked Jay whom he pictured as his audience or listeners, while creating a track, he responded:

> To me … I don't care what I say, and I don't care who listens. And that's where I'm- that's how I got to where I'm at now- is- I stopped carin? about what was said? and how it was said about me? and I stopped carin who's gonna hear it and who's gonna listen.

"Doin [his] own thing" or "goin [his] own direction," for Jay, implies not being beholden to a particular audience's expectations about how his music should sound or what he should say; he even credits his progress as an underground artist to his decision to "stop caring" about who his audience would be and what others might say about him. Yet his explanation of his crew's desire to "do their own thing" clearly shows that he is aware of the possibility of moral censure should iLL Methods' actions be misinterpreted in light of the prevailing stylistic norms of the Navajo/Native hip hop scene.

To look deeply into Jay's transformative spatial practice here is to realize that he is taking issue with others' definitions of authenticity: He does not have to "try to sound Native" because he *is* Native, and whatever hip hop he produces will, by definition, be Native hip hop. It is not that Jay wishes to downplay or hide his Native identity in his lyrics or choice of style(s): on an earlier version of his crew's website, he introduced himself by declaring, "I believe in my self to become one of the best Native Hip Hop artist[s] ever to touch the mic." Rather, he wants to emphasize that, as a Native hip hop artist, he does not need to try to "sound like anything" in order to represent the skill, intelligence, and distinctive musical contributions of Native MCs and producers within and across translocal style communities (Alim, 2009b). In his artistic life, as in his everyday communicative practice, this amounts to mobilizing his personhood, a "mobile spatial field" (Low, 2009, p. 29), as a form of cultural critique: moving from the periphery of the imagined Global Hip Hop Nation, in Farmington, New Mexico, to a relatively more central position, in order to enact a form of indigeneity that resists classification and preconceptions.

Embodied Space as Cultural Critique, Part 2: "I tell 'em straight up, I didn't do it for Uncle Sam"

In this section, we address Jay's use of embodied space to speak out against historical injustices experienced by Diné, even as he defends his military service as "fightin for the same land" of which the U.S. Army tried to dispossess his ancestors. While Jay does not generally identify himself as a political or consciousness-oriented MC, he does brandish a voice of explicit postcolonial critique on certain tracks. For example, on "Land of the Sun" (2010a), Jay lets loose a stunning barrage of verbal artillery, indicting Euro-American society for the slaughter and exploitation of Native peoples:

> Since we were plasma
> Mother Earth coulda contained her own disasters
> Forget the harassment
> My ancestors shoulda murdered their masters
> This world was ours, even before there was your God
> From the roots we crop to the groups we plot
> My people were warriors of madness
> Sought to own their own soil, savages
> Rainin havoc from the Pacific to the Atlantic
> Screamin sink their Titanic
> We don't need the fanatics, we don't need their habits
> We'd rather feed on the rabbits
> Grueling addicts turnin their greed into flashy badges
> So I run around with the mad fist
> Screamin cut off my head and feed it to the kids
> The freedom I give to this land
> Like the blood my ancestors shed to live this beautiful gift

Here, as in other tracks, Jay plays with the stereotype of Native Americans as "savages," inverting the discourse of savagery: In his version of history, White invaders are the "fanatics" who plague North America with their "habits," while framing their invasion—in reality, an attempt to feed their addiction to greed and power—as a quest for glory, or "flashy badges." Whatever "savagery"

Native people did exhibit, then, is not an inherent quality of Indians, but the only sane response to the brutality of the colonizers. "My ancestors shoulda murdered their masters," he declares, before indulging a fantasy of violent resistance in which the "warriors of madness" live up to the "savage" slur, "rainin havoc from the Pacific to the Atlantic" upon the White "fanatics."

Jay inserts himself into this history near the end of the verse, which wraps up with an unexpected twist, as he cites "the freedom I give to this land"—in his view, through the sacrifices he has made during his military service— "like the blood my ancestors shed to live this beautiful gift." His own military service, in other words, is a tribute to the blood his ancestors shed to protect Navajo lands in the past. Notwithstanding the history Jay cites in "Land of the Sun," military service has long been highly regarded in Diné culture, and there is a strong tradition of patriotism and service to the United States in times of war by young people. Some listeners might see this as a contradiction in terms, but for Jay, the fact that Navajo lands are now part of the United States means that he is still "fightin for the same land," and fighting to defend the freedom of the same people, though on a different side and at a different point in history, when the political and social realities for American Indians have changed.

In "Battleground" (2007), recorded not long after his return from Iraq, Jay expresses awareness of the irony that the government that persecuted his own people during the Long Walk[1] has turned the so-called "savage" into a killing machine for its own purposes, at a time when military violence is often commodified:

> My image, my heritage, no advantages
> Just a savage with plenty habits to ravage ...
> I seen love and peace turn to somethin that bleeds
> Overseas screens castin blastin attractions
> America's sons with the combat action
> Camo ain't a fashion, it's a passion
> Uncle Sam don't pastor my people
> For Long Walk massacre's the factor
> For my long lost ancestors

Jay is aware of the potential contradiction presented by a Native American serving in the U.S. military; in talking about "Battleground," he glosses his verse's first line as follows:

> "My image, my heritage, no advantages" —y'know. I mean, look at us, we were the last people to get the vote, rec- decorated as citizens, y'know.

Jay ridicules the idea that his military service is meant to benefit "Uncle Sam," the colonizer, and clearly states that the U.S. government does not "pastor" Navajo people (a perfectly ironic choice of words, deliberate or not, considering the importance of sheep in traditional Navajo culture). Quoting again from "Battleground," he says:

> And I said "Uncle Sam don't past(or)," and ... I just, y'know I'm just sayin, a lot of people say, y'know, "Why you go work for Uncle Sam? ... You're Indian and–" y'know? That's what I tell 'em straight up, I didn't do it for Uncle Sam, y'know ... I did it cause y'know a lot of people did it before me.

He goes on to explain that the "people" who fought before him were, at times, fighting against the same military forces he now serves, but that circumstances have changed for Navajo people, who are now American citizens. Thus, to "man up for what's going on right now," as Jay says—i.e., to respond to the moral challenges of the present moment—can involve acting in apparently contradictory ways. Again, he uses pervasive syntactic parallelism to make sure that we catch his meaning exactly: just as becoming "prominent to our universe" in hip hop means "expanding outwards" to represent Native artists in a Global Hip Hop Nation, rather than remaining tied to local norms and standards, defending the freedom of Navajos in the 21st century, for Jay, means working together with the same forces his ancestors resisted. The contradiction, as Jay sees it, is due not to inconsistencies in *his* moral code, but to the vicissitudes of history:

> Like—it may go- date back to when
> **Indians were y'know fightin**—the army
> I did it for those people, y'know?
> but still today,
> **they're fightin** for **the same place** y'know
> **the same land,**
> still f– y'know?
> **it's just** that we're on that side y'know it's
> **it's not—it's not like** saying that
> **I'm not hatin on nobody** y'know
> **I'm just sayin** basically that it's—
> you gotta man up for what's goin on right now y'know?

It would be too easy to dismiss Jay's actions as a manifestation of "false consciousness" because he does not subscribe to a particular understanding of the relationship between present-day American Indians and the U.S. government, whether or not we share his understanding. Such an analysis would ignore his real critical awareness of the genocidal past and the myriad identity "traps" into which he is always at risk of falling, both as a Native hip hop artist and a Native veteran. As in Jay's explanation of how iLL Methods are "goin [their] own direction," his co-speech gesture in Figure 3.2 provides a window into how he envisions—and indeed, embodies—moving beyond what is, for him, the false binary of "being Indian" versus "working for Uncle Sam":

Sequence 2: "They're fightin for the same place y'know"

(1)	J	like- it may go- date back to when Indians were
(2)		y'know **(1a)** fightin- the **(2a)** army
(3)	B	right
(4)	J	I did it for **(3a)** those people, y'know?
(5)	B	uh huh
(6)	J	but still to**(4a)**day,
(7)		they're fightin for the **(5a)** same place y'know
(8)		the same **(6a)** land,
(9)	B	right
(10)	J	still f- y'know?
(11)		it's just that we're on that **(7a)** side y'know it's
(12)	B	right
(13)	J	it's not- it's not like saying that
(14)		I'm not **(8a)** hatin on no**(9a)**body y'know
(15)	B	right
(16)	J	I'm just sayin basically that it's-
(17)		you gotta man up for what's goin on right now y'know?

As in Sequence 1, Jay's gestures in Sequence 2 place entities or actors in contrasting metaphorical spaces. He begins by saying, "It may … date back to when Indians were y'know fightin the army," using a similar gesture (right arm extended in front of him, palm perpendicular to the table, arm pivoting on the elbow) to place "Indians … fightin" away from him to his left (line 2, gesture 1a), and "the army" away from him to his right (line 2, gesture 2a). Again, as in Sequence 1, the metaphorical space to Jay's left seems to denote "back home" or "Indians/Natives"; in the space to his right, by way of contrast, he seems to place non-Native entities, like the *historical* U.S. Army, which did not include Indians at the time he is discussing. To give another example: in line 4, he sweeps his right arm across the table to the left (gesture 3a) to place "those people"—i.e., Navajos fighting the U.S. Army in the past—in the appropriate metaphorical space.

But this analysis is overly simplistic. After all, in Sequence 1, it is not that the actors in one space are Native and those in the contrasting space are not; the other Native MCs and Jay/iLL Methods are *all* Native, but differ in their degree of involvement with the Global Hip Hop Nation beyond the local scene. Likewise, in Sequence 2, "Indians" and "the army" were mutually exclusive categories in the past, but are not any longer. And so, when Jay says, "they're fightin for the same place y'know/the same land" (lines 7–8), his gestures *collapse* the outdated (for him) "Indians vs. Army" binary. On "the same place," he brings both arms close together, still pointing outward and slightly left, at his center (gesture 5a); then, on "the same land," he broadens the previous gesture

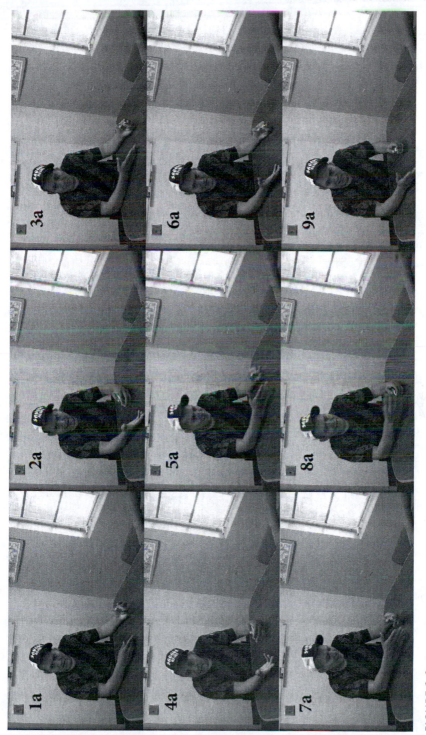

FIGURE 3.2 Gestural strokes in sequence 2.

by keeping his arms parallel and moving them further apart, so that they now point straight ahead (gesture 6a). In other words, the "place" that Navajos fought to protect in the past has, like Jay, "expanded outwards" to encompass a bigger "land"—including, but not limited to, Navajo lands—which Jay now fights to defend. Jay's metaphorical spatialization, then, does not represent a rigid opposition: what seemed to be a contradiction—an Indian serving in the U.S. military—based on the contrasting metaphorical spaces, is resolved, as the categories organizing the spaces are shown to be deceptive.

Conclusion

Through the "relations arising from the interaction of [his] semiotic choices" (O'Halloran, 2011, p. 121), Jay embodies a way of being-in-the-world that makes space, or place, for youth to "recreate themselves while maintaining claims to indigeneity" (McCarty & Wyman, 2009, p. 285). Our multimodal analysis has demonstrated that the "intersemiotic relations" (O'Halloran, 2011, p. 121) evident in the interview data echo and reinforce themes from Jay's lyrics—namely, his contention that seeking to broaden the reach of Navajo hip hop does not make it, or him, any less Navajo, and his recognition of the historical irony of his military service and concurrent insistence that it be seen as a morally coherent, authentically Diné endeavor. All in all, Jay's example is a strong argument for "considering spacetime as a symbolic nexus of relations produced out of interactions between bodily actors and terrestrial spaces" (Munn, 1996, p. 449), which is to say, for expanding *our* sense of what "sense of place," and the linguistic practices associated with it, might mean for Indigenous youth.

For Jay, tracks like "Land of the Sun" and "Battleground" are opportunities to unsettle the dominant narrative of U.S. history, past and present, and, in doing so, to shed light on the borderlands of identity (Gupta & Ferguson, 1992) many young Native people inhabit. They are also opportunities to explore the dilemmas of identity he encounters in everyday life—as when others comment, "You guys don't sound Native!" or ask him, "Why you go work for Uncle Sam?" Jay's response to these questions has been to engage in a transformative spatial practice that invites us beyond the binaries: in his music and talk, he "produces place" (Low, 2009, p. 29), with reference *both* to traditional Navajo senses of place and his own movement through the world, urging us to consider how things "might [be] different from what others have supposed" (Basso, 1996, p. 6).

Our case study of Jay is not meant to downplay the importance of culturally meaningful places for Indigenous peoples, or the importance of Native young people's advocacy for their community languages, but to underline the necessity of thinking carefully and critically about space and place in relation to what García (2009) calls Indigenous youth's dynamic bilingualism. Recently,

Jay enrolled and excelled in a Diné language class at San Juan Community College in Farmington. Afterwards, he told Gilbert that he was interested in co-authoring a Diné language book with him one day. Clearly, for Jay, there is no contradiction between being involved in hip hop and committing oneself to language revitalization; whether the two will ever be connected, for him, remains to be seen.

Acknowledgments

We are profoundly grateful to Jay for his openness and enthusiasm throughout this project, and, most of all, for inspiring us to undertake it. We hope we've done justice to your music, words, and actions. Many thanks to Leisy Wyman, Teresa McCarty, and an anonymous reviewer for generous and incisive feedback on early and successive versions of this chapter. Thanks also to Nate Dumas for helpful comments on a very early version. Perry Gilmore and Norma Mendoza-Denton encouraged us to pursue this topic when we were just getting started. Finally, we would like to thank both our families for their love and support.

Note

1 With "Long Walk massacre," Jay is referring to the deportation of Diné from their traditional lands to Fort Sumner, New Mexico, from 1864–1868, which resulted in extreme cultural disruption and the deaths of many Diné, and has lived on as a significant source of historical trauma for Navajos.

References

Alim, H. S. (2006). *Roc the mic right: The language of hip hop culture.* New York, NY: Routledge.
Alim, H. S. (2009a). Straight outta Compton, *Straight aus München:* Global linguistic flows, identities, and the politics of language in a global Hip Hop Nation. In H. S. Alim, A. Ibrahim, & A. Pennycook (Eds.), *Global linguistic flows: Hip hop cultures, youth identities, and the politics of language* (pp. 1–24). New York, NY: Routledge.
Alim, H. S. (2009b). Translocal style communities: Hip hop youth as cultural theorists of style, language, and globalization. *Pragmatics, 19*(1), 103–127.
Alim, H. S., Ibrahim, A. & Pennycook, A. (Eds.). (2009). *Global linguistic flows: Hip hop cultures, youth identities, and the politics of language.* New York, NY: Routledge.
Ballivían, R., & Herrera, L. (2012). Schools of the street: Hip-hop as youth pedagogy in Bolivia. *International Journal of Critical Pedagogy, 4*(1), 172–184.
Barnhardt, R., & Kawagley, A. O. (2005). Indigenous knowledge systems and Alaska Native ways of knowing. *Anthropology and Education Quarterly, 36*(1), 8–23.
Basso, K. (1996). *Wisdom sits in places: Landscape and language among the Western Apache.* Albuquerque: University of New Mexico Press.
Brayboy, B. M., & Deyhle, D. (2000). Insider-outsider: Researchers in American Indian communities. *Theory Into Practice, 39*(3), 163–169.
Cutler, C. (2003). Keepin' it real: White hip-hoppers' discourses of language, race, and authenticity. *Journal of Linguistic Anthropology, 13*(2), 211–233.
Deloria, V. (2003[1973]). *God is Red: A Native view of religion.* Golden, CO: Fulcrum.

Enfield, N. (2009). *The anatomy of meaning: Speech, gesture, and composite utterances*. Cambridge, England: Cambridge University Press.

García, O. (2009). En/countering Indigenous bilingualism. *Journal of Language, Identity, and Education, 8*(5), 376–380.

Goodwin, C. (2000). Practices of seeing: Visual analysis: An ethnomethodological approach. In T. van Leeuwen & C. Jewitt (Eds.), *Handbook of visual analysis* (pp. 157–182). London, England: Sage.

Gupta, A., & Ferguson, J. (1992). Beyond "culture": Space, identity, and the politics of difference. *Cultural Anthropology, 7*(1), 6–23.

Haviland, J. (2004). Gesture. In A. Duranti (Ed.), *A companion to linguistic anthropology* (pp. 197–221). Malden, MA: Blackwell.

Henze, R., & Davis, K. (1999). Authenticity and identity: Lessons from Indigenous language education. *Anthropology and Education Quarterly, 30*(1), 3–21.

iLL Methods. (2007). Battleground. On *iLL Methods: Phrase, Jay, Knowbody*. PinkyThink Music: Farmington, NM.

Jay. (2010a). Land of the sun. [featuring 22spinx and Shannon Walker]. On *Jus me & my life*. PinkyThink Music. Farmington, NM. Available online at http://www.reverbnation.com/pinkythinkmusic/songs

Jay. (2010b). Livin all seasons. [produced by AngryMonk]. On *I Pinky swear*. PinkyThink Music. Farmington, NM. Available online at http://www.reverbnation.com/pinkythinkmusic/songs

Jay. (2010c). Play school [featuring and produced by SampleCentric]. On *Jus me & my life*. PinkyThink Music. Farmington, NM. Available online at http://www.reverbnation.com/pinkythinkmusic/songs

Keeler, W. (2009). What's Burmese about Burmese rap? Why some expressive forms go global. *American Ethnologist, 36*(1), 2–19.

Kendon, A. (1997). Gesture. *Annual Review of Anthropology, 26*, 109–128.

Lee, T. S. (2009). Language, identity, and power: Navajo and Pueblo young adults' perspectives and experiences with competing language ideologies. *Journal of Language, Identity, and Education, 8*(5), 307–320.

Low, S. (2009). Toward an anthropological theory of space and place. *Semiotica, 175*(1/4), 21–37.

Massey, D. (1993). Power-geometry and a progressive sense of place. In J. Bird (Ed.), *Mapping the futures: Local cultures, global change* (pp. 60–70). London, England: Routledge.

McCarty, T. L. (2003). Revitalising Indigenous languages in homogenising times. *Comparative Education, 39*(2), 147–163.

McCarty, T. L., Borgoiakova, T., Gilmore, P., Lomawaima, K. T., & Romero, M. E. (2005). Indigenous epistemologies and education — Self-determination, anthropology, and human rights. *Anthropology and Education Quarterly, 36*(1), 1–7.

McCarty, T. L., Nicholas, S. E., & Wyman, L. T. (2012). Re-emplacing place in the "global here and now" — Critical ethnographic case studies of Native American language planning and policy. *International Multilingual Research Journal, 6*(1), 50–63.

McCarty, T. L., & Wyman, L. T. (2009). Indigenous youth and bilingualism: Theory, research, praxis. *Journal of Language, Identity, and Education, 8*(5), 279–290.

McNeill, D. (1992). *Hand and mind: What gestures reveal about thought*. Chicago, IL: University of Chicago Press.

McNeill, D., Quek, F., McCullough, K-E., Duncan, S., Furuyama, N., Bryll, R., Ma, X-F., & Ansari, R. (2001). Catchments, prosody and discourse. *Gesture, 1*(1), 9–33.

Mendoza-Denton, N., & Jannedy, S. (2011). Semiotic layering through gesture and intonation: A case study of complementary and supplementary multimodality in political speech. *Journal of English Linguistics, 39*(3), 265–299.

Mitchell, T. (2000). Doin' damage in my native language: The use of "resistance vernaculars" in hip hop in France, Italy, and Aotearoa/New Zealand. *Popular Music and Society, 24*(3), 41–54.

Morgan, M. (2009). *The real hiphop: Battling for knowledge, power, and respect in the LA Underground* (pp. 47–84). Durham, NC: Duke University Press.

Munn, N. (1996). Excluded spaces: The figure in the Australian Aboriginal landscape. *Critical Inquiry, 22*(3), 446–465.

Newman, M. (2007). "I don't want my ends to just meet; I want my ends overlappin": Personal aspiration and the rejection of progressive rap. *Journal of Language, Identity, and Education, 6*(2), 131–145.

Nicholas, S. E. (2009). "I live Hopi, I just don't speak it" — The critical intersection of language, culture, and identity in the lives of contemporary Hopi youth. *Journal of Language, Identity, and Education, 8*(5), 321–334.

O'Connor, B., & Brown, G. (2008). Not for your average brain: The social meaning of metaphor in an underground hiphop community. In A. Brown, K. Feyh, & J. Iorio (Eds.), *Texas Linguistic Forum, 52* (pp. 205–213). Austin: Texas Linguistic Forum.

O'Halloran, K. (2011). Multimodal discourse analysis. In K. Hyland & B. Paltridge (Eds.), *The continuum companion to discourse analysis* (pp. 120–137). London, England: Continuum.

Paris, D. (2011). "A friend who understand fully": Notes on humanizing research in a multiethnic youth community. *International Journal of Qualitative Studies in Education, 24*(2), 137–149.

Pennycook, A. (2007). Language, localization, and the real: Hip-hop and the global spread of authenticity. *Journal of Language, Identity and Education, 6*(2), 101–115.

Pennycook, A., & Mitchell, T. (2009). Hip hop as dusty foot philosophy: Engaging locality. In H. S. Alim, A. Ibrahim, & A. Pennycook (Eds.), *Global linguistic flows: Hip hop cultures, youth identities, and the politics of language* (pp. 25–42). New York, NY: Routledge.

Smith, L. (1999). *Decolonizing methodologies: Research and Indigenous peoples.* London, England: Zed Books.

Stavrias, G. (2005). Droppin' conscious beats and flows: Aboriginal hip hop and youth identity. *Australian Aboriginal Studies, 2*(2), 44–54.

Tannen, D. (1989). *Talking voices: Repetition, dialogue, and imagery in conversational discourse.* Cambridge, England: Cambridge University Press.

Tarifa, A. (2012). Hip hop as empowerment: Voices in El Alto, Bolivia. *International Journal of Qualitative Studies in Education, 25*(4), 397–415.

Teves, S. (2011). "Bloodline is all I need": Defiant indigeneity and Hawaiian hip-hop. *American Indian Culture and Research Journal, 35*(4), 73–101.

Tuan, Y-F. (1977). *Space and place: The perspective of experience.* Minneapolis: University of Minnesota Press.

Wyman, L. T. (2012). *Youth culture, language endangerment, and linguistic survivance.* Bristol, England: Multilingual Matters.

4

"BEING" HOPI BY "LIVING" HOPI

Redefining and Reasserting Cultural and Linguistic Identity: Emergent Hopi Youth Ideologies

Sheilah E. Nicholas

Despite having been immersed in the Hopi culture throughout their lives, many of today's Hopi youth do not understand or speak their heritage language. However, this ethnographic case study of three Hopi young adults' cultural and linguistic experiences revealed that through active participation in their Hopi world, youth learn to act, think, and feel Hopi, an identity cultivated though the myriad practices that comprise the Hopi oral tradition. I examine the emergent ideologies of these youth—how they expressed their lived experiences in their heritage culture, one undergoing significant sociolinguistic change—as sites of potential movement toward positive language shift.

> Yeah it's important to speak, but that's not all that counts. Because a *Pahaana* (Anglo) can learn how to speak it, speak the language, but they don't know the meaning behind it, or the actual culture, the in-depth stuff; [so] then they're not Hopi. They don't practice our religious ceremony[ies] and they don't *live* (emphasis added) Hopi; [so] then they're not Hopi. ... I just don't speak.
>
> *(youth interview, April 25, 2003)*

Dorian, Jared, and Justin, were three youth participants in this ethnographic study which investigated the role of the Hopi language in the contemporary lives of Hopi youth. All were 19 years of age at the time of the study, had been born into Hopi culture, raised on the Hopi reservation in northern Arizona, had actively participated in cultural traditions from early childhood, and, as young adults, expressed a strong affinity for their heritage culture. By birthright, these youth acquired cultural markers of identity—maternal clan identity, maternal village affiliation, birth and ceremonial names—and the privileges of participation in myriad cultural venues: song, dance, ritualized practices, social institutions, and religious ceremonies of Hopi culture.

Dorian's testimonial, which opens this chapter, is evidence of language shift especially visible among the youth, and describes contemporary Hopi society as confronting significant sociolinguistic change. Many Hopi youth, like Dorian, often find themselves positioned on the fringes of their heritage speech community. This sociolinguistic situation raises compelling questions about the vitality and continuity of the Hopi culture conveyed through language: How is language shift manifested in contemporary Hopi society? What is the impact of language shift on the identity formation of Hopi youth? Are youth still learning the social and cultural knowledge and the cultural ethics essential to becoming competent and contributing members of Hopi society? What is the effect of language shift on how Hopi youth view their heritage language? And, more importantly, how will today's Hopi youth ensure cultural and linguistic continuity for future generations of Hopi?

However, Dorian's words also convey a strong cultural identity developed through a life immersed in the Hopi culture, drawing attention to the notion of living Hopi, a posture, or *emergent ideology* (Kroskrity & Field, 2009) underlying how contemporary Hopi youth are redefining and reasserting their personal and social identities as culturally competent members of Hopi society. According to Kroskrity and Field (2009), communities undergoing sociolinguistic change give rise to emergent or contemporary ideologies, shifting away from or modifying pre-Western traditional ideologies (pp. 18–19). In turn, ideologies determine when and how community members will respond, and/or when and how they might choose to participate in language reclamation efforts and initiatives (see discussion in Wyman et al., this volume).

Hopi youth expressions, such as Dorian's testimonial, examined as emergent ideologies offer opportunities for critical insight into the ways in which these youth were modifying or shifting away from traditional ideologies, to negotiate and respond to sociolinguistic changes as well as to family and community perceptions of their linguistic and cultural competencies as young adults.

"Living Hopi," a traditional ideology, is embedded in the Hopi phrase, *"Hak sinmuy amumum Hopiqatsit ang nùutum hintsakme, Hopisinoniwtingwu"* (When one participates along with others in the Hopi way of life, one becomes Hopi), and which I refer to as the Hopi identity formation process (Nicholas, 2008). The emphasis is on active participation and proper conduct in the Hopi traditions, customs, and religion—the Hopi way of life—through which youth acquire the cultural standards of conduct and behavior in everyday life while moving toward a deeper, collective and personal understanding of the purpose and meaning of the Hopi way. Because Hopi remains primarily an oral society, I maintain that language, in numerous forms of use, is inherent in the myriad social, cultural, and religious practices of Hopi life, conceptualized as language as cultural practice (Nicholas, 2008). "Living Hopi," then, establishes the link between culture, language, and identity. Thus, in spite of the fact that, as Dorian stated, "Most of the time when you're growing up, it's English [that is used to learn the culture]," Hopi youth internalize the expected ways of thinking, feeling, and acting that define them as Hopi individuals.

Nevertheless, Dorian, Jared, and Justin contend that the Hopi language is a fundamental aspect of living Hopi; language was described as the "missing piece" in their lived experiences, particularly for Dorian and Jared. Dorian's receptive and productive proficiencies in Hopi were limited to "just some words." Jared maintained he had a receptive ability but would be unable to respond in a conversation, whereas Justin described himself as a speaker-user of Hopi.[1] Dorian noted, "In Hopi, everything [knowledge, ceremonies, song, traditions] is passed down orally," so language "plays a big key ... in the learning process [of Hopi culture]." These youth's perceptions of language became more acute as they assumed adult status, and their Hopi linguistic shortcomings came under increasing scrutiny by family and community members. In the Hopi world, the transition from adolescence to young adulthood signaled a new perception and level of expectation for youth associated with adult independence and greater privileges of participation and cultural competency.

In this chapter, I examine the emergent ideologies of these youth to illuminate the salient notions of and links between "living Hopi" and "language as cultural practice" that Hopi youth have internalized and hold. I contend that articulating youth's lived experiences as ideologies can serve as the catalyst to move us toward what King (2001) terms positive language shift—a process that initiates a (re)focus on language and culture. For Hopi, positive language shift directs a (re)focusing on the collective traditional ideologies conveyed in the Hopi terms *numi'nangwa, sumi'nangwa,* loosely translated to mean to live with mutual love toward one another, and in this mood, united in a common purpose, proceed in the manner of togetherness (Nicholas, 2005, p. 31). This (re)focusing, in turn, serves as a means to re-engage the community, and to re-connect older and youth generations toward "recouping or reinvigorating the use of the native tongue" (King, 2001, p. 12) in both traditional and contemporary contexts.

I begin with a brief overview of contemporary Hopi—the Hopi people, their geographic location, the vitality of the Hopi language as well as a description of contemporary Hopi youth. Next, I describe the research methodology, including my position as an "insider" researcher. I follow with ethnographic portraits of the three Hopi youth. A glimpse into Hopi epistemology provides the cultural context for the examination of youth emergent ideologies emanating from the practices of Hopi naming, planting corn by hand, and songs in ritualized performances. According to Heath, these practices are identified as examples that stand "within an array of other communication forms ... [and as] symbol systems [that] hold different levels and types of influence in different societies" (cited in Ochs, 1988, p. ix), all of which work to ensure the individual becomes a competent member of society.

Contemporary Hopi Society

Hopisinom, The Hopi People

The Hopi people are the westernmost of the Puebloan groups (Rushforth & Upham, 1992). A kinship-based matrilineal society, the Hopi continue to occupy a portion of their aboriginal lands known to them as *Hopitutskwa* in northeastern Arizona. The Hopi reservation encompasses 1.6 million acres situated on and around the three southernmost fingers of Black Mesa. Just over 7,000 of the 13,000 Hopi reside permanently on the reservation and live in or on the outskirts of the 12 villages located on top or at the base of the three mesas referred to as First Mesa, Second Mesa, and Third Mesa. The village of Munqapi is located at the northwestern boundary of the reservation.

Traditionally, the residential unit included the immediate and extended family members (maternal grandparents); today's Hopi households are mostly comprised of nuclear family units. Vehicles and school buses crisscrossing the reservation carrying residents to work and school are evidence of the incorporation of a cash economy and Western education into the Hopi way of life. Yet, each village continues to function largely as a socially, politically, and ceremonially autonomous unit. Village life revolves around a ceremonial calendar of ritual activities and events with everyone working to summon the rains that will nourish the crops as well as the physical and spiritual well-being of the Hopi people.

Hopilavayi, the Hopi Language

Most speakers regard the language as having three dialects: First Mesa Hopi, Second Mesa Hopi, and Third Mesa Hopi, all mutually intelligible across the mesas. The technical description situates the Hopi language as a member of the Uto-Aztecan language family, but Hopi stands as "a separate branch within Northern Uto-Aztecan" (*Hopìikwa Lavàytutuveni;* Hopi Dictionary Project, 1998, p. xv) that depicts four distinct language varieties. Hopi continues to be the viable medium of intergenerational interaction between speakers, in *kiva* (ceremonial chamber) activities, at traditional performances, and additional cultural practices. Thus, Hopi remains a language still spoken by all generations, including children, but is undergoing a rapid change evident in its diminishing use as a language of interaction between generations, ambivalent attitudes toward the language, and the incorporation of English into speech. Marie and Clara, grandparent study participants, described the visible and disconcerting consequences of these changes respectively:

> *Itàalavayiy namiqwriwni'yyungwa. Pahanlavayit enang hakim pu'yangwu. Itàa pu' oovi pu' pas alöngöt yu'a'atota. Pu' piw itam qa natuwi'yungwa sùupan pan Hopiyu'a'atotaniqe. Put pas haamanyaqe ... Itam son as qa panyungwe' put ngu'yungni.*

> Our languages [of use, Hopi and English] are mixed together. We are now interjecting English into our Hopi. Therefore, we are speaking a truly different language. And then we are no longer accustomed, it seems, to speaking the Hopi language. It appears as though we are embarrassed [of our language].... If we were not like that, we would be holding on to it.
>
> *(Elder interview, October 15, 2003)*

> *Anaave alöngti. Pahankwasa yu'a'atot[a].* It [the prominence of the Hopi language] has really changed. They [the Hopi people] are always speaking English.
>
> *(Elder interview, October 15, 2003)*

At a series of village forums held during January 1997, older Hopi speakers voiced their observations of language shift, especially among younger Hopi. As active participants in traditional practices, community members, grandparents, and parents pointed out that youth participants lacked the preparedness to attain a deeper, or spiritual level of understanding of these practices. More troubling were the behaviors and attitudes of youth perceived as *qa hopi*, unhopi—they were no longer behaving humbly, or having "respect for anything," associated with increasing influences from and involvement in activities—substance abuse, gang membership, and domestic violence—that violated principles of the Hopi way of life. Many had become "strangers" in their communities and to their families. Hopi youth were often described as *tsàatsayom*, children, who, despite their chronological age, had not yet learned the precepts that guide one to think maturely and behave in a distinctively Hopi manner.

A 1997 reservation-wide language assessment confirmed that a significant language shift had occurred. English was the primary language in at least half the 347 households surveyed (representing 1,293 individuals), particularly among younger Hopi (Hopi Language Assessment Project [HLAP], 1997, p. 6). The survey also identified schooling as a significant contributor to the rapid language shift.

Hopitsatsayom, Hopi Youth

Many of today's Hopi youth are born and grow up in their village communities. Raised among their immediate and extended families, youth participate from birth in the myriad activities associated with Hopi cultural institutions—baby namings, weddings, traditions—planting corn by hand, social dances, and religious rites of passage and ceremonies made possible with the construction of a junior/senior high school on the reservation in 1986. Previous generations endured lengthy durations away from home, family, and culture as students at distant boarding schools (Qoyawayma, 1964; Sekaquaptewa, 1985; Simmons, 1971; Yava, 1978), experiences that now exist as memories; for some, they are memories of severe loneliness and disconnection. Most youth today attend one of seven elementary schools in the village communities and transfer to Hopi Jr./Sr. High School for grades 7 through 12. Western education is highly valued; its acceptance and integration into the Hopi way of life is premised on an understanding that the benefits of an education will enhance the lifeway of the individual as well as the collective.

Hopi youth are familiar with mainstream society due to increased mobility, media, technology, and regular off-reservation family and school excursions. Following commonly held expectations associated with Western education (e.g., economic opportunities), most youth will venture into the wider society for varying durations of time. Of those who remain on the reservation, most will actively participate in the traditional practices and activities.

Research Methodology

An "Insider" Researcher

Hopi was my first language, but at the age of eight and coinciding with a humiliating school experience brought about by a lack of proficiency in English, I ceased speaking Hopi. I retained a receptive ability in Hopi, but as an adult, I struggled to express myself in the language I had spoken with ease as a child. An especially harsh realization came through my mother's words as she observed my attempts to use the Hopi language in conversations with her: *"Um tsayniiqe as paas Hopiningwu."* "When you were a child, you were fully Hopi," she stated. Conveying a strong link between language and cultural identity, my mother's words struck deeply. Moreover, my children, who are biracial and were raised for the most part in an urban, interracial, monolingual English household, did not acquire the Hopi language. Conceding my role in contributing to their feelings of alienation and estrangement from their Hopi community remains difficult.

Investigating Hopi language shift with a focus on youth came about as I assisted Emory Sekaquaptewa, research anthropologist in the Bureau of Research and Anthropology at the University of Arizona, in providing Hopi literacy lessons to Hopi youth in reservation schools. I was intrigued that despite being immersed from birth in the Hopi environment and culture, these youth were nonspeaker-users of Hopi. Further, given the history of linguistic oppression in Anglo-American schools, I found it ironic that these youth sought to learn their heritage language in school. Recalling my own Hopi linguistic experiences, I now asked, what is the role of the Hopi language in how Hopi youth define and assert their identities as members of Hopi society and as Hopi citizens in the broader sense?

Thus, I was involved in the Hopi social world (cf. Mason, 1996, p. 61). Further, as a researcher in my own community, I was epistemologically privileged because of these shared experiences with the study participants (Seidman, 1998/2006) including language shift in my own life.

Multiple, Intergenerational Case Study

A multiple, intergenerational case study approach was employed for the larger study of which this chapter is part. My goal was to understand the impact of modernity and rapid change on Hopi language ideologies and practices as experienced across three generations and households. Data were collected using Seidman's (1998/2006) tripartite phenomenological interview model, which combines focused life histories with in-depth interviewing and participant observation. This interview sequence provided an effective and culturally appropriate venue—collecting oral stories—for establishing the context and source of participants' "memories of injustice" and "diversities of truth" (Smith, 1999, pp. 144–145). My frequent travels to Hopi to participate in cultural and ceremonial activities and to visit extended family were highly conducive to participant observation of the "daily routines, conversations, language and rhetoric used, [and] styles of behaviour (including non-verbal)" (Mason, 1996, p. 61) practiced in homes, the village, ritual performances, and community events.

Study Participants

My previous work with students enrolled in Hopi language classes at the Hopi Jr./Sr. High School and my frequent visits to Hopi netted the participation of the three Hopi youth at the center of this study, former students in Hopi language classes, as well as their parents and grandparents—a familial intergenerational model for examining language shift. This focus changed with the passing of Dorian's and Justin's maternal grandmothers and the withdrawal of Jared's grandmother as data collection began. Pseudonyms are used for all participants with the exception of Dorian and her parents, who preferred that their actual names be used.

Ethnographic Portraits: Dorian, Jared, and Justin

At the time of the study (March 19–October 25, 2003), each of these youth was 19 years of age, a recent graduate of Hopi High School, and adjusting to young adulthood. Like their mainstream counterparts, their schooling experiences followed a progression of preschool, elementary school, and junior and senior high school, and an array of academic and extracurricular activities that related to their career and academic goals: Dorian had an interest in the performing arts or working with children; Jared wanted to pursue his passion for music as well as computer graphics; and Justin hoped to follow his interest in the field of "healing." Attending school on the reservation provided each with the opportunity to remain intimately involved in their respective village community, and Hopi cultural practices which I highlight in the following portraits.

Dorian

I described Dorian as a petite, vivacious, and precocious young woman, self-assured and confident in manner. She was a member of the high school cheer-leading squad, the cross-country track team, and one of the first females in the school's wrestling program. The second of three children, Dorian, a younger brother, and her mother comprised the immediate household. Her parents, although divorced, assumed an active and integral role in their children's lives. At the time of the study, Dorian was the reigning Miss Indian Arizona, an experience she described as expanding her knowledge about other tribal people, and at a personal level, connecting her more intimately with her heritage and identity including the language.

Her mother's home village of Supawlavi, on Second Mesa was the hub of the cultural activities, and where she spent much of her early childhood and later learned about her female role and responsibility—"to nourish the people"—in the preparation of food. Her maternal grandmother was a prominent figure in her life, and was someone from whom she learned how to make a sifter basket, traditional parched corn, and received important advice about how to treat others—essential in a communal society. Dorian participated as a dancer in numerous social dances, and was also a member of the women's religious *Lalkont* society. Preparation for both required nightly attendance and practice by all participants learning the songs and choreography in the kiva over several weeks prior to the performance in the village plaza. Although challenged in fully understanding the cultural messages conveyed through the practice of these traditions, Dorian intuitively sensed their purpose, that "you're doing it for rain, prayers, for life." Her kiva experiences left a lasting impression about the importance of understanding and speaking Hopi: "If you don't know it [the Hopi language], you don't really understand [Hopi culture]."

Jared

Jared's physical stature and reserved demeanor veiled a sensitive but serious nature. He was the youngest of four children. At the time of the study, Jared was experiencing his first semester at a community college, and his first time living away from family, community, and culture.

Jared's childhood experiences of accompanying the whole family to tend to the fields instilled the desire and obligation to carry on the tradition. It was the Hopi male's role and responsibility; a married man's symbolic demonstration of the economic commitment to his family associated with being a good husband and father. During adolescence, Jared was routinely reminded by his grand-mother, mother, and maternal uncle of his cultural role and responsibility—to "help out"—in the kiva activities; "helping out" would prepare him for his later ceremonial obligations in his maternal village, and in assuming his roles as a maternal uncle to his sister's children, and as a clan uncle to others through clan and ceremonial relationships. Helping out as a singer also nurtured his developing interest in music. He learned that the song words described and painted images of a beautiful world with rain-bearing clouds, bountiful fields, happiness, and prosperity; images that would instill a desire in the people to pursue this kind of world. These experiences impressed upon him the essentiality of participating with a strong personal conviction in order that every ceremony would be beneficial to and for all the people.

Jared's limited proficiency with the Hopi language impacted his ability to participate fully in the kiva activities, and he was made keenly aware of the expectation that he should already "know this;" he stated that often he "felt left out" and frustrated. Nevertheless, his experiences generated a strong desire to pursue initiation into the *Wuwtsim* society—one of the men's priesthood societies for which knowing the language would allow him full participation in the more esoteric realm of the Hopi way of life.

Justin

Justin's soft-spoken demeanor cloaked his strong sense of responsibility, work ethic, and self-discipline. He was living with his parents and his 11-year-old sister, and all were awaiting the birth of another sibling. Although self-identifying as a proficient speaker of Hopi, Justin preferred to use English in the interviews. At the time of the study, he was busy tending his own and his family's fields, working alongside his stepfather on construction projects, and continuing to be actively involved in the kiva (ceremonial) activities in his maternal, paternal, and maternal grandfather's villages; he put his plans to attend college on hold to continue tending to these responsibilities.

Justin's life experiences were centered in his mother's Third Mesa home village. He spent much of his childhood in the company of his maternal grandmother, and later joined his male kin in going to the fields, and in the kiva activities. Going to the cornfields began early in his childhood. While acquiring the knowledge and specialized skills of Hopi dry farming, he learned that tending to the corn was fundamental to the Hopi way of life; that planting was foremost a personal endeavor symbolized in using a single, hand-held planting stick, *sooya*; and that individually, and from personal conviction and commitment, each Hopi male contributed to this tradition. Concern for the well-being of the plants was incessant. He likened sustaining one's corn plants—one's "corn children"—to that of providing for and nourishing one's biological children physically, emotionally, and spiritually; this involved language, spoken words of encouragement as well as song words. Through these experiences the significance of planting corn and being a Hopi farmer were implanted.

The Hopi language was central in these activities, "singing and just talking [in Hopi]." Justin described his Hopi language proficiency at "about 75%," but added that there was much more to learn through the language as well as continuing to develop more sophisticated uses of the language.

Summary

These brief ethnographic portraits demonstrate how contemporary Hopi youth were "living Hopi," a process by which each gained varying degrees of cultural and linguistic competency in socially defined contexts (Schieffelin & Ochs, 1986) while developing a strong orientation to the Hopi way of life. The youth's collective cultural and linguistic experiences confirm the efficacious and affective nature of the traditional Hopi identity formation process: *Hak sinmuy amumum Hopiqatsit ang nùutum hintsakme, Hopisinoniwtingwu.* When one participates along with others in the Hopi way of life, one becomes Hopi. By "living Hopi" one can experience and learn Hopi culture through song, dance, cultural institutions, ritualized practices, traditions, and ceremonies that comprise the Hopi oral tradition. Hopi oral tradition has transported the origin and philosophy of the Hopi way of life across time and continues to connect the Hopi people to their ancestral past. In order to explain how this is reflected in the emergent ideologies of these Hopi youth, I pause to consider aspects of Hopi philosophy and values conveyed through oral tradition.

The Origin and Philosophy of The Hopi Way of Life

The origin and philosophy of the Hopi way of life are embedded in the Hopi Emergence story. The Emergence story is still recounted with the words, *I hapi tutavo* ... This is our teaching [regarding the Hopi way of life] ... The essence of the Hopi Emergence story is encapsulated in the following excerpt from the Emergence story:

> *Itam haqam pötskwanit makiwya, hintaqat qatsit itamumi màataqna. Qaa'öt, natwanit akw itam yesni; pu' haqé it hintsatskyaniqat itamuy aa'awna. I' qatsi áne tumala; kyaananvotpi. Nikyangw i' himu yep tuptsiwni, put akw pay hak itamuy ookwatuwni; itamumi paalay tsölöknani.*

We, [the Hopi people] at that place [of Emergence] received our life path; what kind of life we [the Hopi people] were to lead was made known to us. It was by means of corn, cultivating corn that we would survive and where [the environment] we were to undertake this life sustaining practice. This way of life would be one of hard work; survival would be a struggle. However, by means of our belief [in this way of life], and because of our faith, a greater power [the Creator] would take pity on us and bestow upon us drops of rain.

> *(E. Sekaquaptewa, personal communication, November 10, 2003)*

The Hopi way of life is guided by principles of *humility* and *reciprocity*; if Hopi people live properly, following a moral and spiritual path, moisture in the form of rain—a precious commodity in this high desert landscape—will be ensured and they will attain physical and spiritual fulfillment. Inherent are the values of hard work, self-discipline, and faith. This teaching is reinforced in the religious and secular activities of the Hopi people through the transmission mechanisms (Fishman, 1996) of *ritual, ritualized practices,* and *ceremony.* Whiteley and Masayesva (1998) state, "Hopis regard ritual, if *performed properly* [emphasis added]—the cardinal values are pure intentions and good hearts in harmony with each other—as instrumentally efficacious" in preserving, communicating, and transporting the philosophical principles that continue to give purpose and meaning to the lives of the Hopi people (p. 191).

Youth Emergent Ideologies

"They Don't Teach Us to Introduce Ourselves ... in Hopi for Nothing": Language as Cultural Identity

> I'm Squash [Clan]. ... My mother is Pumpkin or Squash [Clan] and my father [is] Corn Clan ... My mom's from here, Supawlavi [Village] and my dad's from Hotvela [Village].... My baby name, the one I go by is, *Samimana*, which means Corn Girl.
>
> *(Dorian interview, April 23, 2003)*

The Hopi identity formation process begins at birth. The process is encapsulated in the following Hopi expression:

> *Hak tiitiwe, yuy angq sinomuy'yvangwu, pu' tungniy akw námu'yvangwu, ti'amniwtingwu. Hak tungniy akw sòosok hìita ep makiwa'yvangwu.*

> When one is born, through the mother one gains [a community of] clan kin, and through one's name, one gains fathers, becomes their clan child as well [thus gaining an extended community of kin]. By means of one's name, one establishes connection and secures a role in all ritual practices.
>
> *(E. Sekaquaptewa, personal communication, November 9, 2009)*

By birthright, the Hopi child acquires cultural markers of identity—maternal clan identity, maternal village affiliation, and one's birth names—and the privileges of participation and increasing involvement in Hopi culture through social roles established through the clan-kinship system. At birth, the female infant is ascribed the role of *kya'a*, maternal aunt, to the children of the male members of her clan. As well, the male infant, *na'amtingwu*, becomes a father to all children whose fathers are members of his clan. Along with a variety of privileges, this

birthright and clan membership brings with it duty (conduct owed) and obligation (socially imposed duty) to an increasingly expanding community of kin
acquired through naming rituals accompanying rites of passage.

Hopi Naming Rituals

Hopi naming rituals are a means for sustaining the reciprocal relationships
"between individuals and groups in the human world" which begins at infancy
(Sekaquaptewa & Washburn, 2004, p. 467). In turn, these kinship connections are defined through specific kinship terms: *itangu*, our mother; *itana*, our
father; *itàaso*, our grandmother; *itàakwa*, our grandfather; *taha*, maternal uncle,
and *kya'a*, paternal aunt and their respective responsibilities and obligations
encompassing secular and ceremonial Hopi life. The Hopi individual receives
numerous names beginning in infancy as a participant in a series of initiations
that mark significant rites of passage throughout life.

In their responses to interview questions about their Hopi names, Dorian,
Jared, and Justin referenced a "baby name" and an "initiation name," indicating
that each had experienced the naming ritual as part of her/his initiation into
the *katsina*[2] society. Dorian elaborated further: "[M]y baby name, the one I go
by is, *Samimana*, which means Corn Girl. And then for my initiated name, I go
by *Soovenmana*, Star Girl."

Soovenmana (Star Girl) reflects the clan totem of Dorian's chosen sponsor for
initiation into the katsina society was a member of the *Qalngyam* or Sunforehead
Clan. Dorian's "baby" name, Samimana or Corn Girl, indicates her father's clan
family, the *Qa'öngyam*, Corn Clan. Through her baby name, the connection to
her father's clan family is established. Her role and obligations to this clan family are twofold: (1) as a child of her father and therefore the male members of
this clan, *ti'am*, or *mööyi*, niece/granddaughter, her female responsibility is that
of a female child to her fathers—preparing food for them in various contexts
(home, ritualized practices, and religious ceremonies); (2) to her father's sisters
and female clan members, who are her *kyamat*, paternal aunts/grandmothers, she
must demonstrate the Hopi attribute of industriousness by grinding corn. This
relationship is limited in daily life, and is therefore formally acknowledged at
the *Powamuy*, Bean Dance ceremony. Here, as a child of her father's clan family,
she will receive a plaque as a gift from the *katsinam* (pl.), a symbolic reminder to
grind corn—be industrious—and take it to her paternal aunts.

Use of kinship terms obligates people to one another, as manifested in the
concepts of duty (conduct owed) and obligation (duty imposed socially)—a
learned sense of duty and moral obligation toward family. The underlying prin-
ciple of reciprocity in the use of these kinship terms reinforces the concept
of community in the Hopi sense, especially as the immediate family circle
expands to include a wider family network through marriage and initiation

into religious societies. Elders' words of wisdom spoken frequently reinforced and instilled these principles as well, as these youth quotes show:

> Always help people because ... all their [one's] life, somebody will help you. And that's just what I'm doing, helping my dad and helping my mom's side, my other tahas, and just helping 'em as much as I can.
>
> *(youth interview, October 10, 2003)*

> Don't be mean to anybody ... [because] you never know if that person might help you out. [Or] you might need that person's help later on.
>
> *(youth interview, April 23, 2003)*

These relationships are also acknowledged in the *social* way one acts toward certain kin, and are formally acknowledged through ritualized performances and social dances discussed later in this chapter. They serve to establish allegiance to the larger Hopi community, further promoting a sense of communalism. However, adherence often exerts undue pressure, as Jared expressed:

> We're all related, [by] clans, [and it involves] certain responsibilities that our clans have to do [ceremonially for each other].... We have to come out here [and help].... When I don't come [or] take part, I feel guilty and then feel sorry about it later.
>
> *(youth interview, March 19, 2003)*

Nevertheless, a "sense of belonging and responsibility" is attained, a strong component in the development of *affect* and a *sense of aesthetics* for the Hopi way of life; a process I call "affective enculturation"—the development of an emotional commitment to the ideals of a communal society" (Nicholas, 2008, p. 338). Each of these youth had been encouraged and guided by significant kin in conducting themselves according to Hopi standards. Playing the part of one's kinship role in the described social arenas of the kinship network is as important as the ability to use the language. One Hopi elder at a public forum stated, "If you are Hopi, you will never forget your culture because you know who you are, and you ... know what your responsibilities are [to your family, community, people, and the world]" (January, 1997).

"Since You're Hopi, You're Brought Up That Way, You Can't Let It Go. It's Gonna Be Too Hard": Language as Cultural Practice

The Ritualized Practice of Planting Corn by Hand

> The language and that [planting], that was the most [of what] I learned when I was growing up ... how to plant with a stick [*sooya*], on your own

instead of having somebody else doing it for you.... Way back then, that's how we survived—[by] planting the corn. We ate from what we planted and that's what kept us alive.

(youth interview, March 19, 2003)

Justin's statement underscores the notion that "words have a home in the context of culture—in the course of daily activities, in social institutions … they have meaning within these contexts" (Sekaquaptewa, cited in Nicholas, 2005, p. 31). Justin and Jared each confirmed that planting corn by hand—traditionally part of the practice of making a living by farming, preparing for one's family economic responsibilities, and as upholding a spiritual duty—remains basic to the contemporary Hopi way of life.

Whiteley (1998) describes the practice of planting corn by hand, *natwani*, as "a worldly reflection on one's self-practice and conduct" in reference to the successful growth of "crops, children, or other fruits of personal effort; if they turn out well they accrue to the individual's virtue" (p. 41). Justin's statement, "You can talk to the plants; they're just like your children. So, [you tell them] 'Just be strong as you're growing up. Don't let anything bother you.' And they'll hear you," exemplifies the role of language in practicing culture.

Black (1984) adds, "A symbiotic and complementary relationship is seen to pertain to corn and humans. Young plants are cared for as children by people; if they are properly cared for, encouraged and prayed for, they are able to mature …" (p. 286). The Hopi language as spoken words, nurturing words, is integral to the proper care of one's corn children: *"Uma hapi ö'qalyani. Uma qa tsaak-wiwyungni. Uma kyaktaytotini; su'qawyani."* "You [my corn children] desire to be strong. You are not to wither. You have a speedy growth; be confident" (E. Sekaquaptewa, personal communication, May 25, 2004). Justin confirmed the use of this oral tradition in tending to his corn children. Song words also convey these messages. A grandparent study participant, Clara, recalled this practice vividly in memories of her childhood:

Hisat taataqt pasve taatawtinumyangwu, ispi uuyiy songawnen tiitavtotangwu. Haalaykyaakyang amumi unangtavi'yungngwu.

At that time, the men at their fields, would go along singing, because, in effect, they were taking care of their plants [as if they were children]. With much happiness, they were tending to them [the corn children].

(Elder interview, October, 15, 2003)

Among contemporary Hopi youth, Justin is one of few who have accompanied male kin to the fields since early childhood, describing himself as a speaker as well. As such, Justin stated that he was "born and raised" to become a Hopi farmer. This belief figured significantly in his plans following graduation from high school. He stated:

> For me, leaving this place and my farming, [and involvement in] the cultural [activities], that just got to me. [I thought], that's [schooling] way down there [far away from Hopi], so I just left that [put thoughts of further education aside] just to [stay] out here.
>
> *(youth interview, October 10, 2003)*

His case provides strong support for the notion of language as cultural practice and the *affective* nature of involvement in such ritualized practices. In contrast, for Jared the practice of caring for his "corn children" was disrupted by the absence of his biological father as well as the premature deaths of his maternal uncles, the male kin who pass this tradition on to the young. He described himself as a non-speaker of Hopi.

"It's What Your Thoughts Are ... What's Inside of You That Counts": "Being" Hopi in Heart, Thought, and Conduct

Song in Ritualized Performances

> For awhile, I kinda stepped away from it [dancing] ... [and then I said], "Mom, I need to dance."... When that drum goes, you don't hear it, you feel it.... You don't know what they're [men singers] saying, but you still get that feeling [of connection and common purpose] that you go by.
>
> *(youth interview, April 25, 2003)*

Each of these youth attached particular importance to Hopi songs as part of the ritualized performances (Sekaquaptewa & Washburn, 2004) they attended throughout their lives, indicating that songs still emit a powerful influence on Hopi people. Often referred to as "dances," these include social, women's and men's societies, and katsina ritualized performances.

The cultural practice of social dances is the means by which Hopi children learn their kinship connections in a formally acknowledged way. From an early age, they also begin to gain awareness of the religious aspects of Hopi culture through songs and song words. Preparation takes place in the kiva and involves learning Hopi songs that accompany the dances as well as the dance steps and motions choreographed by the men through nightly rehearsals over several weeks prior to the public performance in the dance plaza. The messages relayed through song words "paint images of a beautiful world, prosperity, with the rains bringing all of that [beauty] so that people can feel good about seeing this image as something that they all would want"—affirming a sense of aesthetics for the Hopi way of life (E. Sekaquaptewa, personal communication, May 25, 2004).

Through their performance, the dancers enable community members, who participate as members of the audience, to conjure up these images. Despite their limited proficiency in Hopi, Dorian and Jared expressed an understanding of Hopi songs and ritualized performances as both powerful and significant. For Dorian, it was a "good feeling" to be consumed—physically, emotionally, mentally, and spiritually—by the "awe-inspiring drama and intensity projected in these performances," imparted through the whole "complex of performance features— [song] words, ritual, dance, clothing, and associated objects and images" (Sekaquaptewa & Washburn, 2004, p. 462). "It's what your thoughts are ... what's inside of you that counts," Dorian stated. In fact, these youth were being socialized into Hopi society through the Hopi language in its most "spiritually powerful forms ... [and] through which [the Hopi people] come in touch with the preordained world of Hopi" (E. Sekaquaptewa, 1997, n.p.).

However, the "missing piece—the language, understanding and speaking"—was brought to the forefront by Dorian's experience as a participant in the women's *Lakòntikive*, Basket Dance. She described her conscientious efforts to understand the Hopi songs which accompanied this female ritualized performance:

> Right now, I don't know what the songs mean, but I'm still at that stage of learning [memorizing with limited comprehension] the words and the rhythm and how it's put together. Then once I learn a full song, I'll ask ... my aunt, she's in the Basket Dance, "What does it [the song] say?" And she'll tell me.
>
> (*youth interview, April 25, 2003*)

Although she recognized isolated words, Dorian further stated, "The rest, it's like a puzzle, and I don't have the missing pieces." The missing pieces that eluded both Jared and Dorian are also the meanings embedded in the Hopi language. The Hopi principles of life are embodied in the "metaphorical words and phrases" (Sekaquaptewa and Washburn, 2004, p. 458) of songs, the "same conceptual metaphors that are found in Hopi songs [in the] historic and prehistoric past" that are "perfectly clear" to Hopi who understood the language intimately (p. 460).

In early childhood, participation was about going out and having fun. During adolescence and young adulthood, participation was in part to fulfill their familial and community responsibility. The youth now felt a strong pull to participate from a desire to feel good, important, and connected to something significant to the Hopi people; they sought personal and spiritual fulfillment. Young adulthood brings with it a new perception of youth, as expressed in the adage: *Puma hooyi*—They have "come of age," reached adulthood, gained independence. As these youth widened their social roles in the community, pursuing greater involvement in religious activities, they were keenly aware that Hopi linguistic competence was essential to full participation in the adult social and religious realms.

Emergent Youth Ideologies of Continuance, Persistence, Commitment, Responsibility, and Hope

Adulthood is a status that implies reaching the age of maturity, and in the Hopi perspective, *wuwni'yva*, cognitive maturity, associated with awareness, a consciousness of the responsibilities accompanying increased cultural and ceremonial privileges. Adulthood also presented the essentiality of the Hopi language in assuming these privileges, and to which these youth responded with a new attentiveness expressed in emergent ideologies of continuance (Ortiz, 1992; see also McCarty et al., this volume), persistence, commitment, responsibility, and hope.

Continuance

Jared, in looking to the future with a measure of confidence in the strength and influence of Hopi traditions, predicted, "I don't think it will be gone.... People are gonna always want to have butterfly dances and kachina dances ... that's gonna involve Hopi [language], singing Hopi songs. That's just how it's gonna keep going." These youth, "affected" by living Hopi, will carry on the traditions.

Persistence

While challenged in meeting the community expectation for cultural continuity, Dorian acknowledged, "A lot of our elders and our parents ... are counting on us to keep the traditions going, and that heritage, that culture." Nevertheless, these youth have embarked on this trajectory by their active participation in Hopi culture; their hearts are firmly rooted in the Hopi world, and they have acted on addressing their linguistic shortcomings collectively—as members of a growing cohort of youth taking Hopi language classes, and as individuals. Dorian, as Miss Indian Arizona, advocated strongly for heritage language reclamation, imploring youth, "If you know it [heritage language], speak it, use it." Each asserted that she or he will persist in pursuing a linguistic proficiency: Dorian "'cuz I'm set on [learning] it;" Jared because, "I need to speak Hopi" in the Wuwtsin male society; and Justin "still learning it" in its esoteric forms. Albeit at seemingly individual levels, the effort of each will contribute to the whole.

Commitment

Justin, "born and raised" to become a Hopi farmer, is likely to be among the few contemporary youth with the acquired deeper knowledge and skill of the traditional practice of planting corn, an upbringing cultivated and nurtured by kin and constant reminders. Thus, he will do the same for the children he might have one day: He stated, "If I do have kids, I just wanna keep telling 'em to do this just the way my ... *so'o* [grandmother] told me,... put it on *them* and have 'em learn it too, keep it going, and just don't let it go." This trajectory entailed a lifetime of sacrifice, hard work, self-discipline, and faith: He poignantly stated, "I just want to keep this [tradition] alive.... I didn't learn and work all of this for nothing."

Responsibility

Highly cognizant of her impending role as parent, mother (to her own as well as extended kin/clan children), Dorian asserted, "The language is supposed to be on the parents' efforts...., [A]s a parent, that's what we're here for, and this is how it's always been passed on, from parents to child, for forever!" In Justin's words, the combined cultural experiences of these highlight the inclusive nature of one's parental inherited duties: "... For boys it's planting, and for girls it's preparing food."

Hope

In the kiva, Justin's continued participation was both a demonstration and assurance of continuity and hope. He reflected, "I guess it feels good to them [elder men] 'cuz we're learning, and we're the future for them...." The hope is that the strength of the Hopi way of life has not wavered, but is renewed and re-energized by each generation of youth. The hope resonates in the following expression from Hopi oral tradition, *"Haqàapiy yaw qatsi qatuvostini. Hak yaw pas somatsinen, sùuput namortamantani."* "It is said, that in a time when life becomes difficult [complicated], one who has acquired the powers of discernment, will choose the right way [the Hopi way]" (E. Sekaquaptewa, personal communication, October 25, 2000).

Conclusion

Although the most visible evidence of change is in the customary way that Hopi youth acquire their heritage language in the home and community, the emergent youth ideologies examined here illuminate the promise for cultural and linguistic continuity. These youth employed a *re*emphasis on "practicing living Hopi" by which they were gaining competency as members of their Hopi world, and subsequently, *re*defining and *re*asserting their cultural and linguistic identities. These youth ideologies revealed that the Hopi traditional ideology, emphasizing and linking identity to the acquired knowledge of cultural activities (Kroskrity & Field, 2009, pp. 18–19, citing Hensel, 1996) rather than language, resonates for contemporary Hopi youth. This emphasis is premised on the notion of language as cultural practice; that "words [language] have a 'home' in the context of culture—in the course of daily activities, in social institutions; ... they have meaning within these contexts" (E. Sekaquaptewa, cited in Nicholas, 2005, p. 31), and further, that the *spoken* language is only one of the many ways to experience and learn one's culture (E. Sekaquaptewa in Nicholas, 2008, 2011).

Justin's assertion, "Since you're Hopi, you're brought up that way; you can't let it go. It's just gonna be too hard," poignantly encapsulates and bridges Hopi traditional and youth emergent ideology. This ideology suggests that members of the younger generation, particularly those raised in the Hopi cultural environment, will hold tightly to the Hopi way of life; they are bound to it by habit, intellect, and choice. He also asserted, "It [cultural and linguistic continuity] won't just fall on me.... [I]t's gonna have to be everybody ... the Hopi people ..." who must recommit to a collective effort in assisting Hopi youth apply the relevance of the words of older Hopi, *wuklavayi*; Hopi teachings, *tutavo*; and cultural knowledge, *navoti*, to the circumstances of today's and tomorrow's Hopi society. The emergent ideologies of these youth constitute the hope that the Hopi culture and language will remain viable in the hands of each succeeding generation of Hopi. The hope has been cultivated and nurtured through a merging of Hopi traditional and youth emergent ideologies and practices.

Notes

1 I use the term "speaker-user" to distinguish between individuals who have a proficient receptive and productive ability in the Hopi language and use this proficiency to interact with other speakers, in cultural activities, and predominantly in daily life, from those with the same proficiency who do not use this proficiency in daily or cultural life.

2 In Hopi belief, *katsina* (singular) is a spirit being and *katsinam* (plural), are spirit beings who come in the form of rain, to provide the essential moisture for the corn and "for their part, have control over the rains" (*Hopi Dictionary*, 1998, p. 134). They come with the promise of all things—bountiful harvest, harmony, life—to be realized.

References

Black, M. E. (1984). Maidens and mothers: An analysis of Hopi corn metaphors. *Ethnology, 23*(4), 279–288.

Fishman, J. (1996). What do you lose when you lose your language? In G. Cantoni (Ed.), *Stabilizing indigenous languages* (pp. 80–91). Flagstaff: Northern Arizona University Center for Excellence in Education.

Hopi Dictionary Project. (1998). *Hopi dictionary/Hopìikwa lavàytutuveni: A Hopi-English dictionary of the Third Mesa dialect.* Tucson: University of Arizona Press.

Hopi Language Assessment Project. (HLAP) (1997). Presentation of Hopi language survey results. Report prepared for the Hopi Culture Preservation Office, Hopi Tribe. Tucson: Bureau of Applied Research and Anthropology, University of Arizona.

King, K. A. (2001). *Language revitalization process and prospects: Quichua in the Ecuadorian Andes.* Clevedon, England: Multilingual Matters.

Kroskrity, P. V., & Field, M. C. (Eds.). (2009). *Native American language ideologies: Beliefs, practices, and struggles in Indian Country.* Tucson: University of Arizona Press.

Mason, J. (1996). *Qualitative Researching.* London, England: Sage.

Nicholas, S. (2005). Negotiating for the Hopi way of life through literacy and schooling. In T. L. McCarty (Ed.), *Language, literacy, and power in schooling* (pp. 29–46). Mahwah, NJ: Erlbaum.

Nicholas, S. E. (2008). Becoming "fully" Hopi: The role of the Hopi language in the contemporary lives of Hopi youth—A Hopi case study of language shift and vitality (Unpublished doctoral dissertation). American Indian Studies Program. University of Arizona, Tucson.

Nicholas, S. E. (2011). "I live Hopi, I just don't speak it."—The critical intersection of language, culture, and identity in the lives of contemporary Hopi youth. *Journal of Language, Identity, and Education, 8*(5), 321–334.

Ochs, E. (1988). *Culture and language development: Language acquisition and language socialization in a Samoan village.* Cambridge, England: Cambridge University Press.

Ortiz, S. J. (1992). *Woven stone.* Tucson: University of Arizona Press.

Qoyawayma, P. (1964). *No turning back: A Hopi Indian woman's struggle to live in two worlds.* Albuquerque: University of New Mexico Press.

Rushforth, S., & Upham, S. (1992). *A Hopi social history: Anthropological perspectives on sociocultural persistence and change.* Austin: University of Texas Press.

Schieffelin, B. B., & Ochs. E. (Eds.). (1986). *Language socialization across cultures.* New York, NY: Cambridge University Press.

Seidman, I. E. (1998/2006). *Interviewing as qualitative research* (3rd ed.). New York, NY: Teachers College Press.

Sekaquaptewa, E. (1997, July 7). Paper for living Hopi language. Unpublished manuscript.

Sekaquaptewa, E., & Washburn, D. (2004). They go along singing: Reconstructing the Hopi past from ritual metaphors in song and image. *American Antiquity, 9*(3), 457–486.

Sekaquaptewa, H. (1985). *Me and mine: The life story of Helen Sekaquaptewa (as told to Louise Udall).* Tucson: University of Arizona Press.

Simmons, L. W., with Talayesva. D. (1971). *Sun Chief: The autobiography of a Hopi Indian.* New Haven, CT: Yale University Press.

Smith, L.T. (1999). *Decolonizing methodologies. Research and Indigenous peoples.* London, England: Zed Books.

Whiteley, P. (1998). *Rethinking Hopi ethnography.* Washington, DC: Smithsonian Institution Press.

Whiteley, P., & Masayesva, V. (1998). Paavahu and Paanaqso'a: The wellsprings of life and the slurry of death. In P. M. Whiteley (Ed.), *Rethinking Hopi ethnography* (pp. 188–207). Washington, DC: Smithsonian Institution Press.

Yava, A. (1978). *Big falling snow: A Tewa-Hopi Indian's life and times and the history and traditions of his people.* Albuquerque: University of New Mexico Press.

5

YOUTH LINGUISTIC SURVIVANCE IN TRANSFORMING SETTINGS

A Yup'ik Example

Leisy T. Wyman

This chapter traces how wide-ranging processes placed Yup'ik youth at the center of a community-wide "language tip" (Dorian, 1998) into English in "Piniq" (pseudonym), an Alaskan village, over the course of a decade. Analyzing young men's reflections and storytelling about seal-hunting, I highlight how the first youth in village history to speak mostly English negotiated uneven linguistic repertoires and mediated their learning of an Indigenous knowledge system in interaction. During language tip, youth natural- ized linguistic insecurities and were losing forms marking a linguistic orientation to land. Adult responses to youth innovation also fed cycles of reduced resources for and increas- ing doubts about bilingualism. Nevertheless, youth demonstrated linguistic survivance by translanguaging (García, 2009), and forging connections to community, place, and local knowledge in the face of rapidly accumulating pressures of language shift/endangerment. The chapter discusses youth's challenging positions and bilingual possibilities in radically- transforming sociolinguistic settings.

Within many Indigenous communities in North America, youth live in rapidly changing linguistic ecologies, yet little research has examined how Indigenous youth use changing linguistic resources to mediate language shift and the learn- ing of community knowledge systems. This chapter draws from a longitudinal study of young people's bilingualism in Piniq (all names are pseudonyms), a Yup'ik village of 600 in southwestern Alaska from 1992–2001 (Wyman, 2012, 2013). The study compared two consecutive "cohorts" of youth as the commu- nity experienced a *language tip* (Dorian, 1989), or rapid language shift to Eng- lish. Both groups of youth used Yup'ik, their Indigenous language, and English to construct complex identities as they came of age in a unique sub-arctic set- ting. Most youth in the older group spoke Yup'ik as the main language of peer culture from 1992–1995. Most youth in the younger group spoke English as the main language of peer culture, but also used bilingualism to "get by" with peers and adults in 2000–2001.

From 1992–2001, Piniq youth increasingly spoke English, and transformed patterns of local language socialization. Young people's rapidly changing language practices also threatened to disrupt the intergenerational sharing of *qanruyutait*, important socializing genres of Yup'ik-dominant elders. In this chapter, I briefly overview how a reduction of Indigenous language programming in the local school and increasing migration eroded local resources for heritage language learning in Piniq, placing youth at the center of village-wide sociolinguistic transformation. I also compare how educators, community members, and young people themselves interpreted young people's changing language practices in ways that further naturalized language endangerment as inevitable.

I then compare the ways that youth in the younger "Get By" group talked about their experiences with language loss and locally-valued subsistence practices. Examining young men's storytelling about seal hunting, in particular, I discuss how youth were losing linguistic "forms whose possibilities of use ha(d) been explored and learned for many generations," (Woodbury, 1998, p. 256). At the same time, building on Vizenor's notions of survivance (1994, 2008), I show how youth demonstrated what I call linguistic survivance by negotiating uneven linguistic repertoires and translanguaging in the process of learning and sharing a Yup'ik way of life, navigating the tensions of language shift/endangerment in interaction.

By situating young people's ideologies and everyday language practices in relation to their individualized and shared language learning trajectories, and examining the ways youth use communicative repertoires to engage with community-based learning over time, we can critically highlight how societal forces like schooling shape the maintenance and/or disruption of unique languages and knowledge systems. We may also gain key insights into young people's bilingual possibilities by looking closely at their emerging forms of linguistic survivance in transforming sociolinguistic settings.

Yup'ik Language, Subsistence, and Schooling

Central Alaskan Yup'ik in southwestern Alaska (Yup'ik, hereafter) has historically had large numbers of child speakers for the Circumpolar North. From 1980–1995, however, the number of Yup'ik speakers dropped from 13,000 to 10,000 (Krauss, 1997). Youth in multiple additional Yup'ik communities have also recently begun speaking English, heightening concerns about language endangerment (Wyman et al., 2010a, 2010b).

Indigenous language issues in Alaska and Canada are "embedded in a political discourse centered on land and the role that land plays in Aboriginal cultures, including their spiritual values and languages" (Patrick, 2007, p. 51). In the face of political, social, and economic transformation and the increasing bureaucratization of the Far North, "subsistence and land rights have been the main line of defense" through which Yup'ik community members have fought against cultural extinction (Morrow & Hensel, 1992, p. 40). Questions abound regarding the ways in which school programs might support the continuation of Yup'ik, related community knowledge systems, and unique mixed economies based on extensive hunting, fishing, and gathering.

Historically, arctic schools attempted to eradicate Indigenous languages and ways of knowing by punishing students for speaking their languages (Krauss, 1997). In mid-20th century, secondary students from Piniq were sent to distant boarding schools where they were submersed in English. After an Alaskan court case in the early 1970s, many Yup'ik communities in southwestern Alaska gained local high schools (see Charles, this volume). Building on a bilingual education movement, small village schools also implemented transitional bilingual programs in which students received three years of primary Yup'ik language instruction. Such programs slowed, but did not stop language shift (Wyman et al., 2010a, 2010b).

Outsiders who only stay in the Yup'ik region a few years are often in positions of power in local schools, creating systemic instabilities and inequities (Lipka et al., 1998; Wyman, 2012). Recently mandated high-stakes English testing has also intensified pressures on Yup'ik bilingual education programs (Wyman et al., 2010a, 2010b). Nevertheless, within rural Alaska Native communities formal education "is still an evolving, emergent system ... leaving it vulnerable and malleable in response to a well-crafted strategy of systemic reform" (Barnhardt & Kawagley, 2004, p. 59). New efforts to strengthen Yup'ik language programs also offer transformative possibilities for reversing language shift and reconnecting education to community knowledge. To take advantage of these opportunities, however, language planners, educators, and community members must understand the ways that language programs and young people's practices situate within linguistic ecologies.

Drawing on a unique longitudinal data set collected from 1992–2001, this study is among the first to provide a detailed portrait of how wide-ranging processes combine to shape Indigenous youth language ideologies, linguistic practices and identity performances, how youth negotiate their positions as icons and agents of language endangerment, and how young people's negotiations, in turn, shape local linguistic ecologies.

Studying Youth in Language Shift/Endangerment Settings

Theoretical Framework

Language shift is a notoriously complex phenomenon to document in progress. Multiple internal and external pressures and processes often combine to forward community language shift (Fishman, 1991; Gal, 1979; Kulick, 1992). Individualized forms of bilingualism are also shaped by wide-ranging dynamic language learning processes and life circumstances (Valdés, 2005; Zentella, 1997).

The "choice" to abandon a language involves social assessments about the possibilities and purposes of bilingualism, as well as value judgments about the role of the home language in maintaining community. While choices may appear to occur suddenly, often the groundwork for language shift is laid in *language ideologies*, seemingly commonsense assumptions about languages relating to communities' sociohistorical circumstances (Woolard, 1998) before language shift is apparent (Dorian, 1989; Gal, 1979). Language ideologies may also proliferate quickly when individuals try to maintain or document an endangered language, or make sense of language endangerment (Hill, 2006).

Language shift studies must also identify the ways that *assumptions about* and *resources for* bilingualism change hand in hand as youth are socialized by adults, as youth socialize one another and younger children, and as adults interpret and respond to young people's practices over time (Garrett & Baquedano-López, 2002; Kulick, 1992; Schieffelin & Ochs, 1986). Currently scholars are reconceptualizing how language learners integrate heterogeneous sets of linguistic resources and experiences across historical and shorter timescales, and local and translocal spaces with implications for linguistic practice, identity formation and language contact (Blommaert, 2010; Collins, Baynham, & Slembrouck, 2009; see discussion in Wyman, 2013). Scholars have also begun documenting how individualized, yet overlapping *language socialization trajectories* account for similarities, differences, and dynamism in young peoples' linguistic and cultural repertoires, and social and academic identities (Wortham, 2006). In the study, I examined adults' and young people's assumptions about language use, learning and loss in light of sociohistorical changes and power relationships in and out of Piniq. I also compared the language socialization trajectories of individuals, peer groups, and families in Piniq to see how youth developed and used their linguistic repertoires under varying circumstances, and how, over time, youth took up and enacted positions as non-speakers vs. speakers of Yup'ik, with consequences for community-wide language shift.

Through a third analytical lens, linguistic survivance, I considered Piniq youth as members of a particular Indigenous community engaged in enduring struggles. Vizenor theorizes survivance as a complex combination of survival and resistance that supports Indigenous people's "continuing presence over absence, deracination, and oblivion" (2008, p. 1). In education, the term "survivance" has been used to raise profound questions about how teaching and learning relate to collective identities and contribute to community growth under deeply threatening circumstances (Brayboy, 2005). Building on these ideas, I identified what I came to call *linguistic survivance*—the use of communicative practices to connect to community knowledge, express Indigeneity, and/

or to exercise self-determination in the face of societal inequities and related challenges including language endangerment. Considering young people's linguistic survivance, I avoided simplistically labeling Indigenous youth as "speakers" or "nonspeakers" of endangered languages, I focused, instead, on the wide-ranging ways that youth and adults in Piniq used multiple languages and symbolic practices, as well as bilingualism and translanguaging—the moving across or intermixing of languages and language varieties (García, 2009)— as they shared Indigenous commentary, engaged in community-connected learning, and celebrated and defended a Yup'ik way of life under the tremendously difficult circumstance of rapid language shift and endangerment (Wyman, 2012).

By longitudinally documenting the changing contours of local peer culture in Piniq, and tracing the typical and atypical language socialization trajectories of individuals, peer groups and families in ethnographic detail, I highlighted the *layered simultaneity* of youth discourse, or the "historical accumulation of policymaking, power and sociolinguistic change, as individuals negotiate[d] multilayered, face-to-face interactions and 'regimes of language use' within social networks and spaces" (Blommaert, 2005, p. 130; Wyman, 2013). I also documented young peoples' strengths as they took up new responsibilities with adult mentors and one another, learned a unique community knowledge system, adapted local practices and contributed to their families and community in spite of the ways they were wrestling with linguistic insecurities, and the ways that youth culture itself rapidly became a driving force of language shift and endangerment.

Researcher Positioning and Methodology

Most researchers of language shift arrive once language shift has already taken place, or once all youth under a certain age no longer speak a heritage language (e.g., Kulick, 1992; for an exception see Zentella, 1997). This study, in contrast, grew out of a teacher-researcher effort to connect youth to local knowledge in a village that happened to be experiencing a language tip to English. My relationship with Piniq started when I took a job as a secondary English teacher in the local school. From 1992 to 1995, I taught a 7-year span of students ($n = 75$), which included youth that Yup'ik educators later referred to as the last "Real Speakers" of Yup'ik and a 3-year span of younger students who I referred to as the "Get By" group, who were leading a language tip in local peer culture. During this time I worked with Yup'ik teachers, community members, and youth on an intergenerational project in which students interviewed community elders as the basis for academic work in English and Yup'ik, and on a language documentation project sponsored by the Traditional Council. In the mid-1990s adults and students were already voicing concerns about language endangerment. As a teacher-researcher, I documented students' metamessages and language use, and worked with the youth group to critically consider language shift. From 1995 to 2000, I lived elsewhere, yet continued to work on the documentation project, track students' lives, and discuss language shift with educators.

In 2000–2001 I conducted 14 months of ethnographic research on young people's peer culture and linguistic survivance in Piniq. In the 5 years I had lived away, language shift had progressed rapidly. Community members quickly identified which young people were the last to use primarily Yup'ik (the "Real Speakers"), and which were the first to speak primarily English in local peer culture (the "Get By" group). Yet young people's language uses and experiences also varied tremendously within both groups. My research focused on identifying how linguistic assumptions and resources were changing, how these changes were influencing young people's trajectories of language learning and everyday linguistic practices, and how youth culture was intersecting with family and community language socialization.

Veteran Yup'ik educators shared a wealth of information concerning young people's backgrounds and changing language practices, helping me trace how multiple contingencies affected the language learning opportunities of individuals, peer groups, and families in Piniq. Interviews and informal conversations with parents of school-aged children, participant observation, and two case studies of young families also helped me identify emerging patterns and variation in family heritage language maintenance/shift.

To determine students' language proficiency levels in 2000–2001, I compared (a) district Yup'ik and English test scores; (b) informal language assessments of teachers, parents, and students; and (c) youth observations from wide-ranging settings. To identify how adults spoke with "Get By" group members and the ways youth interacted with one another, I also volunteered daily in a seventh grade class taught by a Yup'ik teacher, shadowed other classes, and used participant observation and selective taping of school-related events (class parties, sports practices, high school prom preparations, etc.) and out-of-school activities (community programs, feasts, church activities, subsistence practices, etc.).

To further document young people's emic perspectives and language practices, I conducted 24 taped informal interviews with 19 secondary students, and many non-taped interviews with additional youth. From 1992 to 2001, I positioned myself as a Yup'ik language learner. In 2000–2001, I also followed young people's linguistic leads in interviews with individuals, pairs and small groups of youth, using Yup'ik when possible with the few students who spoke mostly Yup'ik to peers, mirroring local patterns of code-switching with many others, and switching to "village English" with youth who spoke primarily English, while taping the interactions of youth with varying language proficiencies. Later I worked with Yup'ik language consultants to transcribe, translate, and interpret youth discourse samples. Excerpts below come from interviews in 2000–2001.

From 2001 to the time of this writing, I have discussed findings with educators and community members including youth in Piniq. I have also used the Piniq study with Yup'ik educators and others to investigate bilingualism and education in the school district serving Piniq and surrounding Yup'ik villages. My insider-outsider positioning and collaborative work inform my analysis and are described elsewhere (Wyman, 2012; Wyman et al., 2010a, 2010b).

Situating Schooling in Linguistic Ecologies

Dominant discourses frame the loss of minority languages as a natural, perhaps regrettable, but unavoidable phenomenon, obscuring local meanings of bilingualism and rhetorically sanitizing inequitable histories leading to language endangerment (May, 2005). Below I will critically compare adults' emerging interpretations of young people's changing linguistic practices in Piniq to: (a) local practices and efforts to maintain bilingualism at the time of the study, and (b) long-term processes that laid the groundwork for rapid language tip.

From 1992 to 2001, rotating White administrators and educators made up the majority of local school staff. Outside educators generally knew very little about individual or community bilingualism, though they were aware of the history of linguistic oppression and that Piniq had maintained Yup'ik until recently. As children increasingly entered school speaking mostly English, most outsiders and some local educators assumed that parents and community members simply weren't using Yup'ik enough out of school. As one administrator commented:

> People are very concerned about the loss of language, and some people are looking to the school to save the language. But the school can't save it. Those people need to speak the language at home, and in the business of the community, when they go to the store, and when they work at the council.

The administrator's overall point, that schools, *on their own*, cannot maintain or reinstate community languages, is established in the reversing language shift literature (Fishman, 1991, 2001). Nevertheless, schools play important roles in supporting heritage language maintenance in the contemporary Indigenous communities (Hornberger, 2008). Educators send powerful messages about language learning, ability and linguistic possibility, for instance, in the ways that they discuss schools, individuals, families, and communities. Throughout the 1990s, most Piniq educators ostensibly supported bilingualism, sending home "separate but equal" messages that English was the language of the cash economy, and Yup'ik was the language of elders, subsistence, and traditional ways. Local work in Piniq, however, was bilingual work. For many adult community members, monolingual elders' *qanruyutait,* oral teachings in Yup'ik, represented a "cumulative knowledge on a timescale and spatial scale that no individual could match" (Lemke, 2000, p. 282), and a heritage that had only been partially passed down to bilingual adults who attended boarding schools. Middle-aged adults translanguaged to involve elders and integrate elders' *qan-ruyutait* into new village institutions as a means of negotiating social, political, and economic change. Youth who got good jobs in the local economy also commonly worked with Yup'ik-speaking elders (Wyman, 2012).

As many youth stopped using Yup'ik beyond simple Yup'ik words and phrases, community members expressed concern that youth might be cut off from elders and elders' *qanruyutait*. In 2000–2001 educators also worried that parents had shifted responsibility for Yup'ik language maintenance to the school. Other local adults assumed that youth were orienting toward white-stream society by speaking English, and criticized young people's English use and presumed ethnic identity loss with comments like, "*Yugtun, kassauguci-qaa?*" ("Speak Yup'ik, what are you, whites?").

When educators or community members narrowly focused on single causes of shift, however, this obscured (a) the ways historical and contemporary processes of schooling undermined community efforts to maintain Yup'ik; and (b) how other long-term processes additionally produced language shift at the individual, peer group, and family levels in the complex local linguistic ecology. In the 1970s, Piniq had one of the first Indigenous bilingual programs in Alaska, yet the program was reduced in the 1980s when a non-Native administrator questioned the program's effectiveness. After that time, English became the core language of elementary instruction. The children who first used English as a peer language were the first to receive primary elementary instruction in English in the 1980s. In 2000–2001, most families started out speaking Yup'ik with their children, and the eldest children of these families used Yup'ik productively with peers. Many parents, however, noted how their children started using mostly English after attending school.

In the 1980s and 1990s in southwestern Alaska, increasing village–urban and intervillage movement, and the accompanying modern dislocation and relocation of family life (Fishman, 2001) placed additional pressure on young people's language learning networks in Piniq, shaping young people's language learning opportunities in concert with ongoing schooling practices. Adults from Piniq increasingly moved back and forth between urban and rural Alaska in a strategic effort to take advantage of jobs and education elsewhere, while maintaining villages as touchstones of Yup'ik identity (cf. Fienup-Riordan, 2000). Increasing numbers of second-language Yup'ik speaking adults married into Piniq as well, to raise their children in a safe community where they could be close to elders and practice subsistence.

Further complicating an uneven picture, some young people's Yup'ik skills were fostered and activated by migration to strong Yup'ik-speaking villages and stints in schools with relatively strong Yup'ik programs elsewhere. When children in immigrant communities migrate to heritage language speaking countries, their mobility supports heritage language development and maintenance

(Zentella, 1997). Unlike heritage language learners connecting to countries with stable heritage languages, however, children in Piniq migrated to and from villages in an Indigenous region where language shift already affected three out of four villages (Krauss, 1997). During the study many more children from Piniq moved to English-speaking places than Yup'ik-speaking places (Wyman, 2013).

As the processes described above influenced Piniq's linguistic ecology, local peer culture also became a driving force of language shift. Youth in the "Get By" group maintained a common base of receptive and limited productive skills in Yup'ik, like many immigrant heritage language learners elsewhere (Valdés, 2005). Yet a majority of GB youth "tipped" into using English stand-alone words in lieu of verbal post-bases and word endings that form the heart of the Yup'ik morphosyntactic system (Jacobson, 1995). In 2000-2001 families whose young children had cousins or friends with strong Yup'ik productive skills generally maintained Yup'ik at home. Families without such support in children's peer networks, however, began to evidence a common family-level pattern elsewhere, using increasing amounts of English with younger children after their oldest children attended school.

Thus, within a brief window of time, Piniq moved dramatically towards language shift. Young people's Yup'ik language learning opportunities eroded and diverged as a seemingly stable bilingual setting transformed into a highly uneven linguistic landscape. Next we will consider how youth interpreted and negotiated their positions vis-a-vis emerging dynamics of language shift/endangerment.

Looking Within Youth Culture

Peer Dynamics and Diverging Linguistic Repertoires

Elsewhere I document how youth in the study innovatively combined symbolic resources ranging from a Yup'ik-influenced regional dialect of English to translocalized media-related references and styles as they navigated particular experiences and situations in and out of school (Wyman, 2012). At the same time, youth in the study were very aware of community desires for them to speak Yup'ik and a local language ideology linking Yup'ik with ethnic identity, vibrant land use practices, discourse expectations, and socializing genres of elders' strong talk. Most youth also expressed particularly powerful and positive associations with Yup'ik language, ethnicity, local practices, and local knowledge. From 1992 to 2001, young people in Piniq additionally grew up with a strong sense of who was and wasn't "really speaking Yup'ik." In 2000–2001, roughly a third of secondary students were identified as "fluent Yup'ik speakers," a third as "minimal Yup'ik speakers," and a third as "non-Yup'ik speakers" on school assessments. Among the shrinking sub-group of youth who had life contingencies align in favor of developing strong Yup'ik skills, Yup'ik remained an everyday language of peer culture. Stronger Yup'ik-speaking students also used Yup'ik to communicate in front of or with peers with more limited Yup'ik productive skills. However, students who (a) spent part of their childhoods in English speaking places, (b) had second language Yup'ik speaking parents, and/or (c) were younger siblings with English-speaking childhood friends described and evidenced linguistic insecurities speaking Yup'ik.

Emerging Logics of Language Loss and Endangerment

In the older "Real Speaker" group, youth who spent time in urban areas or English-speaking villages reported that they felt like they could no longer speak Yup'ik when they moved back to Piniq. These youth stood out as exceptions and rarely linked their own individual stories of language loss to concerns about community language endangerment. In contrast, as community members increasingly anticipated full-scale language shift in 2000–2001, young people in the younger "Get By" group described a wide range of life circumstances related to personal language loss. Some youth implicitly or overtly critiqued the ways local schooling in English undermined their parents' efforts to maintain Yup'ik at home. One girl, for instance, described how both she and her younger siblings first "tipped" into using English when they attended the local school.

Youth also shared "emergent narrative logics" (Ochs & Capps, 2000, p. 200) of the ways unexpected life events were tied to community language endangerment. In many instances youth brought up the possibility of language shift, using "free flowing temporal border crossings" (Ochs & Capps, 2000 p. 200) to partially articulate how their personal experiences related to the developing linguistic situation in Piniq. Before the following interview segment with two secondary students in 2000, I asked students what they thought Piniq would be like in the future:

1. *LTW:*   What kinds of things will be the same, what kinds of things will be different?
2. *Nathan:* Our Yup'ik language might be the same, or might be different, I don't know.
3. *Mike:*   I heard one village lost their language.
4. *LTW:*   What do people say about, like, Yup'ik and English?
5. *Nathan:* When I used to be small, I used to speak Yup'ik language, but when they were (inaudible) we lost that language.
6. *Mike:*   Me, too.
7. *Nathan:* When I played with … when my mom brought me to Anchorage, I forgot how.
8. *Mike:*   Me, I forgot how from uh, playing with a boy who talked English too much. When I try speak Yup'ik I speak it wrong.

Above, both students indirectly bring up local concerns about language endangerment, first with Nathan's reference to how "our Yup'ik language … might be different" (line 2), and in Mike's report that "one village lost their language" (line 3). In response to my question about "what people say" about Yup'ik and English (line 4), Mike and Nathan then move back in time to share individual stories of language loss, indirectly linking their personal trajectories to the emerging possibility of community language endangerment. Sharing brief childhood stories, they describe points in time when they "knew" Yup'ik and were Yup'ik speakers, and seemingly explain why they no longer spoke or felt insecure about their Yup'ik use. In line 5, Nathan speaks as part of a group with a unique relationship to Yup'ik, and briefly recaps how "we lost that language" in a one-way process.

Mike and Nathan emphasize how unexpected experiences, such as Nathan's stint in a distant city (line 7) and Mike's friendship with an English-speaking peer (line 8) influenced their non-use of Yup'ik. Relating contingencies to language "forgetting," Mike and Nathan highlight the ways diffuse processes were contributing to students' linguistic insecurities. Yet Mike and Nathan overlook how longer-term processes and relationships contributed to their identities as Yup'ik language "forgetters." Stories of how personal friendships "caused" personal language loss, like Mike's above, for instance, became common only in 2000–2001 after the local peer culture started "tipping" into English, and after changes in schooling and patterns of migration eroded young people's collective resources for learning Yup'ik. By framing their stories in terms of individual language "forgetting" in lines 7 and 8, Mike and Nathan leave open the possibility that changing circumstances and their own actions might allow them to "remember" how to be confident Yup'ik speakers. Yet as they narrate their language trajectories, Nathan and Mike also align to create seemingly logical outcomes of unexpected life events including linguistic insecurity, language forgetting, and collective language endangerment.

Importantly, in their spontaneous descriptions, Mike and Nathan obscured how they themselves *used* Yup'ik in 2000–2001 to "get by" and participate in local life. Similar to many of their peers, Mike and Nathan expressed linguistic insecurity about speaking Yup'ik, and did not use advanced Yup'ik post-bases and word endings in extended Yup'ik utterances. Nevertheless, many youth like Mike and Nathan, who spent years in Piniq, grew adept at combining listening skills with simple statements and phrases in Yup'ik. After returning from Anchorage, for instance, Nathan used Yup'ik at home to interact with siblings who never left Piniq, as well as with grandparents, aunts, and uncles. As the younger child of a shifting family, Mike, as well, used Yup'ik with relatives, and could translate when local elders exchanged pleasantries with White teachers. Like others in the first group to use primarily English in local peer culture, Nathan and Mike also used Yup'ik receptive skills, token phrases, and simple statements to learn practices central to community life, as we will consider here.

Negotiating Connections to Place, Community, and Indigenous Knowledge

Historically, Indigenous youth have been socialized through language practices ranging from stories to naming practices, catechisms, and lectures, as well as activities including observation, imitation, practice, and gendered apprentice-style learning (Lomawaima & McCarty, 2006). Youth who did not comfortably speak Yup'ik in 2000 integrated various forms of heritage language learning with the learning of *yuuyaraq* (the way to be human), a local knowledge system connecting the Yup'ik language with human–animal and human-to-human relationships, local activities, and ecological knowledge (Fienup-Riordan, Rearden, & Meade, 2005). In the same interview as above, Nathan and Mike describe learning how to hunt seals:[1]

1. *Nathan:* Sometimes, me, me and my *apii* (granddad) only go alone … It's fun when we go spring hunting.
2. *Mike:* For seals.
3. *Nathan:* Yup.
4. *LTW:* What's your favorite kind of hunting.
5. *Nathan:* Seal=
6. *Mike:* =Seal hunt, everybody.
7. *LTW:* What's it like?
8. *Mike:* It's cool, cold, really
9. *Nathan:* /Fun/
10. *Mike:* /Really/ … close, real.
11. *Nathan:* Yup.
12. *Mike:* You'll catch *maklaar* (bearded seal), big=
13. *Nathan:* =Really big, really fat, blubber.
14. *Mike:* And sometime the adults say, they'll cut 'em up, "*tangvauriqluci*" (watch carefully, be ever vigilant). [See discussion below]
15. *Nathan:* They cut, cut, cut their head?
16. *LTW:* Um hmm.
17. *Nathan:* If they cut their head, put it in the water, say "*Cali taikina*, come back again." Throw it in the water.
18. *LTW:* Um hmm.
19. *Mike:* I did that at, uh, fall.
20. *Nathan:* I did that when we cut a *maklaar* (bearded seal).

Nathan and Mike describe how they used the simple Yup'ik prayer "*Cali taikina*" ("Come back again") and returned seal heads to the water (lines 17, 19, and 20), enacting the belief that seals treated with respect will return to hunters. Nathan and Mike also use Yup'ik terminology to reference specific seal types (line 12, 19 *maklaar*—bearded seal), and terms of endearment for older relatives (line 1 *apii*—grandad).

Youth in Piniq often recounted interactions with adult mentors, reenacting the ways they used Yup'ik in learning gendered subsistence activities. Above Mike voices an adult mentor's teaching (line 14), and his seeming quote, "*tangvaur-i-qluci*," highlights both the challenges and strengths of heritage learners who may evidence linguistic errors yet still be acquiring heritage language phrases, vocabulary, and skills through participation in community activities (e.g., Valdés, 2005). "*Tangvaur-i-qluci*" echoes a common refrain used when adults instruct youth to pay careful attention—"*Tangvaur-a-qluci*" or "Be vigilant."[2]

Mike's offhand comment about seal hunting being "everybody's" favorite hunting (line 6), and the pacing of the segment stand in marked contrast to local worries that English-speaking youth "wanted to be like whites." Mike and Nathan overlap their speech (lines 9, 10), and latch onto one another's statements (lines 5, 6, 12, 13) as the excitement of recalling seal hunting speeds the interaction. Overall in the segment, Mike and Nathan counter the common assumption that youth who speak dominant languages in endangered language communities are simply orienting away from local practices, physical spaces, or marginalized identities. They also complicate their earlier self-descriptions as Yup'ik language "losers" or "forgetters" who "speak Yup'ik wrong." Importantly, Mike and Nathan offer contrasting evidence of their agency as Yup'ik language *users* and *learners* using Yup'ik prayers, ecological terminology, endearments, and teachings to learn their community's knowledge system.

Socializing One Another through Storytelling about Subsistence

Yup'ik adults may orient toward ethnic identities and local epistemologies in discourse about subsistence (Hensel, 1996; Morrow & Hensel, 1992). Throughout the decade-long study, Piniq youth regularly told one another stories about their experiences with gendered subsistence practices, underscoring and distributing the knowledge they were gaining about the environment, their community, and co-interpreting what it meant to take on adult roles over time. Villagers commonly noted in 2000–2001 that one of the last regular places to hear storytelling in Yup'ik among youth was young men's land-related adventure stories. Both young men and women in the Get By group were particularly likely to use extended Yup'ik in telling land-related adventure stories (Wyman, 2012). In another taped group interview, Mike from above shared seal hunting stories with Evon and Tom, two strong Yup'ik speakers and experienced hunters his age. [Terms in bold discussed below.]

1. *Mike:*   *Kavialuq* caught *maklaar* (bearded seal) at Friday.
2. *Tom:*   Did they go out Friday?
3. *Mike:*   Kavialuq and Ned's dad.
4. *Evon:*   *Cikigaq?*
5. *Mike:*   Ned's dad.

6. *Evon:*   Cikigaq.
7. *Mike:*   Who's Cikigaq?
8. *Tom and Evon:*   Ned's dad.
9. *Mike:*   Yeh. Cikigaq caught *maklaar* (bearded seal).

 You know when we **go down**, we go **that** way?

 I mean, that- **this** way?

 And then, **there** was a *maklaar* (bearded seal) **right there**.

 Issuriyagaq (1-year-old spotted seal), Peter said took 'em, and then ... We were shooting **that** one, and then they went **that way**. And they xxx **this way**, and then they shot it. It went "Qrr ch: ... vvuu tksh;" on the second one. Almost/ sink./

10. *Evon:*   /Was it in/ the water? Under water? When they harpoon it?
11. *Tom:*   Evon-**am pugtangraan nutenqiggluku** (shot it again even though it was floating)
12. *Evon:*   Neh, it was gonna *kit'aq* (sink) it was like this, its back,

 very big, and it was going down. First it went like this "ch:" / staying on the water/.
13. *Tom:*   /And then it was/ it was floating.
14. *LTW:*   Hmm.
15 *Mike:*   *Tegullruan?* (Did you take it with your hands?)
16. *Evon:*   Harpoon.

As in other Yup'ik villages, Piniq community members received multiple Yup'ik and English names, comprising "webs of many... strands weav(ing) each person inextricably and uniquely into the community" (Fienup-Riordan, 2000, p. 194). Yup'ik names tied living individuals to community members who had passed on, and harkened to ongoing relationships with living relatives and friends of the namesakes. As Piniq youth were mentored into subsistence, they entered into new relationships of responsibility with older community members and commonly socialized one another to recognize adults by their Yup'ik names and/or nicknames. In the excerpt above, lines 1–9, we see how Tom and Evon socialized Mike to use the correct Yup'ik name of an adult hunter in lieu of the more childlike English description "Ned's dad," before allowing Mike to describe a hunting event he witnessed.

Strong Yup'ik speakers like Tom and Evon also used Yup'ik to emphasize their relative positions of power with peers as they negotiated the floor in every-day storytelling sessions (e.g., Jørgensen, 1998). Youth who reported linguistic insecurities additionally used simple phrases in Yup'ik to position themselves as knowledgeable participants in subsistence conversations. Above, after Evon asks Mike for clarification about the seal hunt he witnessed in line 10, Tom gains the floor by using a relatively complex combination of morphemes in Yup'ik, "*pugtangraan nutenqiggluku*" (shot it again even though it was floating). In doing so, he temporarily shifts the conversation from strong Yup'ik speakers and hunters (Tom and Evon) listening to a minimal Yup'ik speaker with less hunting experience (Mike), to strong Yup'ik speakers sharing an in-joke about a different story. In the lines immediately following, Evon and Tom discuss the subsequent story in English (lines 12–13). To regain the floor, Mike uses a clarifying question in Yup'ik in line 15:

Example:	*Tegu-llru-an?*
Translation:	'Take'-PAST TENSE-2sSUBJ/3sOBJ
Gloss:	Did you take it?

Here Mikes combines a single, common verbal post-base to mark tense, *-llru*, with a transitive word ending marking subject and object, *-an*, demonstrating his knowledge of how to make simple Yup'ik statements. However, Mike sticks to the type of simple Yup'ik construction that was becoming common among youth in 2000–2001.

Losing Language, Losing Direction ...?

As we have seen, in an early, uneven phase of rapid language shift, youth in Piniq who expressed linguistic insecurities about speaking Yup'ik used Yup'ik tokenism to maintain and negotiate connections to community members and local knowledge, as well as their positions in local peer culture. However, in 2000–2001, young people's stories also evidenced how youth were losing the linguistic awareness of a community orientation to land. Often scholars point out the richness of a specific worldview and knowledge system that disappears with each endangered language (Harrison, 2007; Woodbury, 1993, 1998). One Yup'ik feature that interests linguists is an extensive system of demonstrative pronouns, adverbs, and related verb stems meaning "to go" (in some specific direction). The Yup'ik demonstrative system, with its related forms, elegantly marks a highly tuned orientation to the physical surroundings of the speaker (Jacobson, 1995; Woodbury, 1993, 1998). Yup'ik demonstratives distinguish, for instance, whether an object is near or far, up or down (in the air or down below, up or down the slope of the land), in or out (upriver or downriver), over or across from the speaker (as in across a body of water or trail), moving towards, moving away, spread out, or contained.

Elders who are fluent speakers of Cup'ik, a dialect of Yup'ik, use demonstratives to achieve "broad artistic and communicative goals" (Woodbury, 1993, p. 10). Observing that speakers do not or only partially tend to translate form-dependent expressions like demonstratives into English, Woodbury argues that many aspects of cultural continuity transfer across languages, but that "the continuity of intricate, complex, delicately tuned, deeply interwoven systems" can also be dramatically disrupted in language tip (1998, p. 256). We see an example of this in the excerpt above, where Mike tells a short hunting story in English starting at line 9. As Mike summarizes where he went in a single hunting trip, he uses multiple instances of the demonstratives "this," "that," or "there," and two instances of the verb "go" (identified in bold in the excerpt above).

In similar interactions there was little evidence that young people could not follow one another, and additional evidence that youth were using gestures and shared references to get their meaning across in the absence of Yup'ik demonstratives. While telling the story above, Mike used hand gestures and oriented his listeners by calling up shared experiences and knowledge of land, asking in line 9, "You know when we **go down**, we **go that way**?" Nevertheless, it is easy to imagine how Yup'ik demonstratives and related verb stems might dramatically affect the level of detail of the story, or any similar description of navigating on land. During the study elders, parents, Yup'ik teachers, and students noted that Yup'ik demonstratives and related verb stems were disappearing from young people's Yup'ik use. As one parent described:

> And <u>everything</u> to them is *tageq* **(go up an incline)**, <u>everywhere</u>, like they don't have the meaning of direction. If they don't ... like, toward the river? *Wani* **(Here)**. Toward the airport? *Piani* **(Up, away from the river)**. Toward the [*Name*] building? *Agaani, agaani.* **(Across there, across there)**. *Man'a-ll' tuai, un'gaani* (And **this one, downriver, extended**). *Tua-i-ll', agaani?* (Then, **across there extended**?) If you're talking about *agaani*? (**across there extended**?) My generation: "*Qaqa-tartua* [*Building Name*] building-*amun* (I'm going to **go to the** [*Name*] building). *Atra*qatartua kuigem tungiinun. (I'm going to **go down** in the direction of the river.) *Tagqatartua elitnaurvigmun.* (I'm going to **go up** to the school). *Un'gaavet, waten, uterteqatartua* (**Downriver**, like this, I'm going to go back home)." ... *Ellait-llu tua-i* (And then they), if our kids talk? "*Tagqatartua.*" ("I'm **going up**.") That's <u>all</u> they say, "*Tagqatartua.*" ("I'm **going up**.") "*Tagqatartua*" *kiingan*. (Only "I'm **going up**.") That's the <u>only</u> word they started using from Wes's generation.

The flattened Yup'ik demonstrative system in young people's speech raised questions about the significance of youth's losing the ability to mark linguistically a physical orientation to land. Yet perhaps more importantly, adults described how, in at least some cases, young people's loss of demonstratives was causing intergenerational miscommunication in everyday interactions, contributing to vicious cycles of increasing doubts about and reduced resources for Yup'ik maintenance in homes (Wyman, 2012, 2013). The parent quoted above, for instance, described how she had easily maintained Yup'ik with her older children in the "Real Speaker" group without consciously trying to use Yup'ik or realizing "how bad our language was going to be dropped, later on." She reported that she found herself switching into English to accommodate her younger children in the "Get By" group when they seemingly couldn't understand directives using demonstratives. An elder, as well, described how her granddaughter could not understand simple requests involving Yup'ik demonstratives. As a result, the elder said, she had started using her minimal English, versus Yup'ik, with her granddaughter.

Conclusion

Young people's experiences of language maintenance and endangerment are deeply rooted within local relationships, practices, knowledge systems, and geographical places. Even in very small communities, they vary among individuals, peer groups and families within cornerstone generations of language shift. They are also continuously negotiated within the interactional moments of everyday life. At the same time, young people's linguistic performances and opportunities for learning or losing heritage languages are shaped by forms of schooling and flows of people, policies, and discourses negotiated across time and geographical spaces. Changes in young people's peer cultures can accelerate tidal waves of sociolinguistic transformation in endangered language communities (e.g., Harrison, 2007). Yet as we have seen here, in early settings of language shift, these waves can happen in spite of the ways youth may value their heritage languages, and how they socialize one another and are socialized by adults to maintain connections to unique communities, knowledge systems, and local spaces.

Schools are embroiled in the historical and contemporary sociolinguistic transformation of Indigenous communities. Even after the overtly oppressive period of Alaska Native education, the Piniq school maintained "social and linguistic hierarchies [that were] remarkably persistent" (Jaffe, 2007, p. 73), undermining heritage language programming and community heritage language maintenance. Yet as history sped up in the margins (Hill, 2006), and language endangerment became evident, educators, community members, and youth generated an array of assumptions about bilingualism that often pointed to single root causes of language shift out of school in community life. Together, these emerging logics of shift obscured ongoing effects of schooling on language practices, meanings of heritage language maintenance, and possibilities for bilingualism.

Indigenous educators and community members face tremendous challenges maintaining heritage languages in radically changing sociolinguistic settings. In early language tip, young people's linguistic repertoires may diverge, leaving educators with the task of developing new forms of local language planning, programs, and pedagogies as the proportions of youth with low and high productive skills change very quickly (Wyman, 2012; Wyman et al., 2010a). Youth may lose unique linguistic forms in heritage languages, challenging everyday intergenerational communication. While youth often initially maintain considerable heritage language receptive skills, they may also quickly take up positions as heritage language listeners vs. speakers, expressing and evidencing linguistic insecurities.

Schools are not set up to foster heritage language learning or to "recognize (the) multiple norms and mixed codes" of youth in dynamic shift settings (Jaffe, 2007, p. 73; see also Jørgensen, 1998). In general, teachers who work to reverse language shift must strategically develop students' heritage language competencies so that they can interact comfortably with older generations. However, if youth feel embarrassed about their mixed language practices, they are likely to shift further towards dominant languages (García, 2009).

Understanding how young people's in- and out-of-school experiences, learning opportunities, and everyday discourse practices mediate connections among Indigenous languages, local relationships, unique local ecologies, and land-use practices may also be discouraging for Indigenous language educators. Local processes like peer language socialization and interactions in homes, or translocal processes such as patterns of migration understandably seem like they are out of local educators' control. Single events and short-term processes can also have long-term effects on heritage language maintenance, as well as young people's positions as speakers or non-speakers of endangered languages.

Yet the ways in which specific events and short-term processes play out also depend upon how long-term processes of language learning and subsequent events and relationships integrate with broader learning processes in schools, peer groups, families, and communities over time (e.g., Lemke, 2000; Wortham, 2006). The seemingly short-term change in school programming in Piniq in the 1980s, for instance, had long-term effects on community heritage language maintenance efforts. The ongoing impact of the language programming decision was also shaped by the ways that language learning opportunities eroded through changing patterns of migration, the ways educators, community members, and youth focused outside of school for straightforward explanations of language shift, the ways youth tacitly and explicitly positioned themselves as Yup'ik language "forgetters" in interactions with peers and adults, and the ways adults responded to young people's changing linguistic practices over time.

Language shift, linguistic forms, local knowledge, heritage language learners' identities, and community members' future sense of direction are also contingent, and subject to the actions of educators, community members, and others. Young people's positions as speakers or non-speakers of their heritage languages can also be reshaped given changes in their exposure to individuals, situations, and linguistic processes, especially if their language learning is sustained over time through relationships and community practices (see Wilson & Kamanā, this volume).

As youth teach us, even in rapid language shift settings, there can exist new forms of linguistic survivance and windows of opportunity for connecting individuals, peer groups, and generations to linguistic resources, local relationships, and community knowledge systems. Situating youth language in time and place, and engaging with contingency and hybridity in young people's linguistic practices can help language planners, educators, and community members tease apart the complexities of language shift, recognize a potential school role in supporting community knowledge systems, and understand how youth negotiate varying linguistic competences and language ideologies as they position themselves in relation to community members and (trans) local practices; and strategically rebuild heritage language-learning opportunities in settings of radical sociolinguistic change. In-depth consideration of young people's linguistic practices can also help counter damaging discourses and binary assumptions that Indigenous community members simply orient towards local or global practices, Indigenous languages or English, subsistence versus cash economies, or traditional versus modern worlds. Such countering is crucial for disrupting the damaging essentialisms that are imposed on youth and Indigenous peoples worldwide. It is also essential for grounding language planning and for creating sustained ideological and implementational spaces (Hornberger, 2008) within which Indigenous community members can work through the types of complexities described above, demonstrating linguistic survivance as they create multilingual futures for youth and their communities over time.

Acknowledgments

Quyanaqvaa to the youth and adults in "Piniq" for sharing their insights and experiences. I also thank Shirley Brice Heath, Penny Eckert, and Guadalupe Valdés for valuable research guidance. This research benefited from National Science Foundation, Spencer Foundation, and University of Arizona College of Education financial support. I am additionally grateful to Walkie Charles, Perry Gilmore, Patrick Marlow, Teresa McCarty, Phyllis Morrow, Brendan O'Connor, the University of Alaska Fairbanks SLATE program summer 2007 Language Policy and Planning class, and two anonymous reviewers for comments on a previous version of this chapter. All mistakes are my own.

Note

1   Transcription key: In transcripts, slashes (//) are used to indicate the overlapping talk of speakers. Equal signs (=) are used to indicate sentences where speakers' statements followed quickly after one another without a pause.
2   From the verb stem *tangvaur(ar)*, to stare or to watch intently, with the plural second person subordinative mood ending—*luci* as an imperative. I thank Walkie Charles for clarifying this term, and for insights regarding adult uses of the phrase with youth.

References

Barnhardt, R., & Kawagley, O. (2004). Culture, chaos, and complexity: Catalysts for change in Indigenous education. *Cultural Survival Quarterly, 27*(4), 59–64.
Blommaert, J. (2005). *Discourse.* New York, NY: Cambridge University Press.

Blommaert, J. (2010). *The sociolinguistic of globalization*. New York, NY: Cambridge University Press.

Brayboy, B. (2005). Toward a tribal critical race theory in education. *The Urban Review, 37*(5), 425–446.

Collins, J., Baynham, M., & Slembrouck, S. (2009). *Globalization and language in contact: Scale, migration, and communicative practices*. London, England: Continuum Press.

Dorian, N. (Ed.). (1989). *Investigating obsolescence: Studies in language contact and death*. Cambridge, England: Cambridge University Press.

Fienup-Riordan, A. (2000). *Hunting tradition: Yup'ik lives in Alaska today*. New Brunswick, NJ: Rutgers University Press.

Fienup-Riordan, A., Rearden, A. & Meade, M. (2005). *Yup'ik words of wisdom: Yupiit qanruyutait*. Lincoln: University of Nebraska Press.

Fishman, J. A. (1991). *Reversing language shift: Theoretical and empirical foundations of assistance to threatened languages*. Clevedon, England: Multilingual Matters.

Fishman, J. A. (Ed.). (2001). *Can threatened languages be saved? Reversing language shift, revisited: A 21st century perspective*. Clevedon, England: Multilingual Matters.

Gal, S. (1979). *Language shift: Social determinants of linguistic change in bilingual Austria*. New York, NY: Academic Press.

García, O. (2009). *Bilingual education in the 21st century: A global perspective*. West Sussex, England: Wiley-Blackwell.

Garrett, P. & Baquedano-López, P. (2002). Language socialization: Reproduction and continuity, transformation and change. *Annual Review of Anthropology, 31*, 339–361.

Harrison, D. (2007). *When languages die*. Oxford, England: Oxford University Press.

Hensel, C. (1996). *Telling ourselves: Ethnicity and discourse in southwestern Alaska*. New York, NY: Oxford University Press.

Hill, J. (2006). The ethnography of language and language documentation. In J. Gippert, N. Himmelmann, & U. Mosel (Eds.), *Essentials of language documentation* (pp. 113–128). Berlin, Germany: Mouton de Gruyter.

Hornberger, N. H. (Ed.). (2008). *Can schools save Indigenous languages?: Policy and practice on four continents*. New York, NY: Palgrave Macmillan.

Jacobson, S. (1995). *A practical grammar of the Central Alaskan Yup'ik Eskimo language*. Fairbanks: Alaska Native Language Center, University of Alaska.

Jaffe, A. (2007). Contexts and consequences of essentializing discourses. In A. Duchêne & M. Heller (Eds.), *Discourses of endangerment: ideology and interest in the defence of languages* (pp. 57–75). London, England: Continuum Press.

Jørgensen, J. (1998). Children's acquisition of code-switching for power-wielding. In P. Auer (Ed.), *Code-switching in conversation: Language, interaction and identity* (pp. 237–261). London, England: Routledge.

Krauss, M. (1997). The Indigenous languages of the North: A report on their present state. *Northern Minority Languages: Problems of Survival. Senri Ethnological Studies, 44*, 1–34.

Kulick, D. (1992). *Language shift and cultural reproduction: Socialization, self, and syncretism in a Papua New Guinean village*. Cambridge, England: Cambridge University Press.

Lemke, J. (2000). Across the scales of time: Artifacts, activities, and meanings in ecosocial systems. *Mind, Culture, and Activity, 7*(4), 273–290.

Lipka, J., with Mohatt, G. & the Ciulistet Group (1998). *Transforming the culture of schools: Yup'ik Eskimo examples*. Mahwah, NJ: Erlbaum.

Lomawaima, K. T., & McCarty, T. L. (2006). *"To remain an Indian": Lessons in democracy from a century of Native American education*. New York, NY: Teachers College Press.

May, S. (2005). Language rights: Moving the debate forward. *Journal of Sociolinguistics, 9*(3), 319–347.

Morrow, P., & Hensel, C. (1992). Hidden dissension: Minority-majority relationships and the use of contested terminology. *Arctic Anthropology, 29*(1), 38–53.

Ochs, E., & Capps, L. (2000). *Living narrative: Creating lives in everyday storytelling*. Cambridge, MA: Harvard University Press.

Patrick, D. (2007). Indigenous language endangerment and the unfinished business of nation states. In A. Duchêne & M. Heller (Eds.), *Discourses of endangerment: Ideology and interest in the defense of languages* (pp. 35–56). London, England: Continuum Press.

Schieffelin, B., & Ochs, E. (1986). *Language socialization across cultures*. Cambridge, England: Cambridge University Press.

Valdés, G. (2005). Bilingualism, heritage language learners, and SLA research: Opportunities lost or seized? *The Modern Language Journal, 89*, 410–426.

Vizenor, G. (1994). *Manifest manners: PostIndian warriors of survivance*. Hanover, NH: Wesleyan University Press of New England.

Vizenor, G. (2008). Aesthetics of survivance: Literary theory and practice. In G. Vizenor (Ed.), *Survivance: Narratives of Native presence* (pp. 1–23). Lincoln: University of Nebraska Press.

Woodbury, A. (1998). Documenting rhetorical, aesthetic, and expressive loss in language shift. In L. Grenoble & L. Whaley (Eds.), *Endangered languages: Current issues and future prospects* (pp. 234–258). Cambridge, England: Cambridge University Press.

Woodbury, A. (1993). A defense of the proposition, "When a language dies, a culture dies." *Proceedings of the First Annual Symposium about Language and Society-Austin (SALSA). Texas Linguistic Forum, 33*, 101–129.

Woolard, K. (1998). Introduction: Language ideology as a field of inquiry. In B. Schieffelin, K. Woolard, & P. V. Kroskrity (Eds.), *Language ideologies: practice and theory* (pp. 3–47). Oxford, England: Oxford University Press.

Wortham, S. (2006). *Learning identity: The joint emergence of identification and academic learning*. Cambridge, England: Cambridge University Press.

Wyman, L. T. (2012). *Youth culture, language endangerment and linguistic survivance*. Bristol, England: Multilingual Matters.

Wyman, L. T. (2013). Indigenous youth migration and language contact. *International Multilingual Research Journal, 7*(1), 66-82.

Wyman, L., Marlow, P., Andrew, C. F., Miller, G., Nicholai, C. R., & Rearden, Y. N. (2010a). Focusing on long-term language goals in challenging times: Yup'ik examples. *Journal of American Indian Education, 49*(1& 2), 22–43.

Wyman, L., Marlow, P., Andrew, C. F., Miller, G., Nicholai, C. R., & Rearden, Y. N. (2010b). High stakes testing, bilingual education and language endangerment: A Yup'ik example. *International Journal of Bilingual Education and Bilingualism, 13*(6), 701–721.

Zentella, A. (1997). *Growing up bilingual: Puerto Rican children in New York*. Oxford, England: Blackwell.

6

"I DIDN'T KNOW YOU KNEW MEXICANO!"

Shifting Ideologies, Identities, and Ambivalence among Former Youth in Tlaxcala, Mexico

Jacqueline Messing

Youth in historically Mexicano-speaking communities in Tlaxcala, Mexico have multiple ideologies about language use and local identities. Young adulthood is a particularly crucial time in which ideological positions on Indigenous language and identity are in flux, thus having important consequences for language shift and revitalization. Drawing on ethnographic observation and interviews, I focus on youth and young adult ideologies about Indigenousness and modernity, influenced by globalizing forces and societal discourses that denigrate Indigenous languages and identities. To the outside observer, ambivalence is at the center of youth ideologies of language and identity, yet ideologies governing language shift can change over time. Reflective narratives offer evidence of these changing ideologies and hope for language revitalization. Ambivalence needs to be studied further as part of a sociohistorical response to minoritized status and interpersonal conflicts about authenticity.

Introduction: Youth and Language Shift

Youth in historically Mexicano-speaking communities in the state of Tlaxcala, Mexico have multiple ideologies about language use and local identities. They are socialized to actively use Spanish, while their socialization in Indigenous language is often passive.[1] My research has shown that ideological positions vary and can change over time, with young adulthood being a crucial time in which ideological positions on Indigenous language and identity can change (Messing, 2003, 2009). These shifting ideologies have important consequences for language use and language shift (cf. Campbell, 1994; Dorian, 1989; Gal, 1979; Grenoble & Whaley, 1998; Mufwene, 2004), and language revitalization (Hinton & Hale, 2001; Hornberger, 1996; McCarty, 2008; McCarty & Zepeda, 2006; Wilson, 1998, this volume). This chapter focuses on Mexicano youth—children, teens, and early 20-year-olds—through the vista of young adults' ideologies, which, as I demonstrate below, are characterized by ambivalence about Native language use and identity.

I want to explain upfront that although youth rarely state ambivalence in Tlaxcala, it is observable through ethnography, and explicit in the reflective narratives of young adults I interviewed, mostly teachers in their 20s and 30s, who looked back on their changing perspectives over time. Several young adult interviewees changed their perspectives, actively seeking to improve their Native language skills over time. These reflective narratives are instructive. Regional use of Mexicano (the local name for Tlaxcalan Nahuatl) provides for a sociolinguistic situation of great ideological complexity (Hill, 1993; Hill & Hill, 1986; Messing, 2007a).

Ambivalence is a slippery topic to study. The importance of ambivalent ideologies has not otherwise been studied in depth, with the notable exception of Hornberger's (2000) work on ideological paradoxes in language revitalization. Through ethnography and analysis of taped interviews, a researcher can gain great insight into the myriad ideologies of language and identity among youth that are the driving forces behind language shift, and into the strong potential for Indigenous language revitalization. Indigenous Tlaxcalans are immersed in ideological struggles of identity and economics that emerge in everyday discourse and symbolic representation among youth. This chapter underscores the importance of observing and understanding *ambivalence* as part of language shift. My data from interviews with young Indigenous teachers also suggest that ideological orientations are alterable over time in endangered language situations, and at least some young adults change their ambivalent or anti-Indigenous positions, seeking to activate passive linguistic knowledge.

I begin by describing the ethnographic setting and ideological configuration of multilingualism in this Mexicano region of Tlaxcala, followed by a discussion of explicit and implicit ideologies of language, identity, and modernity in the young adults' discourse, including excerpts from interviews and general ethnographic observations. Themes include linguistic respect, purism and authenticity, use of English, and ambivalence among youth. Finally, I give examples of young people who shifted to a positive perspective on their Native language in their 20s, showing how language can indeed shift in favor of Native languages.

Methodology and Researcher Positionality

Since 1996 I have been conducting ethnographic and linguistic-anthropological research in the Malintzi volcano region of Tlaxcala intermittently, where I have collected over 100 hours of audio and video recordings, and conducted 45 interviews. Although I first visited the region in 1993 as a high school Spanish teacher, bringing six students for homestays in Tlaxcalan Mestizo cities, on future visits I met people from the Indigenous Malinche region. As a graduate student, during pilot research and later dissertation research, I focused particularly on the large county of San Bernardino Contla which is known for its textile industry (both industrialized and informal) (Nutini & Isaac, 1974), and drew comparisons from a part of the region where language maintenance is stronger—San Isidro Buensuceso (Francis, 1997; Nava Nava, 2007). I have been studying how people form and express their identities in and through competing discourses of Indigenousness, national identity, and economics in this Mexicano-speaking region of this central Mexican state. My observations and interviews have included people in both regions, and two Indigenous bicultural schools sponsored by the Dirección General de Educación Indígena (DGEI) that were attempting to incorporate a bilingual component in their otherwise standardized, official SEP (Secretaria de Educación Pública) curriculum. I conducted interviews in Spanish, with some in Mexicano, and recorded conversation in both languages.

Much of my contact with youth was through schools in Tlaxcala and through two large families with whom I lived starting in the early 1990s. Knowing I was from the United States, schoolchildren would often come up to me, asking to learn some English words. I conducted a few focus groups among elementary school children and interviewed youth who had been involved in an experimental language revitalization program. Some students reported enjoying spending time with their grandparents to hear stories. Others said they remembered curse words in Mexicano more easily than anything else! (See also Muehlmann, 2008.) The most direct, explicit information about youth came from narratives of Indigenous education teachers and townspeople during interviews and subsequent analysis of interview transcripts long after our conversations about language, identity, and social change had begun.

A key question of youth ambivalence surfaced in my research. I asked myself, what are the implications of placing youth at the center of our research agendas when working in ethnographic settings where shift is already advanced? When I was in the field I did not center my study on youth because the ambivalence I observed made it challenging to directly collect data. Rather, I engaged with "former-youth"—families, teachers, and local language promoters who expressed interest in Mexicano and my research who were in their mid- to late-20s and early 30s. Some made a point to tell local youth that an American anthropologist had traveled a long way to study their culture and language, when so many of them were (seemingly) more interested in learning English; this seemed to be an attempt to lend global validation to their goals of teaching Mexicano and inspiring interest.[2] Many teachers are very talented and motivated language promoters; several have been taping elders' narratives for years and have written their own Mexicano curriculum in their private time.

Ethnography is particularly important when focusing on youth cultures, because youth perspectives are often in a state of flux. I have found that ethnographic observation in communities and schools prior to interviewing individuals (or conducting focus groups) ensures more in-depth responses during taped, formal interviews and yields important information about actual language use and symbolic representation.

Observing Mexicano in Tlaxcalan Communities and Schools

Early in my fieldwork, I observed and was told about youth in some towns using Mexicano as a "code language," although it was rare for them to communicate in Mexicano when anyone outside of their social group could overhear them. For example, one day I overheard a conversation between two teenagers on a bus in Tlaxcala. Running into each other, these friends greeted one another and then one made a reference to Mexicano while the other replied, "I didn't know you knew it!" The ensuing conversation switched from Spanish to Mexicano.

The Mexican census reports that between 23% and 27% of the Tlaxcalan population over age 5 are speakers of an Indigenous language (INEGI, 1997, p. 21), but the accuracy of self-reporting is questionable. Mexicano language socialization does have certain predictable patterns (Hill & Hill, 1986; Messing, 2007b). Active speakers of Mexicano are usually over 40, but many younger people speak or understand much of the language, and many others are passive, semi- or quasi-speakers (Dorian, 1977; Flores Farfán, 1999). Native-language speakers usually converse with their generational peers; it is quite notable that cross-generational communication in Mexicano takes place in only very restricted contexts.

Factors that influence Mexicano and Spanish day-to-day speech in Contla vary and depend on the context, particularly who is talking to whom, when, and where. There is a greater likelihood that one will hear Mexicano in private, intimate contexts where there is greater trust (*confianza*). Such contexts include with family, with *compadres*, and in town or religious sodality (*cofradía*) or meetings. With these exceptions, the language of public meetings outside people's homes is most often Spanish. In addition to the need for *confianza*, Mexicano language use is also a matter of habit between speakers. A speaker must be certain that his or her interlocutor understands Mexicano, which is a subjective decision (Messing, 2003, 2007b). Communication with or among older community members can often be in Mexicano if interlocutors know each other well. Sometimes Contla residents use Mexicano with people who hail from other regions and are Mexicano-dominant.

My primary research goals were to study language use, linguistic ideology, and language shift in Mexicano communities, and to address the question: Is language revitalization possible via schools in Mexico? I found that the sociolinguistic situation in Indigenous-intercultural schools reflects that of the community and government, with a multitude of perspectives on language and identity, while adding the restriction of predominantly nationally standardized

Spanish-language curriculum. In Tlaxcalan public elementary schools with a bilingual component, speakers mainly use Spanish to communicate and Mexicano plays primarily a symbolic role. Furthermore, Spanish literacy instruction has traditionally been discordant with the oral tradition of speaking Mexicano (and other Mexican Native languages), thus creating another disjuncture when Native language education is modeled on Spanish teaching. Mexicano conversations take place occasionally among individuals; however, no "official" conversations are held in Mexicano. Language revitalization efforts have been ongoing in three contexts: (a) on a very small scale through local DGEI schools, (b) on a slightly larger scale through town cultural centers (*Casa de Cultura*), and (c) as institutionally independent efforts (teachers producing textbooks with their own time and resources).[3]

Multiple Ideologies of Language, Identity, and Modernity

In Tlaxcala, local residents take up ideological struggles of identity, language, and economics in everyday speech, which is organized through three dominant discourses. All Spanish speakers in Mexico (and much of developing Latin America) tap into a hegemonic *salir adelante* (to forge ahead and create a better socioeconomic future) discourse in some form. I see *salir adelante* as a broadly circulating metadiscourse of modernity. It can be heard in many parts of Latin America and the phrase is used in Indigenous and non-Indigenous settings when people talk about creating a better economic and professional future for their families. Locals call upon this metadiscourse of *salir adelante* through two microdiscourses of language, identity, and economics: *menosprecio* (denigration) or a pro-Indigenous (*pro-indígena*) discourse. These two ideological orientations compete for dominance in Malintzi residents' conversations (Messing, 2003, 2007a).

The ideological stances that surface in these discourses determine whether individuals will speak in Mexicano and actively inform the language socialization of children, and children's choices to use or not use the language in their presence. Children also take active roles in their socialization of Mexicano based on whether they are interested in learning the language. A young person might be the single family member to learn Mexicano, seeking out conversation with a Mexicano-dominant older relative (Messing, 2007a). The ideological stance or orientation is likely to be either *pro-Indígena* (pro-Indigenous), one of *menosprecio* (denigration), or a combination of the two.

Children are raised hearing and learning about these local views of Indigenousness, modernity, and economics within the context of being citizens in a developing nation. The children and their families' choices regarding who learns Mexicano and who speaks it when and to whom are often governed by these ideologies surfacing in the discourses identified above. For most youth, particularly semi-speakers, linguistic insecurity in Mexicano is common, and the desire to orient toward identities external to the community is strongly influenced by national and international media messages and local racism. Many interviewees explained that anti-Indigenous racism has been internalized in their communities, negatively affecting people's attitudes toward the main symbol of Indigenous identity in Mexico: language.

My understanding of the relationship between language and identity is informed by sociolinguistic and linguistic-anthropological theories of language as a symbol of identity (Greymorning, 2004; Kroskrity, 2000; McCarty & Zepeda, 2006; Schieffelin, Woolard, & Kroskrity, 1998), ethnic boundary marking (Barth, 1969), and that speech/conversation is an activity through which identities can be created and projected (Gumperz & Cook–Gumperz, 1982; Hymes, 1972; Mannheim & Tedlock, 1995). In particular, the "repertoire of identities" proposed by Kroskrity (1993) in his description of Arizona Tewa identity advances a multifaceted conceptualization of alternating identities, aspects of which surface in certain contexts. The complexity of the Tlaxcalan contemporary Indigenous sociolinguistic situation is captured by Kroskrity's discussion of identity as being communicated, interactive, and primarily situational, yet also a reflection of historical circumstances. For González (1992, 2001), the historical, socioeconomic, and political factors combine with affective factors. To understand how experiences with *menosprecio* or denigrative attitudes ultimately affect language use and ideology through identity, we must focus attention on what González (1992) called "the emotion of minority status":

> Because of a history of economic deprivation and second class citizenship, *the child is a receptacle for a greater number of ambivalent messages from a greater number of caregivers.* The filtering out process becomes exponentially complex ... the process of the construction of self through the exploration of affective parameters is not only an internal, psychobiological endeavor, but an external historically constituted, and particularistic process.
>
> *(1992, pp. 145–146; emphasis added)*

Experiences with multiple languages, identities, and "second class citizenship" in the U.S. borderlands bear a strong resemblance to the linguistic-ideological world of contemporary Indigenous Mexico in which ambivalence has also been observed. González's notion of the "emotion of minority status" suggests that there are cross-cultural dimensions to the affective experiences of children who are socialized as members of societies that have gone through a historical process of being "minoritized" (McCarty, 2002), with identities that are also marked linguistically. Interviewees spoke of the emotional process Tlaxcalan children go through to rid themselves of the "complex of being Indian," as one of my interviewees described the phenomenon (Messing, 2003).

Discourses of Language and Identity: Ambivalence and Linguistic Racism

To understand the relationships between ambivalence, language, and identity among Tlaxcalan youth, one must first have a sense of the larger discourses that circulate within and surrounding these youth's linguistic environment. Linguistic racism also needs to be understood. One example is from Mexico City, where I encountered a college-educated business owner who asked me: "Is Nahuatl really a language? I thought it was just a bunch of sounds."[4] Such *menosprecio* discourse is based on ignorance of what constitutes a language, but also a historical degradation of that which is Indigenous and thus considered inferior by Mestizo Mexico (Alonso, 2004; Bonfil Batalla, 1994; Garcia Canclini, 1994). Much writing on language shift and identity in Indigenous communities has focused on the concept of *stigma*, whereby the Indigenous language becomes viewed as stigmatized due to internalization of outside racism within local perspectives. At stake is the ideological question of what constitutes "authentic Mexican" identity. In Tlaxcalan Mexicano communities, the question becomes, what is an "authentic" Mexicano-Malintzi region identity? Hill (2004) has suggested that Indigenous languages such as Mexicano are becoming "disauthenticated": While Aztec ruins may be lauded by the mestizo public, tourism bureau and others, and Nahuatl proudly inscribed on historical buildings in Mexico City (Alonso, 2004), many actual speakers of Nahuatl are locked in a "struggle for authenticity, which is actively denied to subaltern groups" (Hill, 2004, p. 4; see also Hinton & Ahlers, 1999). The experience of idealizing an Indigenous past while marginalizing present-day Indigenous realities is a phenomenon experienced by Indigenous peoples throughout North America (Brayboy, 2005; Deloria, 1970; Vizenor, 1998). These similarities suggest that there are parallels in the lived experiences of Indigenous peoples in a post-colonial world, regardless of how colonialism has manifested in individual nation-states.

I have encountered many such instances of racism, either observed directly, or recounted to me in conversation or during an interview in Mexico City and other urban and rural settings. One interviewee, a man in his 30s, spoke of experiencing ostracism when he admitted to his classmates in an urban university setting that he could speak a Native language. A 70-year-old woman spoke of the days before running water existed in Contla, when the women from the small towns higher up on the Malinche would bring their clothing down to the river, on donkeys, to wash; she told me how awful it was to see her neighbors—themselves Mexicano speakers washing clothing in the same river—make fun of women who were slightly more fluent and more markedly "Indian" than their neighbors. Youth never spoke to me directly about these experiences, yet these experiences surfaced in conversations and interviews with young adults.

Ideologies of Respect, Purism, and Authenticity

Among speakers of Mexicano, ideologies of "good speakers" and "proper Mexicano" dominate the discourse. Ideologies of respect and purism sometimes include, for example, the ideology of *legítimo Mexicano* (legitimate/true Mexicano), in which speakers' purist attitudes encourage Mexicano speech completely without a trace of its syncretic elements whose source is the Spanish language (note that the salient elements are not necessarily the same for speakers as for linguists) (Flores Farfán, 1999, 2003; Hill & Hill, 1986). *Legítimo Mexicano* can best be understood as "unmixed" speech. There is also a related discourse of nostalgia about earlier times, which includes greater use of this type of legitimate Mexicano (Hill, 1998).

The expression *legítimo Mexicano* is still relevant for today's generations of speakers who also feel that the language spoken today is inferior to that which was spoken in the past because Spanish has been mixed in. The ideologies remain regulating the use of the *o:me tlahto:l* (two languages) through the associations of Spanish with power, social distance, and rudeness, and of Mexicano with intimacy and politeness, but to a lesser extent among semi-speakers. Educators and language activists in and out of the state educational system promote Native language use simultaneously with ideological shift, calling upon the *pro-Indígena* discourse to reauthenticate Indigenous identity by interrogating the racism directed at Indigenousness in *menosprecio* discourses, as Esther does in example 3 below. In doing so, they successfully refocus local ideology of Malintzi identity as a marker of prestige.

Salir Adelante: English, Social Class, and Hairstyles

In Tlaxcala, global influences that affect the desire for modernity and its related cultural and linguistic icons and material commodities are coupled with a fear that Mexicano has no place in such a modern world. Locals respond to circulating discourses of modernity and socioeconomic development—*salir adelante* (Messing, 2007a). The large county of Contla has seen industrialization of its textile industry, and a desire for modern goods has accompanied the surge of factory employment. To achieve desired personal and economic progress, many Indigenous peoples in Tlaxcala believe that the Indigenous remnants of the past should be replaced by more global identities.

Youth are reconfiguring local identities through interaction with pop culture and foreign/globalized styles. Evidence of self-presentation emerges in choices of clothing, hairstyle, and music. Girls of secondary school age, 12 to 15, begin to wear their hair long and loose rather than braided. Wearing two braids, they explain, makes you "look Indian." At 11, one girl tried to avoid "looking Indian" by begging her mother to buy her name-brand clothing for graduation. Here, for parents, the ability to acquire a commodity for their children such as expensive shoes from the city, has come to symbolize access to wage-labor and progress.

English has become a commodity with great symbolic capital, one whose icons can be acquired or displayed, thus making the bearers into citizens of a transnational world that is more global and less local—and somehow less Indigenous and "lower class." In a 2006 interview, two teenage sisters told me that they and their classmates saw the Native language as being "of a low category"—*de baja categoría*—a euphemism for crassness and low social class. Their peers listen to music from the United States and its bilingual borderlands, especially *Reggaeton*, bilingual hip hop. Locally produced clothing is modeled on foreign patterns (e.g., low-waisted jeans). Over the past dozen years, English increasingly appears on youth's T-shirts in Tlaxcala. More recently English has appeared on storefronts, as the urban chain of coffee shops called "The Italian Coffee Company," a Mexican company has encroached upon the semi-urban border towns of the Malintzi Indigenous region. While it is unlikely that area residents other than the rural textile industry or urban elite can afford a drink there, the storefront signs remain an icon of the globalized world that has recently reached this region.

"Se Libre, Aprenda Inglés"—Be Free, Learn English

This slogan advertises a school that combines English language teaching with computing; these professional schools target youth with or without a high school education. It is not clear from what the future student will be "freed" if she or he acquires English; however, it is certain that young people are being challenged to see the importance of acquiring technology and English skills in order to advance—part of the discourse of modernity (*salir adelante*). In my interviews, while asking about bilingual education, several young parents of elementary-age students expressed the view that English acquisition would be "practical," a potentially lucrative skill, whereas increasing knowledge of Mexicano was viewed almost as a luxury, with greater symbolic capital than potential for future economic capital.

Example 1: Valeria. Shortly after a recent trip to Tlaxcala, I received the following email from Valeria (all names are pseudonyms), the daughter of a teacher involved in Contla language revitalization. Her parents are fluent in Mexicano and dedicated educators in monolingual Spanish schools; they were thrilled to be part of efforts to revitalize Mexicano in their community. The email from Valeria is in excellent English.

Subject: HI, KIND REGARDS FROM MEXICO (TLAXCALA)

Hi, I am teacher [X X] and teacher [X X]'s daughter, do you remember us? We live near to the malinche, in Tlaxcala. You were working with my parents, some work about nahuatl. First of all, I am sending this message because my parents and me want to know news from you. Secondly, I am writing because I would like to keep in contact with you, if you do not mind, and send you some messages, because I want to practice my English. I am studying it and that is why I would prefer practice it with somebody who I know. This is a special favor I beg you to help me. Teacher X gave me your e-mail address, because I asked for it.

Kind regards, V.

Valeria was 20 years old when she emailed me, while studying English, French, and linguistics at a university in a nearby city. She was 13 and 14 during our workshops. The implicit ideology expressed here is one that is related to *salir adelante*, indexed by English use. Knowing Valeria's family and hometown, I suspect she has a passive understanding of Mexicano, if not an active one. The implicit ideology in her email is one of value being placed on the languages foreign to the region—on a globalized identity. The use of a particular language over another, in a bilingual community, can be an indicator of an implicit language ideology—as I describe in greater detail in the following sections.

Implicit Language Ideologies and Ambivalence Among Youth

Linguistic ideology has been defined as "the cultural ... system of ideas about social and linguistic relationships, together with their loading of moral and political interests" (Irvine, 1989, p. 255). Language ideologies are ideas about languages and talk, often expressed in speech about speech produced by speakers in particular interested positions (Silverstein, 1979; Woolard, 1998). The focus on studying ideology implies attention to the historical, political, and economic factors that shape power in social life (Philips, 2001). Linguistic-anthropological theory is instructive in understanding language ideologies (Irvine & Gal, 2000; Philips, 1998, 2000) with levels of implicitness and explicitness (Philips, 1998).

Language, identity, and ideology are fundamentally interconnected. Gal and Irvine's ideas on semiotic processes in linguistic ideology (Gal, 1998; Irvine & Gal, 2000) help us understand the relationship of boundaries between speakers, their languages, identities and ideologies, and the articulation of local, nation-state, and global processes. This focus on the semiotic dimension of identity highlights the ways in which individuals use language every day to mark boundaries between their social identities and others'; to understand language shift we must understand the ways in which local people's ideologies of language and identity are organized in their discourses. A study of implicit and ambivalent community ideologies is especially useful in examining the ideological milieu that youth are socialized in—a sort of socio-historical-ideological legacy that they confront as they enter young adulthood.

Teachers in bilingual education programs and local language promoters officially espoused an explicitly *pro-indígena* ideology in which Mexicano is valued, at the same time that many struggled with their language socialization choices for their own children. Little attention is paid to speakers' "process of ideolo-gizing in language use" (Philips, 2000, p. 255), how their choice of language use is part of a process of creating ideologies of language. For example, when a bilingual education teacher fluent in the Native language espouses a *pro-indígena* stance and then does not speak Mexicano to her own children, this can be seen as an instance of dual language ideology and ambivalence, or lack of decisive-ness in the words of *Maestro* (Teacher) Miguel, as we shall see in data following. The ideology implicit in their language use is that Spanish is the important (or dominant) language of the household and for youth, as it is in much of Latin America (cf. Reynolds, 2009).

Indigenous Education Teachers in Their 20s and 30s as "Key Informants"

Ambivalence should be studied where it surfaces, and in this case the informa-tion about youth emerges, rather explicitly, in the narratives of former-youth interviewees, when they reflect on their own changes in perspectives over time. Teachers in the DGEI schools from two Indigenous communities made won-derful interviewees because explicit language ideologies are particularly salient for them and they have reflected upon this since becoming teachers.

Teachers face a great ideological task in bilingual/Indigenous education pro-grams because this challenges them to put the Native language in the public sphere to be used among people who don't know each other well. Their jobs as teachers, and in particular as teachers in an Indigenous education division, offer them experiences which tend to make them especially attuned to and interested in issues of language.

What follows are excerpts from three such interviews.

Example 2: Miguel and Ana.   Miguel is a teacher from San Felipe Cuahutenco who teaches in the bilingual school in San Isidro where all children are socialized in both languages (cf. Nava Nava, 2007). He was 33 years old when this interview was conducted in 1999. By high school he had decided to become a teacher and entered the teachers' "Normal" high school and college. When he went to study in the state capital, classmates teased him because of his Nahuatl family names, which, he explained, indicated his Indigenousness; people asked him about them, and then would ask if he spoke the Native language. In the following interview excerpt, ambivalent language ideologies are apparent, surfacing in examples of *menosprecio* and *pro-indígena* discourses.

As with most of my interviewees, Miguel and I had spoken many times before the formal interview about language and education issues; he believes that people in public in the Contla county speak 95% Spanish, and 5% Nahuatl. Below the reader will see that Miguel states and restates his thoughts about his and his family's language ability; his statements vary, indicating that he has multiple opinions about language use and language socialization.

Ah, una ocasión que yo tuve ahí un cargo, tuve un cargo de ahí de la iglesia, pues también hay de todo, como la mayoría éramos puros jóvenes, pero también hablábamos en náhuatl. También para agradecer, ya ve que luego aquí se utiliza cuando ... Por ejemplo el otro día que fuimos a un convivio, fuimos a entregar un niño, el... que iba adelante de nosotros, el mayordomo es un muchacho que lo habla perfectamente, o sea la versión del Náhuatl, y nos [?]-también, lo poco que pudimos porque son unas palabras un poquito más este, más rebuscadas, sí se habló un poco.

Ah, on one occasion I had an elected duty, I had a duty there in the Church, well there's also a bit of everything, since the majority we were all young people [men], but we would also talk in Nahuatl. Also to give thanks, you see that here what's used when ... For example the other day we went to a gathering, we went to offer a statue of baby Jesus, the one who went ahead of us, the mayordomo [one in charge] is a young man who speaks it perfectly, that is the version in Nahuatl, and we [?]-also, the little that we could do because they are some words a bit more, um, more uncommon, yes it was spoken a bit.

This young *mayordomo* was about 32 years old, according to Miguel's calculation. Miguel explains that, in his town of San Felipe, few speak Mexicano to their families and that most youth age 15 to 20 do not speak it, but that in a few families, Mexicano is spoken, including among children. In his interview Miguel's self-description of language use and ability is flavored by a linguistic insecurity that he describes as "get[ting] tongue-tied." This insecurity is common for second languages acquired in the home, (including in heritage language households elsewhere; see, e.g., King, 2000; Santa Ana, 2004) and is related to an emotion of minority status resulting from the discrimination so many speakers have felt. Miguel, similar to others interviewed, talks about the importance of trust, of *confianza,* for him to speak Mexicano.

When asked if he would like his children to learn Mexicano, Miguel replied that there is interest but a lack of "decisiveness"—not enough of a conscious "push" in his family, and some shame that also stands in the way; this illustrates that *menosprecio* discourse and related ambivalence about promoting Mexicano at home.

Pues sí me gustaría, lo que pasa es que, no nos podemos quitar esa ... ¿cómo se diría? esa, ¿cómo decir? Este, esa pena que sentimos tal vez al hablarnos, casi no. Lo que pasa es que a veces siento a veces que aunque yo y mi esposa nos hablemos en Español, eh que diga en Náhuatl ellos también escucharían hablar en Náhuatl y pues, lo aprenderían, quién sabe. Sí, sería lo mejor, o sea, sí hay ganas, lo que pasa es que no hay decisión.

Well yes I would like it, what happens is that it's, we can't rid ourselves of that ... how to put it? That, how to say it? Um, this shame that we feel maybe as we speak to each other, almost no. What happens is that sometimes I feel sometimes that although I and my wife we speak to each other in Spanish, eh that if it be said in Nahuatl they [his children] would also hear speaking in Nahuatl and then, they would learn it, who knows. Yes, it would be better, that is, yes there is the desire, what happens is that there is not decisiveness.

Miguel's honest reflection about a complex situation highlights the linguistic ambivalence in this region. There is a locally common explicit ideology which this Mexicano semi-speaker articulates, that he would like to increase his children's exposure to the Native language. Yet we also see ambivalence about this mixed with memories of bad experiences with racism and with linguistic insecurity. This reinforces Hill and Hill's insightful assertion:

> The people of the Malinche are not naïve about these ambivalences and complexities. The problem for the scholar is not to reveal the nature of their structural position, but to come to as profound an understanding of it as they themselves have developed. Only if we fully understand the practices which they have developed to manage their situation will we be able to make recommendations which will enhance the constructive effects of these practices and minimize their destructive impact.
>
> *(1986, pp. 53–54)*

My view, based on extensive observation and interviewing, is that the role of respect in social relations in the Malintzi region is so strong that Mexicano speakers exhibit great respect for their languages and ancestors by not wanting the language to be tainted by Spanish. From this interview, I also learned that Miguel's young children understand a bit of Mexicano, although he has thought of taking them to San Isidro so that they could become as fluent as his students there. Miguel's wife Ana came in during the interview, and explained that she didn't think her parents spoke to her in Mexicano as a child. However, she added that her grandparents spoke it to her and her siblings as children. This language transmission from grandparents to grandchildren is an important factor that, in many families, has served to keep the language alive, even when parents actively choose not to socialize their children in the language. I now turn to two more teachers' reflections on their changing ideologies.

Shifting Language Ideologies in University

Example 3: Esther. In her 20s when the interview excerpted below was taped, Esther understands and speaks Mexicano. From observations in her extended family household, I know that her siblings also understand it but appear less interested in using it. Esther told me that having experienced anti-Indigenous discrimination caused her to ignore the value of her linguistic skills until she was in her early 20s. She does not think of herself as Indigenous because to her, the Indigenous ones were the people who spoke legítimo Mexicano and lived in the past. She spoke to me of a shift from her menosprecio orientation, thinking that to use Mexicano was "uncivilized," to a pro-indígena stance that today is actively pro-language revitalization. She said:

> Como que la generación X, ya como que lo sentimos más. Con eso de que viene … ¿cómo te diré? Las modas más bien del extranjero, que son los gringos, entonces como que valoramos más lo que tienen ellos que lo que nosotros tenemos, nos olvidamos de lo que tenemos, pensamos que eso es cosa para nacos ¿no? O sea la gente que no se ha civilizado.

> Como que la generación X—It's like generation X, like we now feel it more. It's that it comes from … How should I tell you? The styles mostly from foreign places, which are the gringo [American] ones, so like we value more what they have than what we have, we forget what we have, we think that that is something for nacos [low class; crass] no? That is, the people that haven't become civilized.

Echoing the teenaged girls quoted earlier, Esther illustrates the link some draw between Indigenousness, marked by language use, and low socioeconomic status. Here my questions about language led to socioeconomic and discrimination concerns, and local desires to salir adelante—become "civilized"—and adopt styles from "foreign places." The ideological stances can vary within a single family, where all children have been socialized together, as in Esther's family, and the stances can change over time, as they have for her. This may be because of affinities between individuals of different generations in the family, or because a child grows up being particularly interested in learning Mexicano, or communicating with older Mexicano-dominant relatives.

In Esther's case a college professor challenged her and her classmates to conduct research in their communities for their undergraduate theses. Esther spoke of experiencing anti-Indigenous discrimination to the point that she didn't value her linguistic skills and local knowledge within the context of her university education until she finished her coursework. It wasn't until she and a classmate were in the final year of university that they decided to do research in and about their own communities. In her interview she asked of herself, "How is it possible that we didn't do anything [before that time]?" Esther ended up writing a thesis based on local legends that she had collected in Mexicano and Spanish, earning funding to continue research. Esther clearly illustrates her own process of change with regard to her ideological orientation, and a very individual take on salir adelante, while contextualizing this in what she sees as a common local disregard for Indigenous cultural riches.

Example 4: Jimena.   In another representative example, an elementary school teacher finished her high school education while teaching and had a change of heart about her language after becoming a teacher under the Indigenous education system. She explained:

> *Si yo no lo pude aprender de chiquita porque me negaba siempre, siempre me negué. [...] Porque ese era mi problema para mi. "¿Yo hablar eso? No. ¿Qué me van a decir mis amiguitas?" Yo decía eso y si lo recuerdo porque siempre me insistian mis papás. "No, no. A tal lado me van a escuchar hablar, no." "Me da pena," o "me da vergüenza hablarlo delante de otra gente que no es de mi familia." Entonces yo lo tomaba así y yo quiero que ellos [los niños] no lo tomen así.*

> If I couldn't learn it as a child, it's because I negated myself always, I always negated myself. [...] Because that used to be my problem for me. "Me speaking that? No. What are my friends going to say?" I used to say that and I remember it because my parents always used to insist with me. "No, no. In some place they're going to hear me speaking, no." "I'm embarrassed," or "I'm ashamed of speaking it in front of other people who aren't my family." So that I took it that way and I want that they [her children] not take it that way.

Conscious of her former rejection of Mexicano, Jimena is now becoming a language promoter, challenging her students if they tap into the *menosprecio* discourse by telling them, "*No me hagas sentir vergüenza porque es una lengua muy bonita*" (Don't make me feel shame because it's a very pretty language). Her siblings have started coming to her for Mexicano translation assistance. These comments suggest that some young people may understand or speak Mexicano without anyone but their closest family members knowing, keeping this fact from their teachers, neighbors, and friends. Jimena's shift in perspectives is like that of the others, promising because it illustrates that culture change is not always unidirectional.

Conclusions and Implications

Young adult narratives show how former youth are caught up in the nexus of multiple ideologies of Indigenousness and modernity influenced by globalizing forces. This myriad of ideologies most impacts Mexicano youth at a time in which they are making decisions about their educational and employment possibilities, leading to explicitly ambivalent perspectives on their social identities and languages. "Former youth" is an ethnographic category that could lead to insights not otherwise observable with youth directly, although, research directly with youth should also be a research goal.

Ambivalence, to the outside observer, is at the center of youth ideologies of language and identity, and yet ideologies governing language shift can change over time, as the data has shown. Youth communicate both implicitly and explicitly the roles of Mexicano, Spanish, and English and their views on their daily lives. Here further attention needs to be paid to young adults and emerging adult language socialization practices, and to the role of shifting individual language ideologies in this process. This knowledge is key for productive language revitalization (cf. Hinton & Hale, 2001; Wilson & Kamanā, this volume) because if ideological orientations can change over time, then young adults may reactivate their passive linguistic knowledge and outsiders must make an effort to understand the local ideological-linguistic landscape.

I echo Hill and Hill's (1986) call for scholars to "come to as profound an understanding" as the people of the Malinche about the "ambivalence and complexities" (pp. 53–54). In this analysis, I further emphasized the critical need for ethnographic attention to ambivalence and ideological complexity for understanding youth culture and linguistic practice worldwide.

The narratives illustrate that ambivalence is rarely stated, but is observable in practice; ambivalence is implicit in actions of speaking and explicit in reflective narratives of young people and young adults who look back on their youth. Ambivalence such as this should be seen as part of multifaceted post-conquest identities (Bhabha, 1994). An emotional and sociohistorical response, ambivalence is a response to the local ideological situation of minority/minoritized status (González, 1992; McCarty, 2002) and interpersonal conflicts about authenticity. More work on Indigenous post-conquest "structures of feeling" (Williams, 1977) among youth would be instructive in informing the development of culturally relevant, youth-focused, and technologically advanced language revitalization.

Acknowledgments

For support of field research and data analysis I thank the Fulbright Commission, Spencer Foundation, University of Arizona, the University of South Florida, and the Whatcomb Museum. For conversations helpful to this analysis I would like to thank José Antonio Flores Farfán, Refugio Nava Nava, Ramos Rosales Flores, Nieves Ahuantzi Calderon, and Desiderio Lopez Marcos. I am grateful to Susan Philips, Jane Hill, and Norma González for insightful comments on earlier versions of this research. Special thanks to the editors of this volume for their insightful and thought-provoking commentaries.

Notes

1 Many people in the Malinche region, and across Mexico, have a passive understanding of the Native language. That is, children are raised hearing it spoken and they learn to understand it, without always being able to converse in the language (Messing, forthcoming).

2 See the Introduction to this volume, McCarty and Wyman (2009), and McCarty, Nicholas, and Wyman (2012) for parallel discussions of researcher positionality among my colleagues, in the ethnographic context of Indigenous communities.

3 The question of how much of a role schools can play in Indigenous language revitalization is a topic of much scholarly interest. See Hornberger (2008) for related examples and discussion.

4 Mexican Spanish is replete with words that originate in Nahuatl. This business owner ironically likely uses Nahuatl loan words and place names on a daily basis, without knowing it.

References

Alonso, A. M. (2004). Conforming disconformity: "Mestizaje," hybridity, and the aesthetics of Mexican nationalism. *Cultural Anthropology, 19*(4), 459–490.

Barth, F. (1969). Introduction. In F. Barth (Ed.), *Ethnic groups and boundaries: The social organization of culture difference* (pp. 9–38). Bergen-Oslo, Norway: Scandinavian University Books.

Bhabha, H. (1994). *The location of culture.* New York, NY: Routledge.

Bonfil Batalla, G. (1994). *México profundo: Una civilización negada* [Deep Mexico: A civilization denied] (2nd ed.). México: Grijalba.

Brayboy, B. M. J. (2005). Toward a tribal critical race theory in education. *The Urban Review, 37*(5), 425–446.

Campbell, L. (1994). Language death. In R. E. Asher (Ed.), *The encyclopedia of language and linguistics* (pp. 1960–1968). Oxford, England: Pergamon Press.

Deloria, V. (1970). *We talk, you listen: New tribes, new turf.* New York, NY: Macmillan.

Dorian, N. (1977). The problem of the semi-speaker in language death. *International Journal of the Sociology of Language, 12,* 23–32.

Dorian, N. (Ed.). (1989). *Investigating obsolescence: Studies in language contraction and death.* Cambridge, England: Cambridge University Press.

Flores Farfán, J. A. (1999). *Cuatreros somos y toindioma hablamos* [Mistake makers we are and our language we speak]. México: CIESAS Press.

Flores Farfán, J. A. (2003). Nahuatl purism: Between language innovation, maintenance and shift. In J. Brincat, W. Boeder, & T. Stolz (Eds.), *Purism in minor languages, endangered languages, regional languages, mixed languages. Papers from the conference on "Purism in the age of globalization"* (pp. 281–313). Bochum, Germany: Universitätsverlag Brockmeyer.

Francis, N. (1997). *Malintzin: Bilingüismo y alfabetización en la sierra de Tlaxcala (México)* [Malintzin: Bilingualism and literacy in the sierra of Tlaxcala (Mexico)]. Quito, Ecuador: Ediciones Abya-Yala.

Gal, S. (1979). *Language shift: Social determinants of linguistic change in bilingual Austria.* New York, NY: Academic Press.

Gal, S. (1998). Multiplicity and contestation among linguistic ideologies. In B. Schieffelin, K. Woolard, & P. V. Kroskrity (Eds.), *Language ideologies: Practice and theory* (pp. 317–331). New York, NY: Oxford University Press.

García Canclini, N. (1994). *De lo local a lo global: Perspectivas desde la antropología* [From the local to the global: Perspectives from anthropology]. Mexico City. Mexico: Universidad Autónoma Metropolitana.

González, N. (1992). *Child language socialization in Tucson U.S. Mexican households* (Unpublished doctoral dissertation). University of Arizona, Tucson, Arizona.

González, N. (2001). *I am my language: Discourses of women and children in the borderlands.* Tucson: University of Arizona Press.

Grenoble, L. A., & Whaley, L. (Eds.). (1998). *Endangered languages: Current issues and future prospects.* Cambridge, England: Cambridge University Press.

Greymorning, S. (2004). Culture and language: Political realities to keep trickster at bay. In S. Greymorning (Ed.), *A will to survive: Indigenous essays on the politics of culture, language, and identity* (pp. 3–17). Boston, MA: McGraw Hill.

Gumperz, J., & Cook-Gumperz, J. (1982). Language and the communication of social identity. In J. Gumperz (Ed.), *Language and social identity* (pp. 1–22). Cambridge, England: Cambridge University Press.

Hill, J. H. (1993). Structure and practice in language shift. In K. Hyltenstam (Ed.), *Progression and regression in language: Sociocultural, neuropsychological, and linguistic perspectives* (pp. 68–93). Cambridge, England: Cambridge University Press.

Hill, J. H. (1998). "Today there is no respect:" Nostalgia, "respect," and oppositional discourse in Mexicano (Nahuatl) language ideology. In B. Schieffelin, K. Woolard, & P. Kroskrity (Eds.), *Language ideologies: Practice and theory* (pp. 68–86). New York, NY: Oxford University Press.

Hill, J. H. (2004, November). *Discussant's commentary.* Presentation at the Annual Meeting of the American Anthropological Association, Atlanta, GA.

Hill, J., & Hill, K. (1986). *Speaking Mexicano: Dynamics of syncretic language in central Mexico.* Tucson: University of Arizona Press.

Hinton, L., & Ahlers, J. (1999). The issue of "authenticity" in California language restoration. *Anthropology and Education Quarterly, 30*(1), 56–67.

Hinton, L., & Hale, K. (Eds.). (2001). *The green book of language revitalization in practice.* San Diego, CA: Academic Press.

Hornberger, N. H. (Ed.). (1996). *Indigenous literacies in the Americas: Language planning from the bottom up.* Berlin, Germany: Mouton de Gruyter.

Hornberger, N. H. (2000). Bilingual education policy and practice: Ideological paradox and intercultural possibility. *Anthropology and Education Quarterly, 31*(2), 173–201.

Hornberger, N. H. (Ed.). (2008). Can schools save Indigenous languages? Policy and practice on four continents. New York, NY: Palgrave Macmillan.

Hymes, D. (1972[1986]). Models of the interaction between language and social life. In J. Gumperz & D. Hymes (Eds.), *Directions in sociolinguistics: The ethnography of communication* (pp. 35–71). Oxford, England: Basil Blackwell.

Instituto Nacional de Estadística Geografía e Informática (INEGI). (1997). *División territorial del estado de Tlaxcala de 1810 a 1995* [Territorial division of the state of Tlaxcala from 1810 to 1995]. Aguascalientes: INEGI ad Gobierno del Estado de Tlaxcala Aguascalientes: INEGI and the Government of the State of Tlaxcala.

Irvine, J. (1989). When talk isn't cheap: Language and political economy. *American Ethnologist, 16*(2), 248–267.

Irvine, J., & Gal, S. (2000). Language ideology and linguistic differentiation. In P. V. Kroskrity (Ed.), *Regimes of language: Ideologies, polities, and identities* (pp. 35–83). Santa Fe, NM: School of American Research Press.

King, K.A. (2000). Language ideologies and heritage language education. *International Journal of Bilingual Education and Bilingualism, 3*(3), 167–184.

Kroskrity, P. V. (1993). An evolving ethnicity among the Arizona Tewa: Toward a repertoire of identity. In P. V. Kroskrity (Ed.), *Language, history, and identity: Ethnolinguistic studies of the Arizona Tewa* (pp. 177–212). Tucson: University of Arizona Press.

Kroskrity, P. V. (Ed.). (2000). *Regimes of language: Ideologies, polities, and identities.* Santa Fe, NM: School of American Research Press.

Mannheim, B., & Tedlock, D. (Eds.). (1995). *The dialogic emergence of culture.* Urbana: University of Illinois Press.

McCarty, T. L. (2002). *A place to be Navajo — Rough Rock and the struggle for self-determination in Indigenous schooling.* Mahwah, NJ: Erlbaum.

McCarty, T. L. (2008). Language education planning and policies by and for Indigenous peoples. In S. May & N. H. Hornberger (Eds.), *Encyclopedia of language and education. Vol. 1: Language policy and political issues in education* (pp. 137–150). New York, NY: Springer.

McCarty, T., & Wyman, L. (2009). Indigenous youth and bilingualism — Theory, research, praxis. *Journal of Language, Identity and Education, 8*(5), 279–290.

McCarty, T., Nicholas, S., & Wyman, L. (2012). Re-emplacing place in the "global here and now": Critical ethnographic case studies of Native American language planning and policy, *International Multilingual Research Journal, 6*(1), 50–63.

McCarty, T. L., & Zepeda, O. (Eds.). (2006). *One voice, many voices — Recreating Indigenous language communities.* Tempe: Arizona State University Center for Indian Education.

Messing, J. (2003). *Ideological multiplicity in discourse: Language shift and bilingual schooling in Tlaxcala, Mexico* (Unpublished doctoral dissertation). University of Arizona, Tucson, Arizona.

Messing, J. (2007a). Multiple ideologies and competing discourses: Language shift in Tlaxcala, Mexico. *Language in Society, 36*(4), 555–577.

Messing, J. (2007b). Ideologies of public and private usages of language in Tlaxcala, Mexico. *International Journal of the Sociology of Language, 187/188*, 211–227.

Messing, J. (2009). Ambivalence and ideology among Mexicano youth in Tlaxcala, Mexico. *Journal of Language, Identity, and Education, 8*(5), 350–364.

Messing, J. (forthcoming). *Speak to me in Nahuatl, I'll answer in Spanish: Ideologies of language and modernity in Tlaxcala, Mexico.* Unpublished manuscript.

Muehlmann, S. (2008). "Spread your ass cheeks": And other things that should not be said in indigenous languages. *American Ethnologist, 35*(1), 34–48.

Mufwene, S. (2004). Language birth and death. *Annual Review of Anthropology, 33*, 201–222.

Nava Nava, R. (2007). *Linguistic vitality in San Isidro Buensuceso, Tlaxcala* (Unpublished doctoral dissertation). Centro de Investigaciones y Estudios Superiores en Antropología Social (CIE-SAS), Mexico, D.F. [Center of Research and the Advanced Study of Social Anthropology, Mexico City].

Nutini, H. G., & Isaac, B. L. (1974). *Los pueblos de habla Nahuatl de la región de Tlaxcala y Puebla* [Nahuatl-speaking towns in the region of Tlaxcala and Puebla]. Mexico City, Mexico: Instituto Nacional Indigenista y Secretaría de Educación Pública.

Philips, S. U. (1998). Language ideologies in institutions of power: A commentary. In B. Schieffelin, K. Woolard, & P. Kroskrity (Eds.), *Language ideologies: Practice and theory* (pp. 211–225). New York, NY: Oxford University Press.

Philips, S. U. (2000). Constructing a Tongan nation-state through language ideology in the courtroom. In P. V. Kroskrity (Ed.), *Regimes of language: Ideologies, polities, and identities* (pp. 229–257). Santa Fe, NM: School of American Research Press.

Philips, S. U. (2001). Power. In A. Duranti (Ed.), *Key terms in language and culture* (pp. 110–112). Malden, MA: Blackwell Press.

Reynolds, J. F. (2009). Shaming the shift generation: Intersecting ideologies of family and linguistic revitalization in Guatemala. In P. V. Kroskrity & M. C. Field (Eds.), *Native American language ideologies: Beliefs, practices, and struggles in Indian Country* (pp. 213–237). Tucson: University of Arizona Press.

Santa Ana, O. (Ed.). (2004). *Tongue tied: The lives of multilingual children in public education.* Lanham, MD: Rowman and Littlefield.

Schieffelin, B., Woolard, K., & Kroskrity, P. (Eds.). (1998). *Language ideologies: Practice and theory.* New York, NY: Oxford University Press.

Silverstein, M. (1979). Language structure and linguistic ideology. In P. R. Cline, W. Hanks, & C. Hofbauer (Eds.), *The elements: A parasession on linguistic units and levels* (pp. 193–247). Chicago, IL: Chicago Linguistic Society.

Vizenor, G. (1998). *Fugitive poses: Native American Indian scenes of absence and presence.* Lincoln: University of Nebraska Press.

Williams, R. (1977). *Marxism and literature.* Oxford, England: Oxford University Press.

Wilson, W. H. (1998). I ka 'olelo Hawai'i ke ola, "Life is found in the Hawaiian language." *International Journal of the Sociology of Language, 132*, 123–37.

Woolard, K. A. (1998). Introduction: Language ideology as a field of inquiry. In B. Schieffelin, K. Woolard, & P. V. Kroskrity (Eds.), *Language ideologies: Practice and theory* (pp. 229–255). Oxford, England: Oxford University Press.

7

CRITICAL LANGUAGE AWARENESS AMONG NATIVE YOUTH IN NEW MEXICO

Tiffany S. Lee

This chapter draws on research that sought to learn how Native youth negotiate mixed messages of the need for the Native language for cultural continuity and the importance of English for success in American society. Youth strongly critique school structures that inhibit language learning and reinforcement of their cultural identity. Yet, youth still find ways to provide safe spaces in school for learning and strengthening ties to their heritage. Youth perspectives, taken from interviews, focus groups, and reflective writing, demonstrate their critical language awareness and constitute the counter-storytelling that expressed the youths' ideas and experiences across five thematic areas: respect, stigmatization and shame, marginalization, impact on identity, and agency and intervention. The study affirms that language plays an important and complex role in contemporary youth identity and in school success.

> I think school is a culture.
>
> —*Pauline, Pueblo high school student*

Pauline's succinct statement speaks volumes about Native youth perspectives of schooling institutions' influences and impacts on their identity and socially and culturally relevant learning opportunities. High school and middle school students spend the majority of their day in school. Their relationship to school is largely based on the school's efforts to include or exclude the students' lived experiences, rooted in the contexts of their homes and communities. The school place becomes a cultural institution within itself that either supports, ignores, or denigrates its students' heritages and sociocultural backgrounds. To understand students' lived experiences, it is important to recognize how languages are embedded in the context of their homes and communities. Contexts of language include the language(s) used in the home, recognizable language shift within the family from Native languages to English, and family and community ideologies about language. Schooling institutions then become significant because they can help or hinder family or community efforts toward language maintenance and revitalization.

This chapter examines the perspectives of Native youth and young adults on the place of their heritage language in their lives, their schools, their communities, and their future. It shares youth's support for and critiques of the school as a domain for learning their language and strengthening their cultural identity. The chapter is rooted in contemporary Native life, which provides a unique set of circumstances and experiences that shape youth perspectives. Native youth and young adults are cognizant of the nature of language shift and loss in their communities (Lee, 2007; McCarty, Romero, & Zepeda, 2006). They have expressed their concern with their language vanishing, and they are negotiating what it means to be a Native person in today's society with or without their language.

Native youth recognize messages in their communities about the importance of retaining cultural and linguistic knowledge for cultural sustainability, and they recognize messages about the importance of English and Western education for achieving success in life equated with such dominant societal goals as job security and material wealth. Often the two are positioned in opposition, as though one cannot be both successful in the larger society while also maintaining Native language and cultural lifeways. Both positions about retaining Native language emanating from the community and the importance of English emanating from school and society represent powerful influences on Native students' language choices and sense of identity. This chapter presents youth responses to their own communities' and the larger society's messages. In particular, it presents youth experiences in school as a place for retaining language and for preparing for success in society. To this end, youth confront the school by demanding adequate and effective education for language learning, cultural continuity, and preparation for success in society.

Mixed Messages

An abundance of research has examined the nature of language loss, change, and revitalization among Native American and other Indigenous peoples (Crawford, 1996; Hornberger & Coronel-Molina, 2004; McCarty & Zepeda, 1998; Romero-Little & McCarty, 2006; Sims, 2001). Native Americans are not alone in their experiences with language loss as most of the world's heritage languages are also declining (Fishman, 1991, 2001; Hinton & Hale, 2001; Krauss, 1992).

There is less research on Native American young adults' language experiences. In one important study that included many interviews with Native youth in the U.S. Southwest, messages and perceptions regarding language attitudes and language use between youth and adults were vastly different (McCarty et al., 2006). In some cases, the youth seemed to express feelings of linguistic shame. The authors note that many Navajo youth viewed speaking Navajo as an "emblem of shame" and hence, gave the impression they do not have Navajo language skills when in school (McCarty et al., 2006, p. 38). While students in this case exercise their agency by choosing not share their language skills in school, the reasons behind these choices are complex.

For instance, students chose not to speak their language if they felt scolded or teased by their relatives or peers for mispronunciation or grammatical errors of Navajo words and phrases. Students heard rhetoric in school that speaking Navajo was not popular, yet they also received messages from their families and communities about the necessity to speak Navajo to truly identify as a Navajo person. When they were shamed for their efforts, students expressed frustration and a reluctance to keep learning (Lee, 2007). McCarty et al.'s (2006) study demonstrates an added complication. While students may demonstrate frustration and reluctance to learn and practice speaking their Native language because of scolding or for other reasons, teachers viewed their behavior as not caring about their language. Added to this layer of complexity is that students in their study viewed teachers as not caring about them (McCarty et al., 2006). Quijada (2008) found similar sentiments among Pueblo students. She describes how Pueblo students' attachment to their community is often disregarded by their teachers, negatively affecting their relationships. The varied perceptions and misunderstanding between youth and adults create a complex web of messages youth interpret and resolve in multiple ways, but as the present study shows, they nonetheless maintain their sense of agency and power over their decisions to use or not use their language.

Similarly, Nicholas (2005) shared her response to disenfranchising messages about her Hopi language from family and school by "putting aside" her language and culture so that it would not interfere with her educational success. She now works to fill the void left by putting her language and culture aside and in this effort is reclaiming her Hopi identity.

This chapter shows that today Native youth critique the school place for its neglect to make education relevant to their present-day lives. They also condemn it for its hostile environment toward their cultural backgrounds. Yet, students often have no choice but to utilize the school for learning their Native languages. Native language shift has been well documented in Navajo and Pueblo communities making the school context vital for helping to reverse this shift (Lee & McLaughlin, 2001; Sims, 2001). In fact, multiple endangered language communities are turning to the schools to address language revitalization (Hornberger, 2008). To this end, youth locate and create safe spaces with particular teachers or courses for inclusion of their cultural identity. In particular, they develop critical language awareness by acknowledging the challenges to accessing and learning their Native languages and thus, become more demanding for effective language education.

The studies and perspectives shared above outline a common experience of Native youth and adults with the hierarchical positioning of Native languages and English. There is a continuous negotiation by Native youth and adults to determine the place of Native languages in relation to the privileged position of English. Influences on youth's perceptions of their language include what May (1999) asserted as the tendency by the dominant society to associate English with a modern world and Native languages with a traditional world relegated to the past. In addressing Indigenous peoples' rights today, May explains that agendas to create a national identity privilege the dominant group. In the case of the United States, privilege is afforded to an English-speaking society based on Western European values. To create this national identity, May adds, "The language and culture of the dominant group comes to be viewed as the only vehicle of modernity and progress, and the only medium of 'national' identity. Alternatively, other cultural and language affiliations are viewed pejoratively as merely 'ethnic' and relatedly, as regressive and premodern" (p. 45). This ideology can have a potent influence on Native youth's perspectives on the relevancy of their Native language in their lives today.

This chapter attempts to understand how Native youth negotiate the world in which they live that encompasses varied, and often oppositional, expectations from sources in their homes, schools, and communities. It focuses on young adults' reclamation of self with or without the heritage language in all the settings that they negotiate. The chapter explores the power relations and interactions Native youth experience at home, in school, and in the community with regard to learning and using their heritage language. It offers insight into how young people are responding, resolving, and internalizing mixed messages from powerful influences on the status of language located at home, in school, and in the community, the resulting impact on their identity, and the effect of how they define their place and role at home, in school, and in community. As Benally and Viri (2005) suggest, this generation of youth and young adults may be one of the last generations to hear active heritage language use in their communities, making their insights and experiences all the more imperative.

Methods

This chapter utilizes study findings derived from examining youth and young adults' counter-storytelling taken from: (a) written reflection papers from Native college students mostly representing Navajo and Pueblo tribes; and (b) interviews and focus groups with Navajo, Pueblo, and Apache teenagers in several middle and high schools across New Mexico. Counter-storytelling (Solórzano & Yosso, 2002) is a methodology derived from critical race theory (CRT). CRT began as a movement in legal studies that expanded to many disciplines, including the examination of race within the social and political context of schooling. CRT utilizes counter-storytelling to share experiences that have often been ignored or marginalized (Delgado & Stefancic, 2001). The present study utilized the CRT methodology of counter-storytelling as the focus of analysis in order to position Native perspectives at the center of analysis.

Counter-stories offered Native youth and young adults the space to share their perspectives, knowledge, and experiences which actively counter the dominant society's and/or their Native community's narratives of their sub-dominant social place and role (Gilmore & Smith, 2005). The counter-stories were the means by which Native youth voiced their critical language awareness and this included their concerns, values, frustrations, celebrations, and dilemmas with regard to their heritage language and identity. The use of these students' counter-stories was also an exploration of ways to accurately represent their funds of knowledge (González, Moll, & Amanti, 2005; Moll, Amanti, Neff, & González, 1992), also known as home-based and cultural knowledge rooted in students' life experiences and relationships, and their construction of self.

Researcher Relationships

To elicit the personal stories from the students during the interviews and focus groups, it is important to note several aspects of the research methods that coincide with Indigenous research methodologies and that highlight the importance of the researcher's position and relationships with participants (Smith, 2012). My background as a Navajo/Lakota researcher and teacher influenced my interactions, relationships, and interpretations. I conducted this study from the position of someone who is personally affected by language shift and who is working towards language revitalization and sustainability by understanding youth perspectives.

My relationship with the participants in the college course was based on personal connections. I had known many of them from previous courses, but I also related many personal experiences with our topics of study over the semester. I shared my passion for the topic, and I shared my stories with them. In this sense, I developed a relationship with the students which was more than academic. Instead, the relationship was also based on our shared Indigenous heritage and on a shared passion for Indigenous issues such as cultural sustainability, community transformation, and love for Indigenous cultures and people.

In the study with high school students, *Indian Education in New Mexico, 2025,* five out of six members of the lead research team came from the communities of study or had significant experiences in the communities outside of the professional realm. All the graduate and undergraduate assistants were Native. Their perspectives enhanced the research process to create a comprehensive, multidisciplinary research approach rooted in Indigenous methodologies, beliefs, and practices. The Indigenous research approach entailed adhering to tribal community protocols with regard to research in their communities. It also entailed understanding each community's history and nature of interaction at a personal, school, and community level. While much of the understanding derived from the research is based directly on the transcript and context of the situation, it is also derived from the lived experience and knowledge of the Indigenous researchers. This study stood apart from many others in this respect because the researchers' perspectives and relationship to the communities enhanced the analysis. In essence, the study emphasized Indigenous ways of knowing and interacting (for the full study, see Jojola et al., 2011).

Participants

Nineteen Native college students ranging in age from 18 to 30 (with two students older than 30) participated in the first study. A total of 79 Native high school students ranging in age from 12 to 19 participated in the second study. The majority of these students were Navajo, Pueblo, and Apache—all Native peoples whose homelands lie in what is now the southwestern United States. All the participants' life experiences were highly diverse, with some residing within their reservation community, some recently relocated to the city with their families, and others born and raised in cities.

Collection of Counter-Stories

The college students allowed me to analyze their written reflection papers (four each), which were on topics related to their experiences with language shift, loss, revitalization, and intersections of language and identity. To write their reflection papers, I prompted them by asking them to listen, observe, and name what was happening in their families and communities regarding language use and language ideologies. I encouraged the students to reflect on their personal experiences as they related to the topics of the readings and discussions. Many students went beyond the assignment by directly questioning their own family members about historical experiences and current opinions about the role of language in their communities.

In the second study, we investigated "best practices" in American Indian education from the perspectives of Native youth, community members, and teachers. The focus group and interview questions for the students focused on issues in seven key areas: pedagogy, accountability, language, curriculum, successful students, school climate, and vision. The questions asked students to describe what they were learning as it related to their heritage, how they learned, how comfortable they felt in school, and what they envision as an ideal schooling situation. We conducted focus groups and/or interviews in 16 communities and schools across New Mexico with separate groups of students, teachers, and community members. This chapter includes primarily student and some teacher perspectives.

Analysis and Results

I analyzed the reflection papers through an inductive theorizing process (LeCompte & Schensul, 1999) informed by relevant themes in the literature to identify statements that were related to these themes. The literature on Southwest Native-language attitudes and choices has demonstrated four relevant themes I expected to find in the students' statements: (a) the perceptions of respect for one's heritage language; (b) stigmatization and shame toward one's language; (c) marginalization of one's language; and, embedded in all this, (d) the resulting impact on identity (Benjamin, Pecos, & Romero, 1996; Benally & Viri, 2005; Crawford, 1996; Lee & McLaughlin, 2001; May, 1999; McCarty et al., 2006). I expected to find statements that supported these previous research findings with similar populations. In locating statements in the reflection papers that related to these themes, I identified statements that occurred often, statements that were related to one another, statements that were rare or unusual, and statements that were absent despite my expectations for them. One theme, not recognized by previous research, was additionally identified. This was the theme of agency and desire to intervene on behalf of one's heritage language. Students expressed a desire to reclaim their language and their identity for themselves and their community.

Additionally, I have selected quotes from across the seven topic areas utilized in the *Indian Education in New Mexico* study based on how they related to the five themes identified in the first study. There was tremendous overlap and similarity in students' perspectives across both studies in terms of how they expressed their critical language awareness. The participants in the second study had more to say about the role of the school in supporting language education and cultural identity, and thus their desires and critiques of school are included as well. The following sections present the results from both studies according to each thematic area.

Respect

An examination of the students' counter-stories showed that most students did not question the intrinsic value of their heritage language. Many students, from fluent speakers to non-speakers, expressed great respect for their language and heritage. Some acknowledged its necessity for accessing their spiritual beliefs and practices. For example, Kelly (all names are pseudonyms), a Pueblo[1] college student, stated, "I believe that the teachings of our culture, traditions, and beliefs are more meaningful when learned in our native language than when we try to teach our children these beliefs and customs using another language."

In a feedback session with high school students on the Navajo Nation for the New Mexico Indian education study, one student, Martha, discussed (or perhaps lectured) to her classmates the importance of learning Navajo out of respect for what her ancestors endured during the Long Walk (an event in 1864 when 7,000–8,000 Navajo people were forcibly removed from their homelands). She explained to everyone in the room that it is important to respect Navajo language and history for all the hardships Navajo people have suffered and survived, and especially to retain all the knowledge embedded in the stories.

Angelica, another high school student, similarly demonstrated her pride and respect for her heritage language during a focus group session when she stated, "If I could speak Navajo, I'd speak it 24/7." She explained her desire to know her language because of her pride in being Navajo. Her statement expresses the level of her pride, desire, and connection to her cultural identity.

Stigmatization and Shame: Toward Language or Toward Self?

Interestingly, absent from the students' counter-stories were direct expressions of shame for their heritage language. Instead, students revealed expressions of embarrassment for their own limited Native-language ability, not necessarily embarrassment or shame with the language itself. Wyman (2009) found similar results with Yup'ik youth's linguistic insecurities over speaking Yup'ik incorrectly. The youth in this study shared how this impacted their identity and sense of self.

Natalie, a Pueblo college student, conducted a class research project on the impact of language shift in her community and shared this insight about young people's embarrassment with their limited fluency in their Native language:

> Many times fluent speakers believe that the younger generations simply don't want to learn their native Tewa language; however this is not always the case. From my research, there are many young people who respect the language but have a difficult time putting themselves out into the community where they should be speaking the language. Their reasons for not taking part in community activities are due to their own fear of making mistakes and feeling embarrassed in front of elders.

Exemplifying these remarks, Navajo college student Marjorie discussed her embarrassment of her limited Navajo skills and resorted to lying to people about her heritage to avoid the criticism.

> I worked a full-time job as a tax preparer … and I recall some of the times when I needed to get another Navajo to interpret for me, since I was unable to speak Navajo. I remember comments from my clients, especially the elders, words being said such as, "Why don't you speak Navajo? What is wrong with you? Why don't you know your language?" I did get tired of this and started to tell people that I was of a different tribe. It made me feel guilty, but what else was I supposed to say or do?

Marjorie's experience leads to another important point in her comment here, which relates to the importance of bilingualism. Marjorie's experience counters the messages that students hear about the need for English for upward social and economic mobility. In this scenario, she clearly needed to be bilingual in Navajo and English to interpret and translate as part of her job skills. It also counters messages of the Navajo language as a disenfranchised and marginalized societal language. It is undoubtedly of necessity and useful in this present-day activity of tax preparation. Unfortunately, the message Marjorie takes away is one of embarrassment and shame for not knowing how to speak her heritage language.

While McCarty et al. (2006) found that some Navajo youth marked their language as "an emblem of shame," the counter-stories of youth in the present research suggest that the "shame" youth express has more to do with the feelings they attribute to their own limited ability and limited fluency in their Native language. Messages and expectations they encounter with regard to their Native language position these students to blame themselves for their lack of ability. Those that realized the unfairness and injustice in this blaming become resistant and frustrated, such as the many teenagers who stated in their interviews that their tribal government and schools should take more responsibility in providing more and effective opportunities for them to learn. In turn, students redefined and reasserted their sense of Native identity given their personal level of Native language fluency.

Marginalization, Hostility, and Intolerance

As mentioned earlier, May (1999) asserts that by virtue of the dominant society's hegemonic position, the dominant language is the only language that signifies "progress" and is associated with modernity and advancement. In other words, the dominant language is positioned in a place of privilege and higher status in comparison to Indigenous languages. Conversely, non-dominant cultures and languages are relegated to a position in the past, as static and vanishing. This message is perpetuated in school systems through a hidden curriculum and the school's celebrations, holidays, and activities. The students recognized this marginalization of their Native language and cultural heritage within their school systems and were very critical of the school's apathy and often hostile environment. Marginalization for these students included not only language, but also curriculum and pedagogy that were not relevant to their lives. Kerry, a high school student, stated it this way: "If we're learning about Americans we should [also] be, like, allowed to do an activity in our own [cultural] way—like sing a Native song, bead or make jewelry, make pottery, baskets." Similarly, another high school student, Ruben, expressed this last example well in terms of how school can limit students' potential and should be connected to larger community and world issues:

> It's like a different world for me here. It's like school world. It's like your mind's more covered, concealed at school. You're worried about letters

and alphabets. But when you're out there, you're worrying about the whole thing. Not only from A to F, your alphabet, but you're looking for A to Z out there.

Marginalization of Native language and cultural content is indicative of a larger problem with apathy, hostility, and intolerance in school. In a recent national study which examined the impact of high-stakes accountability policies on Native learners, McCarty (2009) found that culturally-based and relevant instruction is neglected in schools because these subjects are considered to be "low stakes" (i.e., not subject to high-stakes tests) and therefore low priority. In the New Mexico Indian education study, when we asked youth about what they felt worked well for their learning, they often had a difficult time expressing "best practices" because they felt their education was inadequate, replete with worksheets and textbook assignments where they worked in isolation. When we asked one group of students how their teachers may have included Native life experiences, language, or cultural knowledge in their courses, Angelica said, "Well we don't really do much here at this high school. We don't go on field trips or … so it's kind of hard to answer something like that. I mean half of the stuff that I do here in school I don't really enjoy." Her statement was similar to those of other students who desire more hands-on learning from teachers who care about them and who understand their daily lives.

The inclusion of Native language education and socio-culturally responsive schooling cannot be achieved in an environment where students' perceive hostility, intolerance, and uncaring educators. These negative perceptions of school were common in the New Mexico Indian education study. A striking example comes from Vern, a high school student who described an incident with a teacher who became angry with his class and accused Vern of giving him "mean stares." Vern explained: "He said, 'I don't care if I leave from this school and leave you guys here.' He said, 'I'll forget about you guys and go teach at some other school.'" While teachers cannot be blamed for being human and having emotional responses on occasion, Vern's statement was one example of many in this school where students felt the teachers did not care about them. In explaining her vision for an ideal education, another student said she would like a school "where there's actually teachers who want to teach instead of just sitting there and doing nothing." Another student indicated a climate that was generally hostile when describing his vision for an ideal education when he said, "Just stop all the fights and have better teachers." These quotes were students' responses to what they would envision for the best educational experience they could receive, and they hoped for basic safe and caring learning environments.

Native youth's desire for culturally relevant and caring learning environments extended to their communities as well. They expressed feelings of marginalization in their communities based on their limited language fluency. Natalie (Pueblo) recognized the marginalization of her participation in the

ceremonial life of her community. She expressed an intense desire to participate through her Native language:

> Cultural reasons greatly motivate me to learn my language. Although I
> practice my culture in many ways, I can't say I truly know my culture
> if I can't speak my language. The two are tied together and one can't
> exist without the other. Because of this interdependency, I feel scared
> not to learn my native language since I will also be losing my culture. I
> no longer want to hear the English version of the meaning behind our
> traditional songs; instead I have a strong desire to understand our songs
> as a Tewa person.

Natalie attributed a discrepancy between her identity as a Tewa person and an
incomplete understanding of her culture because she could not understand or
speak her ancestral language. Youth's counter-stories often shared this desire
to know their language in order to fully understand their culture. Yet they also
expressed frustration with their own communities' differences in priorities.
Danielle, a Pueblo college student, analyzed it this way:

> Personally, I feel that the reason why there has not been a successful lan-
> guage revitalization program in my community is because people have
> ranked other issues such as economic development, infrastructure devel-
> opment, blood quantity requirements,[2] and personal conflicts as more
> important than preserving our language.

Similarly, another student, Don (Pueblo), who is older and a fluent speaker of
his language, shared this insight with regard to his community:

> Every morning, I dread walking out the door of my house for fear of fac-
> ing another day of speaking English to people who should be speaking
> our Keres language. Everywhere I turn, someone is talking in English to
> other Keres speaking people in our community.

Danielle and Don recognized the marginalization their Native languages by
people within their communities based on a lack of language programs and a
preferred use of English. Danielle offered further insights into what Crawford
(1996) hypothesizes as one reason for language shift: that modernity, economic
development, and social integration are more dangerous than the repressive
language policies of schools because the former are signs from within of community change and assimilation. Danielle's observation is indicative of Crawford's position:

> The most obvious cause for our lack of knowledge in our language and
> culture points to the fact that we are no longer spending time at home
> learning traditional aspects of our culture from our grandparents and
> elders; instead we are off learning things about the modern, English-

dominated world around us. The scary thing is that the BIA [Bureau of Indian Affairs] schools are no longer the obvious threat to our survival as a culture—now the danger is internal; it is within us as a community.

Danielle and Don's comments reflect their observations of their communities' internalized assimilation ideologies about language, which result in the marginalization of Native languages by Native peoples. Their perspectives counter and respond to community discourse about the importance of language in identifying oneself as a Native person. They name the internal conflict within their communities to place Native language at the center of learning and family life.

These students' insights, observations, and critical analyses shed light on a new theme identified in the data that has not been widely addressed in the literature. Throughout the students' stories, the youth described experiences of awakening to these issues of language shift and change in their communities and of their ability to create spaces for learning language and culturally relevant content in school. They became conscious of the denial they and their families have felt regarding language loss. They recognize the school as an important domain for reversing language shift in their own lives and hold the school accountable for effective language education. With the awareness of the threat of language loss now more present, they demonstrated a sense of agency and proactive motivation to transform their families, communities, and schools toward language maintenance and revitalization.

Agency and Intervention

Human agency has been discussed in the critical studies literature as encompassing individual motivation and ability to transform social injustices through collective action (Giroux, 1988). I use the term to emphasize the nature of the youth's attitudes and decisions. The realization of language shift in their families and communities empowered these youth to create positive change toward language maintenance or revitalization. In the interviews and their writing, many students articulated their desire to make on impact in their community, such as by bringing more awareness about language shift and by implementing their own strategies to influence young people's mindsets about their Native languages. Kelly (Pueblo) explained how she experienced the denial of language shift in her own family:

> I was freaked out how much I was in denial, and also how much my family is still in denial [about language shift]. I would ask them how they felt about how little our youth and our elders were starting to speak our language. My family was like, that is not true, and we still speak our language. Then I would just start talking about other things going on in my life or some stories about my great-grandmother and other relatives.

> Then I would catch them talking in English, and I would raise my eyebrows and they would snap, too, that they were speaking more and more English. It angered many of my family members that I was being that observant about our use of our Native language.

Another Navajo student, Rose, took seriously the messages regarding the importance of her language as a means to connect to her culture and identity. But she did not allow these messages to diminish her sense of being a contributing member to her community.

> Since I can remember, I have the thought stored in the back of my mind and I have been telling myself: "Yeah, *one day* I will learn my language." One day. The days are bypassing me and as each day elapses, I lose out on my language. When I think about this situation, it makes me feel bad. It almost makes me feel inadequate as a Navajo. Sure, language is like the backbone of a culture but just because I cannot speak my language does not entirely mean that I am not a good Navajo. (emphases in original)

After becoming cognizant of the language shift occurring in their families and across Native communities, these youth expressed a desire to intervene through their own research, language practices at home, and personal efforts to learn their heritage language. They also intervene by taking Native language courses in high school and by demanding effective, rigorous, and engaging pedagogy and curriculum. They critique courses where they feel their education is inadequate or the instructor is uncaring. High school student Nelson remarked, "I took Navajo in my eighth-grade year. It was boring 'cause all the teacher did was just give out worksheets. That's it." Another student, Jenny, felt her teacher could be more engaging and patient. She remarked, "She teaches good stuff, it's just like she doesn't entertain us. She just gets mad and like— 'cause we really don't understand and she doesn't go in more depth like how to pronounce things and stuff."

Their desire for learning their language leads these youth to expect effective teaching. In a feedback session in one of the high schools that participated in the New Mexico Indian education study, I reported what fellow students had to say about their desire for an emphasis on learning oral Navajo communication skills over written skills. They disliked worksheets and learning only nouns. One student, Sharon, remarked that although she felt that was true, she said, "I *really* want to learn to speak Navajo," which included learning to read and write it. She praised her teacher from whom she had taken three sequential levels of Navajo language. This teacher began with basic oral skills and moved into more emphasis on writing and reading skills over the 3 years. Sharon felt learning oral skills along with reading and writing Navajo challenged her and supported her pronunciation and understanding of the language. Several other students in the session agreed with Sharon. These students were appreciative of a teacher that challenged and engaged them through varied pedagogical methods.

Sharon's desire to learn Navajo is indicative of many students' overall desire to learn and be more connected to their cultural heritage. School administrators and teachers may be unaware of this level of desire. In another feedback session at a different high school, the principal of the school sat in on the session. In discussing the number of Navajo language courses available at the school, the principal remarked that there was not a need for more Navajo language teachers because he felt the students did not desire to take these courses. I asked the 25 students in the room how many of them had taken Navajo language courses at their school, and every student raised their hand, to the surprise of the principal. School educators may be largely unaware of the impact these courses can have if they have never asked their students about them.

Native language courses provide a space for Native youth to feel connected, to learn their people's stories and history, and to develop important relationships with adults in the school and at home. In speaking about how her Navajo classes strengthened her relationships at home, Rachel said,

> I learn more words [in class] then I try to use it at home to talk to my parents. I told my dad one time [in Navajo] that I had no gas, and I needed money and then he gave it. They like it when I talk to them in Navajo. I'm not fluent but I'm trying to make myself learn.

Students appreciate it if the school is aware of their heritage and inclusive of it by offering Native language courses. Trevor, a middle school student, expressed this as, "We have two enrichment courses: Navajo and Lakota. Both are teaching us to take back our culture, which is like really excellent." Taking Native language courses is more than simply learning the language; it includes reclaiming a cultural identity or a means to "take back our culture."

Overall, the students' counter-stories demonstrated that awareness of the issues surrounding language loss and the personal impacts on their families and communities can motivate youth to resist and transform these situations. For example, Natalie is continuing her research in her community to inform and implement a language program. Kelly continues to raise her family's consciousness about their language choices with her gentle reminders. In turn she has said her family views her as the "language police." Another student, Jolene (Pueblo), promotes Native language learning and use in her family with games she invented to play with her younger relatives that require them to use their Native language. The older student, Don, has presented his observations and ideas to his tribal council about the nature of language shift in his community. The list of examples goes on and on.

Reflecting a critical Indigenous consciousness, these young people are trying to make a difference. At the same time, they are redefining and reasserting their own personal identity as Native people within the realm of language change. As one student, Doreen, articulated it,

> Our miseducation, and even the loss of many of our Indigenous languages, painful and unjust as these things are, inform who we are now as Indian people, and provide the energy necessary to regroup, revitalize and even, in some respects, reinvent who we are.

Doreen's statement succinctly describes a role many Native youth now feel responsible to fulfill.

Schools can support youth's regrouping and reinvention of their identities. Native language courses create a place in school for a socioculturally responsive education based on Native values and protocols. Teachers of these courses work to build and maintain relationships with students that support their learning but that acknowledge and mirror the values and life ways of Native communities. For example, a Lakota language teacher utilizes relationship building and includes it in his assessment of student learning. He looks for his students to demonstrate respect, compassion, and helpful behavior with others, as these are also attributes associated with the way the Native language is used and the way Native people treat one another.

Understanding the relationships and history of their communities is important for Native language teachers. Through their efforts to share this knowledge base, they create an atmosphere where students see themselves in the content and where they are positioned as important and valuable to their communities. A Keres language teacher discussed her goals in her classroom,

> What I do in the Keres language class is I have them learn their Indian names, and then I normally talk about the history of our people from the community, so the kids will have better understanding why we're doing this. One of the things that I did was panel exhibits; they design a family tree. I was pretty amazed with the students, how much they took an interest in developing that, and they also interviewed their parents about their own educational experiences.... So with that, they need to learn their family relationship and how to respect the members, as well as the community members.

The result is students who enjoy what they are learning and who can connect what they are learning to their lived experiences. In essence, these courses are transferring the goals and tenets of Indigenous education, which supports students in learning their place and role in their communities, and practicing that education in schools. These courses develop students' critical language awareness and support a positive Indigenous consciousness and identity. Their impact is exhibited in students' motivation and efforts for language learning, which is a hopeful sign, as the survivability of Native languages requires youth who are committed to learning, using, and passing on their language.

Implications for Indigenous Communities and Language Revitalization Movements

The implications of this research center on the importance of understanding contemporary Native youth identities—specifically whether learning and speaking their Indigenous language is an integral part of or supplementary to their self-perceptions of what it means to be an Indigenous person. Are their feelings toward their Native language a mixture of shame and pride? These students' counter-stories demonstrate that language is a large part of their identity, but they struggle with how to learn their language and maintain it in a world that often makes such choices difficult. Yet they remain strongly assertive in their sense of self as a member of their heritage language community, even when they feel they are limited in fully accessing and understanding their culture and its associated worldview. So they turn to the school domain as a place to access language education. They critique it when it is ineffective and demand proficient language pedagogy because they really want to learn their language.

The students' counter-stories generate a necessary and broader discussion of the internalized assimilation of Native peoples and everyday functions of Native communities. Native language shift and change are unlike what Native people have ever experienced, and their responses to that shift and change require many layers of negotiation from individuals to institutions within those communities. While the school had an initially dominant role, it is not the only factor that is instigating marginalization of Native languages today (Benally & Viri, 2005; Sims, 2006). The students' perspectives in this chapter can help to initiate those important discussions that need to take place within our Native communities about reclaiming language and reinserting it purposefully and intentionally in everyday community, school, and family life.

Fishman (1996) emphasizes that to maintain or revitalize a language that is not being intergenerationally transmitted naturally within a community, there must be change within that community. He stated that this can be done by a small group of people, and that the more dislocated the speech community, the smaller that group tends to be. This chapter's ultimate purpose is to learn from those small groups of Native individuals who demonstrate a critical Indigenous consciousness and critical language awareness. Related to human agency and Freire's (1993) discussion of critical consciousness, I define critical Indigenous consciousness as an awareness of the historical and broad oppressive conditions that have influenced current realities of Indigenous people's lives. This awareness leads to acknowledging, respecting, and embracing one's role in contributing to and transforming their communities and families. It is also a realization that becoming a complete human being according to Indigenous worldviews is through service to others, family, and community (Cajete, 1994). By serving one's community, one's needs and goals are freed from a dominant, hegemonic position and viewed from an Indigenous perspective, which allows for transformation and is vital for the protection of Indigenous lands, people, culture, and languages (G. Smith, 2003).

Interestingly, if not ironically, many youth must express their Indigenous identity through English. Poet and author Simon Ortiz (Acoma Pueblo) acknowledged this quandary in a public lecture in which he eloquently redefined its meaning in the way these youth have shared. Speaking in first-person as a Native youth, he said, "I may not be fluent in my Indigenous language, but I am fluent in my Indigenous consciousness" (2008). The students demonstrate that defining a Native identity for youth and young adults is not a simple, uncomplicated process, and that youth's Native identity now encompasses multiple levels of cultural access, participation, and knowledge with or even without the Native language. While many youth in these studies realized the inherent value of their language, maintaining and transmitting language is more difficult when they have to live with competing values and needs in their schools and communities. Our Native languages and communities need our youth and young adults not only to realize the intrinsic value of their languages, but to act on that value by committing to their language in a world that often sends them powerful mixed messages that marginalize, stigmatize, and induce feelings of embarrassment or shame with their own limitations in their language. The Native language courses are one step forward for building critical language awareness and supporting student commitment to language learning. These courses challenge students to know themselves, to hold high expectations for themselves, and ultimately, to become contributing members and transformative change agents in their communities and in the world.

Notes

1 Many of the Pueblo students in this study come from very small communities. Thus, to provide for more protection of their anonymity, I only list their tribal affiliation as "Pueblo" without naming their specific Pueblo community.
2 Blood quantum requirements are utilized in many Native communities to determine eligibility to enroll in the particular Indigenous nation. The federal government initiated this form of enrollment and set the standard level requirement at one-fourth blood quantum to enroll. Some Native nations have changed this requirement, while many maintain and enforce the federal standard.

References

Benally, A., & Viri, D. (2005). Diné bizaad (Navajo language) at a crossroads: Extinction or renewal? *Bilingual Research Journal, 21*(1), 85–108.

Benjamin, R., Pecos, R., & Romero, M. E. (1996). Language revitalization efforts in the Pueblo de Cochiti: Becoming "literate" in an oral society. In N. H. Hornberger (Ed.), *Indigenous literacies in the Americas: Language planning from the bottom up* (pp. 115–136). Berlin, Germany: Mouton de Gruyter.

Cajete, G. (1994). *Look to the mountain: An ecology of Indigenous education.* Durango, CO: Kivaki Press.

Crawford, J. (1996). Seven hypotheses on language loss: Causes and cures. In G. Cantoni (Ed.), *Stabilizing indigenous languages* (pp. 51–68). Flagstaff: Northern Arizona University Center for Excellence in Education.

Delgado, R., & Stefancic, J. (2001). *Critical race theory: An introduction.* New York, NY: New York University Press.

Fishman, J. A. (1991). *Reversing language shift: Theoretical and empirical foundations of assistance to threatened languages.* Clevedon, England: Multilingual Matters.

Fishman, J. A. (1996). Maintaining languages: What works? What doesn't? In G. Cantoni (Ed.), *Stabilizing indigenous languages* (pp. 186–198). Flagstaff: Northern Arizona University Center for Excellence in Education.

Fishman, J. A. (Ed.). (2001). *Can threatened languages be saved? Reversing language shift, revisited: A 21st century perspective.* Clevedon, England: Multilingual Matters.

Freire, P. (1993). *Pedagogy of the oppressed: 30th anniversary edition.* New York, NY: Continuum.

Gilmore, P., & Smith, D. (2005). Seizing academic power: Indigenous subaltern voices, metaliteracy, and counternarratives in higher education. In T. L. McCarty (Ed.), *Language, literacy, and power in schooling* (pp. 67–88). Mahwah, NJ: Erlbaum.

Giroux, H. (1988) *Teachers as intellectuals: Toward a critical pedagogy of learning.* Westport, CT: Greenwood.

González, N., Moll, L. C., & Amanti, C. (Eds.) (2005). *Funds of knowledge: Theorizing practices in households, communities, and classrooms.* Mahwah, NJ: Erlbaum.

Hinton, L., & Hale, K. (Eds.). (2001). *The green book of language revitalization in practice.* San Diego, CA: Academic Press.

Hornberger, N. H. (Ed.). (2008). *Can schools save Indigenous languages: Policy and practice on four continents.* New York, NY: Palgrave Macmillan.

Hornberger, N. H., & Coronel-Molina, S. (2004). Quechua language shift, maintenance, and revitalization in the Andes: The case for language planning. *International Journal of the Sociology of Language, 167,* 9–67.

Jojola, T., Lee, T. S., Alacantara, A.M., Belgarde, M., Bird, C.P., Lopez, N., & Singer, B. (2011). *Indian education in New Mexico, 2025.* Santa Fe, NM: Public Education Department.

Krauss, M. (1992). The world's languages in crisis. *Language, 68,* 1–10.

LeCompte, M. D., & Schensul, J. J. (1999). *Analyzing and interpreting ethnographic data.* Walnut Creek, CA: Altamira Press.

Lee, T. S. (2007). "If they want Navajo to be learned, then they should require it in all schools": Navajo teenagers experiences, choices, and demands regarding Navajo language. *Wicazo Sa Review,* Spring, 7–33.

Lee, T. S., & McLaughlin, D. (2001). Reversing Navajo language shift, revisited. In J. A. Fishman (Ed.), *Can threatened languages be saved? Reversing language shift, revisited: A 21st century perspective* (pp. 23–43). Clevedon, England: Multilingual Matters.

May, S. (1999). Language and education rights for Indigenous peoples. In S. May (Ed.), *Indigenous community-based education* (pp. 42–66). Clevedon, England: Multilingual Matters.

McCarty, T. L. (2009). The impact of high-stakes accountability policies on Native American learners: Evidence from research. *Teaching Education, 20*(1), 7–29.

McCarty, T. L, Romero, M. E., & Zepeda, O. (2006). Reclaiming the gift: Indigenous youth counter-narratives on Native language loss and revitalization. *American Indian Quarterly, 30*(2), 28–48.

McCarty, T. L., & Zepeda, O. (Guest Eds.). (1998). Indigenous language use and change in the Americas (Special issue). *International Journal of the Sociology of Language, 132.*

Moll, L.C., Amanti, C., Neff, D., & González, N. (1992). Funds of knowledge for teaching: Using a qualitative approach to connect homes and classrooms. *Theory into Practice, 31*(2), 132–141.

Nicholas, S. E. (2005) Negotiating for the Hopi way of life through literacy and schooling. In T. L. McCarty (Ed.), *Language, literacy and power in schooling* (pp. 29–46). Mahwah, NJ: Erlbaum.

Oritz, S. (2008, April). Keynote address. Native American and Indigenous Studies Annual Conference, Athens, Georgia.

Quijada, P. (2008, March). Tribal critical race theory and educational spaces: (Re)examining schooling experiences of Indigenous youth. Paper presented at the Annual Meeting of the American Educational Research Association, New York, NY.

Romero-Little, M. E., & McCarty, T. L. (2006). Language planning challenges and prospects in Native American communities and schools. Tempe: Arizona State University Education Policy Studies Laboratory, Language Policy Research Unit. Retrieved July 31, 2008, from http://epsl.asu.edu/epru/documents/EPSL-0602-105-LPRU.pdf

Sims, C. (2001). Native language planning: A pilot process in the Acoma Pueblo community. In L. Hinton & K. Hale (Eds.), *The green book of language revitalization in practice* (pp. 63–73). San Diego, CA: Academic Press.

Sims, C. (2006). Language planning in American Indian Pueblo communities: Contemporary challenges and issues. *Current Issues in Language Planning, 7*(2–3), 251–268.

Smith, L. T. (1999). *Decolonizing methodologies: Research and Indigenous peoples.* London, England: Zed Books.

Smith, G. (2003, October). Indigenous struggle for the transformation of education and schooling. Keynote address. Alaskan Federation of Natives Convention, Anchorage, AK. Retrieved June 16, 2005, from http://www.ankn.uaf.edu/curriculum/Articles/GrahamSmith/

Solórzano, D., & Yosso, T. (2002). A critical race counterstory of race, racism, and affirmative action. *Equity and Excellence in Education, 35*(2), 155–168.

Wyman, L. (2009). Youth, linguistic ecology, and language endangerment: A Yup'ik example. *Journal of Language, Identity, and Education, 8*(5), 335–349.

8

IGNITING A YOUTH LANGUAGE MOVEMENT

Inuit Youth as Agents of Circumpolar Language Planning

Shelley R. Tulloch

This chapter explores the role of Inuit youth and their international organization, the Inuit Circumpolar Youth Council (ICYC), in language planning initiatives for the Inuit language. It shows their engagement in language planning as a collaborative, consensus-building process within a particular sociolinguistic context. Through the work of the ICYC, Inuit youth have become deliberate agents of Inuit language preservation, engaging at an organizational level by hosting two youth symposia, participating in international forums, and advocating to local, regional, national, and international bodies for language policies and programs which reflect their needs and priorities. These processes of engagement have increased Inuit youth's voice, choice, and agency in language planning. Discussion suggests how Indigenous non-governmental organizations such as the ICYC can bridge bottom-up and top-down approaches to language planning.

The Honourable Louis Tapardjuk, Inuit Elder and Minister of Culture, Language, Elders and Youth (Government of Nunavut, Canada), greeted Inuit youth gathered for the First Inuit Circumpolar Youth Symposium on the Inuit Language, "I am looking at the generation that the rest of us are depending on to carry the Inuit language into the future" (Tulloch & ICYC, 2005). One wonders if he knew how prophetic his words would be. Youth have not been traditionally considered as powerful language planning agents, and the responsibility is heavy. Most youth feel pressure, overt and covert, to use and pass on a more widely spoken language. Many have insufficient opportunity to learn the Indigenous language and feel dispossessed to carry it on, while others are distracted by seemingly more immediate threats to Inuit youth well-being. Bilingual Inuit youth are de facto agents of language maintenance or loss as they use one language or the other, influence their peers, and, most importantly, socialize their children, the next generation of speakers (for discussion of youth as de facto language planners, see Lee, 2009; McCarty, Romero-Little, Warhol, & Zepeda, 2009; Wyman, 2012). Through the work of the Inuit Circumpolar Youth Council (ICYC), Inuit youth have become deliberate agents of Inuit language preservation, engaging at an organizational level by hosting two Inuit Circumpolar Youth Symposia on the Inuit Language (ICYSIL 1 and 2), participating in international forums, and advocating to local, regional, national, and international bodies for language policies and programs which reflect their needs and priorities. This chapter describes these initiatives, and analyzes how the process of engagement has increased Inuit youths' voice, choice, and agency in language planning (see Hornberger, 2006b, and McCarty, 2006, for discussion of voice and choice in Indigenous language planning). It further shows how Indigenous organizations such as ICYC can bridge grassroots and legislative approaches to language planning.

Academic-Grassroots Collaboration

As a non-Indigenous, English-mother tongue academic, my engagement with Inuit youth language planning dates back to a first field trip to Nunavut in 1999. I had travelled north with the intention of analyzing how the newly formed, primarily-Inuit government would pursue its mandate of implementing the Inuit language as the language of work. After a series of pilot interviews with a wide range of community members, I was floored by the passion and activism expressed by the 18-year-old Inuk[1] in my final pilot interview. Her position contrasted starkly with older pilot interviewees' general descriptions of youth disinterest and passivity. I thus decided to focus on youth experiences with Inuktitut as foundation for understanding the potential of language promotion in Nunavut. I found that Inuit youth presented themselves as capable and motivated learners and users of the Inuit language, who felt threatened by diminished opportunities to expand their competence and by others' judgements of their language use (Tulloch, 2004). Similar contrasts between self-declared youth attitudes, experiences and expectations and adults' taken-for-granted assumptions of their experiences in other Indigenous contexts highlight the need to listen to youth voices in Indigenous language planning (Lee, 2007, 2009; McCarty, Romero, & Zepeda, 2006; McCarty & Wyman, 2009; McCarty et al., 2009; Wyman, 2012).

I first met Miali-Elise Coley, then chair of the ICYC, when I returned to her hometown to share these research results. She had been away and busy with school during my earlier extended field trips, so I had missed her, even though many in her community had recommended her as a key informant on youth perspectives on language promotion. She drew me in as an academic supporter to ICYC's language-related work, where I helped with funding applications, sat in on planning and follow-up conference calls, attended meetings and events, took notes (verbatim, as much as possible) and/or audio or video recorded the above, and helped with the production of minutes and reports. Through Miali,

I met the other 2002–2006 ICYC executive members (Jonathan Epoo and Eric Nutarariaq [Canada], Elizabeth Saagulik Hensley and Lee Ryan [Alaska, U.S.], Upaluk Poppel and Janus Kleist [Greenland], and Lubov Tajan [Chukotka, Russia]). The synergistic relationship continued with the 2006–2010 ICYC executive council (Greta Schuerch, Chair [Megan Alvanna-Stimpfle chaired from 2006–2007], Lee Ryan and Dea Latham [Alaska], Jonathan Epoo and Wynter Kuliktana [Canada], Nuno Isbosethsen and Stina Berthelsen [Green-land], and Galina Seliverstova and Lydia Tutai [Chukotka]). Connections with the Inuit Circumpolar Council (ICC) ultimately led to my collaboration to help organize and facilitate youth components of ICC and Government of Nunavut-hosted language planning meetings.

This chapter combines my outsider observations and analyses with ICYC members' and other youths' insider experiences and testimonies to explore ICYC's role in Inuit language planning. The understandings derive from obser-vation, relationship and dialogue—classic both to ethnographic and Indig-enous approaches to knowledge-making (Battiste, 2008). The analysis takes into account documentation of ICYC's language planning process (notes and records of the conference calls, executive council meetings, language symposia and other events, and the reports that came out of them, supplemented by per-sonal journal reflections). These were created, discussed and interpreted along-side ICYC executive members. In accordance with the spirit of the work—led by youth, for youth—Inuit youth have commented on various versions of this chapter. The former ICYC chairs who led the work described within also approved the publication of this chapter, although they declined to officially co-author. Quotations below are taken from documents approved and distrib-uted by the youth (reports, media releases, and agreed-upon meeting notes).

Inuit Circumpolar Youth Council

The Inuit Circumpolar Youth Council works in a context of threats to Indig-enous well-being (and especially to youth well-being). The parent organiza-tion, Inuit Circumpolar Council, was founded in 1977 as a non-governmental advocacy organization representing all Inuit in Russia, Alaska, Canada, and Greenland. Leading up to and following its creation, modern land claims and movements toward self-government have been achieved for most Inuit groups (Alaska Native Claims Settlement Act 1971; James Bay Northern Quebec Agree-ment 1975; Greenland Homerule 1979 and Greenland Self-Government 2009; Inuvialuit Claims Settlement Act 1984; Nunavut Land Claims Agreement and Nunavut Act 1993; Labrador Inuit Land Claims Agreement [Nunatsiavut] 2003). The Indigenous activism behind these agreements seeks to redress the harms of past colonial and assimilationist policies and create a positive future for Indig-enous peoples. The land claims and self-governments create contexts where Inuit ways of being are privileged, where legislation is passed to protect Inuit rights, and where being Inuk, practicing Inuit values and speaking the Inuit language are valued politically and economically, as well as culturally and socially.

The ICYC was created in 1994 to create space for a stronger youth voice parallel to the parent ICC. Despite positive developments recognizing Inuit and broader Indigenous rights internationally, Inuit suffer gross inequities in their respective countries. The ICYC is mandated to increase Inuit youths' potential for agency (e.g., through information sharing and securing a voice in other international forums), and advocate for and implement initiatives to enhance the Inuit youth's well-being. Every 4 years, youth delegates at the ICYC General Assembly use a consensus-building process to identify youth priorities. Language and culture have figured prominently in these priorities, as they are considered indices of other aspects of well-being alongside celebrating life/ suicide prevention and environmental protection (2002–2006), and promoting healthy communities and education (2006–2010). Youth keep language at the forefront as they consider knowledge and ancestral language use to be advantageous to addressing these other priorities.

Inuit Language Vitality

ICC officially recognizes a single Inuit language spoken across the homeland. Linguists identify 16 dialects and 40 sub-dialects (Dorais, 1990). Intelligibility between varieties is unclear, and speakers commonly identify their linguistic allegiance at the dialectal, sub-dialectal, or even community level. Ethnolinguistic vitality, as measured by numbers of speakers, intergenerational transmission, corpus development, institutional support, language prestige, etc. (Bourhis & Landry, 2008) varies greatly between languages/dialects, between communities, and even within communities. Although Greenland has officially declared Kalallisut "not endangered," studies across the Inuit homeland reflect difficulties in balancing the ancestral language and colonially introduced languages—each with differing associated values and opportunities (for Chukotka, see Morgounova, 2007; for Alaska, see Harcharek, 1992, and Wyman, 2012; for Nunavut, see Aylward, 2006; Aylward, Kuliktana, & Meyok, 1998; Dorais & Sammons, 2002; Tagalik, 1998; and Tulloch, 2004; for Nunavik, see Crago, Annahatak, & Ningiuruvik, 1993; Crago, Chen, Genesee, & Allen, 1998; Louis & Taylor, 2001; Patrick, 2003; for Nunatsiavut, see Anderson & Johns, 2005; for Greenland, see Langgaard, 2001; and for a circumpolar perspective see Dorais, 2010; and Poppel, Kruse, Duhaime, & Abryutina, 2007). As increased knowledge and use of contact languages (Russian in Chukotka, English in Alaska, English or French in Canada, and Danish and English in Greenland) undermines the ancestral language, Inuit youth experience this shift as part of broader social, cultural, and political changes. As reflected in this chapter, youth are also attempting to support the Inuit language in order to shape their desired futures.

Language Planning

I interpret the ICYC's work within the theoretical framework of language planning. Language planning can refer to any attempt to alter or sustain language development and use (Cooper, 1989). Early language planning studies considered that only governments had sufficient power to shape a language's future (Calvet, 1998). Without negating the importance of legislation in creating a context which motivates and enables language choices (e.g., Brenzinger, Heine, & Sommer, 1991), language planning scholars now acknowledge that communities previously considered to be powerless can exert deliberate influence upon their own languages (see case studies in Fishman, 1991; Hinton & Hale, 2001; Lee & McLaughlin, 2001). Indeed, Shohamy (2006) argues that the real power lies with individual speakers: the collective impact of each speaker's everyday choices and behavior ultimately shapes the development and use of a language.

While Hornberger (2006a) points out that a better understanding of agency has led to language planning advances, Tollefson (2006) argues that more research into grassroots agency is still needed: "A key agenda for CLP [critical language-policy] research is to develop better understanding of the factors contributing to successful language maintenance and revitalization programs, particularly the roles of indigenous communities in shaping policies and programs" (pp. 51–52). Although action at the two poles—governmental action and truly grassroots (local, "micro") action—is well studied, the potential of non-government organizations such as the ICYC is not documented. I argue that the language planning efforts of the ICYC show how such organizations can bridge grassroots and governmental action, becoming a powerful middle ground directing a language's future.

The following sections briefly describe five key youth meetings and their outcomes, then analyze how the events, and the interactions leading up to and following them, demonstrate youth voice, choice and agency in language planning.

Description of Inuit Youth Initiatives in Language Planning

First Inuit Youth Symposium on the Inuit Language

The first Inuit Circumpolar Youth Symposium on the Inuit Language (August 15–19, 2005) brought youth together to share information, encourage and inspire each other (described in Coley & Tulloch, 2008), and was the first of its kind. It was organized by Inuit youth for Inuit youth. ICYC conceptualized the meeting, fundraised, and called in help from other experts and facilitators. In the words of Alaskan executive council member Elizabeth Saagulik Hensley, "This gathering is so awesome. It's so cool that youth arranged it, got the funding for it. It makes the statement that youth can do what they want. Of course, we need support from other people but it's pretty huge" (recorded in Broberg, 2005). The objectives of the symposium were to expand youth understanding of Inuit language issues across the Arctic, identify challenges in preserving the language(s), and develop policy recommendations for communities and governments. The 20 delegates from Alaska, Greenland, and Canada (Nunavut and Nunavik) came from diverse walks of life: hunters, artists, students, leaders, parents, and teachers. (The Russian delegate was, at the last minute, unable to attend due to visa issues. However, a Russian elder and an interpreter were present.)

The flexible agenda privileged facilitated, focused dialogue, while also incorporating research presentations from each country's youth delegation and guest speeches by language policy and planning specialists (mainly Inuit adults). On the third day of the symposium, ICC elders (meeting concurrently in Iqaluit) were invited to listen to the youths' dialogue and provide guidance. Beyond the formal agenda, youth ate together, spent time on the land and in private homes, performed for each other and the community, played traditional games and generally listened to, learned from, and built relationships with each other.

Delegates left pledging individual action in learning and using the Inuit language, and continued collaboration with each other and community-based initiatives to enhance others' opportunities to learn and use the language. These actions and initiatives included commitments to "use what you know" and support each other's use; to create Inuit language media; and to take advantage of Inuit language learning opportunities—on the land, using technology, and in the classroom. Youth also developed an Inuktitut "hipification" strategy, which involved embracing historical connections to Inuktitut as a "cool" part of modern Inuit identity and bringing the Inuit language into parts of society that many youth consider "cool" today. Through this strategy, youth strove to overcome tensions whereby some peers saw Inuktitut as belonging only to the elders, promoting it as a positive tool for youth self-expression. The synergy at the symposium and follow-up activities demonstrate that ICYC achieved its goal of "igniting the light" of a youth language movement, centered on the Inuit language as a "hip" way of speaking. The report co-authored by myself and ICYC (Tulloch & ICYC, 2005) presents a synthesis of youth discussions, including their presentation of language issues in each country, youth priorities for action, and a summary of recommended action points.

Second Inuit Circumpolar Youth Symposium on the Inuit Language

The Second Circumpolar Inuit Youth Symposium on the Inuit Language (ICYSIL 2), held in Kotzebue, Alaska, July 6–7, 2007, built on the momentum of the first symposium. The second symposium took as a starting point that youth are eager to learn and use the Inuit language, and worked to identify and share resources to motivate and equip the youth delegation accordingly. In the spirit of sharing best practices, working together, and gaining community support (goals identified in the first symposium), the ICYC organizers (the fourth executive council of ICYC, elected in 2006) invited respected Inuit language activists and leaders to contribute, starting at the planning stages. They invited symposium presenters who have implemented successful language learning/ promotional initiatives (whether grassroots, or partnerships between grassroots and institutions) to learn from those they admire. As they listened to examples of those who had effectively moved forward, in spite of little support from government or any higher level authority, one message the youth heard was to "pave your own way."

The symposium format allowed for morning motivational and informational presentations from activists, leaders, teachers, and others followed by afternoon action-planning brainstorming sessions (agenda listed in Schuerch, 2007). The delegates and speakers represented a cross-generational group of Inuit, sharing experiences on equal footing. The outcome was increased commitment for intergenerational sharing of the responsibility to perpetuate the Inuit language, expressed poignantly when delegates of all ages took an oath to each other, to learn and use the Inuit language, and to teach, have patience, and not to judge or give up on each other. The group workshops also yielded strategies for creating opportunities to see, hear, interact in and speak the Inuit language. The youth left motivated, with resources for strengthening their language. The symposium report, edited by the ICYC chair (Schuerch, 2007), offers a brief synthesis of the event, compiles speakers' original contributions (e.g., Power-Point presentations), and lists action points from brainstorming workshops.

General Assemblies

Between the first and second Inuit Language symposia, ICYC youth met face-to-face in Barrow, Alaska at the 2006 ICYC General Assembly (GA), held concurrently with the ICC General Assembly. Here the executive council updated youth delegates on related initiatives, elected a new executive, set priorities for the next 4 years, and, significantly, met face-to-face to reinforce relationships. The ICYC and ICC General Assemblies intersected only partially, as some ICC speakers came and shared with the youth, youth presented once at the ICC GA, and attended some ICC GA sessions. The final outcome of the General Assemblies was a declaration mandating ICC's priorities for the next 4 years. The 2006 Utqiaġvik Declaration (ICC, 2006, p. 5) stated:

> 31. Instruct the ICC Executive Council to work with and support the Inuit Circumpolar Youth Council (ICYC) to further develop its organization to allow participation of Inuit youth and to more fully participate in ICC governance at the international and national levels;

> 32. Mandate the ICC Language and Communications Commission to participate in international bodies and to promote technological initiatives that will promote linguistic diversity, fight the tendencies of linguicide in Inuit language speaking areas and to promote youth initiatives, such as the Inuit Circumpolar Youth Council's project on hipification of Inuit culture and language.

Youth's determination to gain a stronger voice and influence the future of their ancestral language was having an impact.

Arctic Indigenous Language Symposium

In 2008, ICC invited ICYC chair, Greta Schuerch (Alaska) and executive member Wynter Kuliktana (Canada) to represent Inuit youth at the first circumpolar Arctic Indigenous Languages Symposium (AILS). This symposium was primarily funded by the Canadian Government, jointly hosted by the Inuit Circumpolar Council (ICC) and the Saami Council in Tromsø, Norway (October 19–21, 2008). The symposium involved Indigenous delegates of various ages, including at least one youth, from each Indigenous organization represented on the Arctic Council ("Permanent Participants": Aleut International Association; Arctic Athabaskan Council; Gwich'in Council International; Inuit Circumpolar Council; Russian Association of Indigenous Peoples of the North; and the Saami Council), in addition to government delegates from the Arctic states and a number of observers (academics, media, etc.). The goal of the meeting, in regard to the two ICYSILs, was to share information, best practices, and develop an agenda for preserving Arctic Indigenous languages. Youth were full participants throughout, and held a "youth-only" roundtable one evening, in which they shared their own challenges, priorities, and successes. Schuerch presented a summary of these discussions to the full delegation the following day, challenging more seasoned Inuit leaders to demonstrate with actions as well as words that language is a top priority (Schuerch, 2008). Another youth delegate (Laresa Syverson, Alaskan Aleut) upheld youth positions in meetings of the drafting committee, which prepared policy recommendations directed at national and regional governments, non-governmental and Indigenous organizations, and others with potential influence on the future of Arctic Indigenous languages. The full incorporation of Indigenous youth in the agenda and outcomes, and adult leaders' use of ICYCs ICYSIL reports as background reading indicate the growing respect for and incorporation of Inuit youth in Arctic language planning. A full symposium report, including a summary of youth contributions, was published by ICC following the symposium (ICC, 2008). Schuerch (2008) also published a summary of youth positions.

Nunavut Language Summit

When the Government of Nunavut held its Nunavut Language Summit in February 2010, bringing in experts from across the Inuit homeland, youth were invited speakers alongside such internationally esteemed Inuit linguist–elders as Dr. Edna Agheak McLean, Jose Kusugak, and Dr. Carl Christian Olsen, Puju. Youth delegates attended daily sessions with the full delegation, then met for 1 or 2 hours each day to debrief, discuss youth-specific issues and develop recommendations and strategies for addressing their specific language needs. Youth presented their priorities and strategies to the full delegation on the summit's final day. The summit's purpose was to draw on advice and best practices from across the Inuit homeland to develop a comprehensive plan for the implementation Nunavut's language laws. The youth voice was effectively captured in the resulting report, with a full section dedicated to "Youth and Language" (Nunavut Department of Culture, Language, Elders, and Youth, 2011). Furthermore, concrete outcomes such as the launch of an Inuit language learning application for iPods were pursued and achieved in direct response to youth recommendations.

The above are just a few of the international initiatives ICYC executive members and other Inuit youth leaders have been involved with or organized related to language. They show a progression from "youth-only" events to intergenerational events where youth have a strong voice, and from "Inuit-only" events to those involving a broader spectrum of Indigenous peoples. These progressions suggest that the work of ICYC is succeeding in increasing Inuit youths' voice, choice, and agency in language planning.

Analysis of Outcomes of ICYC's Language Work

Voice

> Our meeting here is so vital toward understanding how youth across the Circumpolar compare and what kind of thoughts they have about our Inuit language. [...] The youth that are participating at the Symposium have lots of knowledge and ideas and thoughts they want to share regarding our culture and why it is significant. Young people's views need to be heard by the general public. (Miali-Elise Coley, co-organizer of the 1st ICYSIL, recorded in Broberg, 2005)

The Inuit Circumpolar Youth Council has deliberately magnified Inuit youth voice in language planning through implicit and explicit strategies. The format of the 1st ICYSIL created a forum that gave youth an opportunity to express themselves and their priorities. "I want to hear about other [Inuit] groups facing same issues and how they're dealing with it" (Kelsi Ivanoff, Inuit youth, quoted in Tulloch & ICYC, 2005). ICYSIL 1 organizers maintained an informal roundtable approach where Inuit youth spoke to and with each other, created a safe context through relationship-building, and minimized the impact of "outsider" influences or "judges" by favoring an almost exclusively Inuit youth delegation. This format, along with the characteristically-Inuit consensus style of decision-making, was repeated in the GA meetings, and the youth forums at AILS and the Nunavut Language Summit. The youth-only meetings followed by larger group presentations helped youth learn and practice exercising a stronger public voice. As a youth delegate to the Nunavut Language Summit reflected, "I realize I used to be really shy but I wanted to overcome it.... [N]ow

I realize that if I want to change things I need to speak out. I realize that practicing in groups like this can make us more comfortable" (draft youth meeting notes, 2010). Time set aside for youth to speak among themselves contributed to them emerging with a strong voice, anchored in relationship and unity.

As knowledgeable, engaged youth came together from diverse backgrounds, with detailed knowledge of and experience in specific local contexts, they produced new understandings of overarching concerns, realities, and future possibilities of the Inuit language. Youth naturally disseminated these back to their local communities: "I'm excited about this sharing of knowledge and bringing it home so that we can start revitalizing our language and bringing up smart beautiful Inupiaq speaking babies" (Elizabeth Saagulik Hensley, quoted in Tulloch & ICYC, 2005). Canagarajah (2005) refers to similar processes as "a new form of grassroots knowledge making" (p. xviii), essential in grassroots language planning. Locally, youth passed on their learning and vision through personal communication, community presentations, press releases, media reports, and appearances. They have reached popular national audiences, at least in Greenland, through a television documentary on ICYSIL 1, created by participants in the first Symposium (Broberg, 2005). Youth have also reached select targeted audiences, such as policy makers (e.g., the Canadian federal government published an article on ICYC's work and priorities in one of their policy journals [Coley & Tulloch, 2008]; an Alaskan delegate used the 1st ICYSIL report to lobby the U.S. government at the Recovery and Preservation of Native American Languages hearing in 2006; the Greenlandic Language Secretariat took up the ICYC's ideas and supported follow-up events in Greenland), international academic audiences (e.g., Coley and Tulloch presented at the 2006 International Inuit Studies Conference), and, as seen already, other Indigenous audiences (e.g., ICYC's priorities and recommendations regarding language have been acknowledged and incorporated by the larger organization, ICC; youth recommendations have been included in Nunavut's comprehensive language plan). By all measures, ICYC has heightened consciousness of youths' vision of the current and desired linguistic situations, which Fishman (1991) recognizes as a necessary first step in influencing language-related change.

Inuit leaders, elders, and others are welcoming Inuit youth's voice in language planning. Carl Christian Olsen, Puju, an Inuk (Greenlandic) linguist and chair of ICC's Inuit Language Commission, urged youth and elder delegates at the 2nd ICYSIL to listen to, speak to, and learn from each other, and encouraged youth to assert their agenda, just as youth in his day, 30 years ago, had done, helping to reverse language shift in Greenland. The Honorable Louis Tapardjuk appealed to youth, at ICYSIL 1 "… the Inuit language … belongs to you just as much as it belongs to your Elders. It is your language to shape and to change so that you are able to talk to each other about what matters most to young people today" (Tulloch & ICYC, 2005). Elder Nina Enminaku (Chukotka, Russia) responded warmly to youth at ICYSIL 1, "Today I've been so joyful hearing youth speak to each other in their mother tongue. […] The interest is up to you—whether you like the language or not." Forums on Arctic Indigenous language revitalization since the two ICYCSIL's have explicitly sought out the youth voice.

This increased voice has been one of ICYC's explicit goals since the first ICYC executive council was formed in 1994, with the mandate to secure a permanent seat on the ICC council. When Coley addressed youth at the 2006 ICYC GA at the end of her term as chair, she opened with, "Being able to speak up is a gift and a blessing. And I encourage you all to speak up—whether it's one-on-one or in public.[…] Speak to each other." As she exhorted youth to carry on and assume responsibility, she also urged the full ICC delegation, in her address to the ICC GA, to listen to and recognize the potency of Inuit youth. By the end of the 2006 ICYC and ICC General Assemblies, the result-ing declaration mandated the incoming ICC executive to work more closely with youth and to support their language planning recommendations. ICC's incorporation of youth as key collaborators in the AILS Symposium, and rec-ommendation that all delegates read the two ICYSIL reports, suggest that the youth voice, organized and amplified through the work of ICYC, is being heard and making a difference within larger Indigenous organizations in addi-tion to going out to local, regional, national and international audiences.

Choice

As McCarty (2006) points out, voice is closely linked to choice in Indigenous language planning. Spolsky (2004) argues that language planning inherently addresses the right to choice. ICYC has established a context where Inuit youth are heard alongside others. As seen in their symposia and participation in other events, ICYC is shaping who they hear from, in which format, and on which topics. While in the first ICYSIL youth focused on establishing youth voice, in the second ICYSIL they chose to solicit input (as planning committee members and as speakers) from a wide range of leaders, activists, specialists—people the youth admired and who had demonstrated commitment to listening to youth. The elders, leaders, Inuit teachers, and others (see list in Schuerch, 2007) hon-ored those choices by coming and acting as invited participants, affirming the young Inuit's choice to be near them, share with them, and learn alongside them. Wide-based funding and in-kind support for both ICYSILs, listed in the reports, further indicates community and outside support for ICYCs choices.

The youth's growing ability to choose is also seen in ICYC's determination to select who will speak for them. In 2006, for example, outgoing executive council members from Alaska resisted pressure to allow ICC Alaska to name the youth delegates to the ICYC General Assembly, asserting their right to help elect the executive council that would represent youth for the next 4 years.

Finally, information sharing is foundational to ICYC's mandate and key to enhancing youth choices. Inuit youth leaders active in ICYC are also active in multiple international arenas, such as the United Nations youth internship program. Through the ICYSILs and other international gatherings, youth have taught each other about their linguistic and Indigenous rights (e.g., the United Nations *Declaration on the Rights of Indigenous Peoples* ratified in 2007) and Indigenous advocacy in much larger forums (e.g., the United Nations Permanent Forum on Indigenous Issues). Tapping into these broader arenas and efforts, youth have strengthened their positions. In the many ways listed above, youth have also emerged as informed decision-makers, shaping the direction of Inuit language planning.

> [...] We need to take part in decision making, be heard and understood. We are the caretakers of tomorrow. Our views need to be considered and taken seriously today. (Miali-Elise Coley, co-organizer of the 1st ICYSIL, recorded in Broberg, 2005)

Agency

The ICYC is collectively impacting the situation of Inuit languages. It is also empowering youth (individuals and peer groups) to proactively take hold of and intentionally shape the future of their language. At the heart of each symposium was a commitment and call to action. Each report includes agreed upon action points for furthering Inuit language knowledge, use and prestige. While ICYC is advocating to (what are supposedly) more powerful organizations and governments, the youth's focus has been on "what can *we* do?" from the inside, rather than waiting on outside contexts and plans for language revival: "Institutions are a place to make things mandatory, but something needs to be done to bring something out from the inside rather than to project it from the outside" (Elizabeth Saagulik Hensley, Alaskan co-organizer of ICYSIL 1). Stina Berthelsen (2006–2010 ICYC executive, Greenland), addressing the 2nd ICYSIL, emphasized speakers of the Inuit language's responsibility to support others' acquisition and use: "We need to bring about the understanding that language is a common responsibility. [...] I can start. When someone doesn't understand, I can translate, explain, help." Joel Forbes, a Yup'ik youth presenter to the 2nd ICYSIL, currently learning his ancestral language, encouraged Inuit youth who do not speak the language as well as they wish to take responsibility for their own learning: "You have to keep reminding some people to talk to you. ... [W]e brainstorm ways to ask people to speak to us ... I try to find those places [i.e., elders' homes, where only Yup'ik is spoken] and bring it out. [...] I try to get my mom to speak Yup'ik ... It's hard work ... but I'm not going to give up and I don't want any of you to give up." Elders affirmed this agency: "This is the first time I've met with youth at this kind of meeting and I know what you want and your statements are in my heart and in my head. [...] I know for a fact that we will have a better future because of you and your actions" (Elders David and Lizzie Mary Angnakak, Nunavut, Canada, quoted in Tulloch & ICYC, 2005). Tulloch (2004) documents similar grassroots commitment among Inuit youth in Nunavut to be agents of language revitalization through their daily actions. Wyman (2012) also demonstrates how Yup'ik youth are de facto agents of language shift or maintenance in Shohamy's (2006) sense, as their everyday actions ultimately shape the language and its use.

While individual agency does not depend on ICYC's organized efforts, it is facilitated by them, as youth are empowered by knowledge and by relationships with others striving for similar goals. The model of agency evidenced in ICYC's work is one of collaborative power—working together for a common goal. Efforts are strongly anchored in home communities and networks, even as the group attempts to reach broader, including international, audiences.

Youth agency is acknowledged in governmental and organizational policies emerging from the initiatives discussed above. For instance, Nunavut's comprehensive language plan dictates that the Department of Culture, Language, Elders and Youth "will support youth in designing their own language promotion programs" (Nunavut Department of Culture, Language, Elders, and Youth, 2011, p. 36). Recommendations from the Arctic Indigenous Languages Summit include mechanisms for youth to take on leadership roles in follow-up actions. The resulting Arctic Council-endorsed Assessing, Monitoring, and Promoting Arctic Indigenous Languages project, led by ICC, incorporates a deliberate youth component. The strength of youth vision, innovativeness, and energy is recognized, and "adult" organizations and governments are concretely creating spaces for youth to move their language agendas and priorities forward.

ICYC is serving as a bridge between individual and institutional action. Discussing globalization, Appadurai (2000) points to the potential of nongovernmental organizations and transnational advocacy in knowledge creation, dissemination, and application. Canagarajah (2005) picks up on these ideas, advocating for reconsidering agency in language planning. Groups like ICYC are made up of grassroots individuals from the communities that language planning efforts seek to impact. At the same time, by their numbers and organization, such groups have the potential to go beyond what individuals can know or do. The knowledge that they can create and disseminate, and the recommendations they generate, are particularly relevant and applicable because the members understand and are affected by local realities. Of course, they are not neutral, but they are free from some governmental constraints, so may have more freedom than governments in their words, plans, and actions. In brief, such groups have strengths that neither individuals nor governments have and models of agency in language planning may do well to consider the potential of non-government organizations.

Social Change

ICYC initiatives have positively impacted youth communities beyond language outcomes. Part of ICYC's rationale in focusing on language is that language-related developments promise to impact broader goals for healthy, empowered communities. A background document to the 2nd ICYSIL asserts: "The ICYC, through the Symposium, seeks to send a strong, positive message to tribal, state, and national leaders that not only are we ready to learn, but our Inuit languages are essential to becoming healthy, confident, and productive members in our communities." As Hornberger (2006a, p. 25) says, "language planning is first and foremost about social change." Language planning is also about social justice, reclaiming rights to identity, to education, to governmental services, to personal and community well-being. Youth have seen positive personal and community changes as a result of their language planning initiatives.

ICYC deliberately targeted language as a tool for building circumpolar unity among Inuit youth. Janus C. Kleist (Greenland) reflected on the impact of ICYSIL 1, "I came here knowing I was part of a community of 50,000 (Greenlandic) Inuit, now I know I am part of 155,000 (Circumpolar Inuit)" (Tulloch & ICYC, 2005). A clear speech community (in Gumperz's [1968] terms) emerged from the symposia and meetings in which youth affirmed shared norms of valuing their language and shared expectations for its use that surpass any individual's or community's capacity or practice. Concrete evidence of this was seen, for example, in the first ICYSIL's roundtable with elders. With limited interpretation available, Inuit youth (speakers and non-speakers of the language) urged each other, and complied, to speak whichever Inuit language variety they knew, insofar as they knew it (and the Eastern Canadian Inuktitut translator kept up as best she could with the Greenlandic, Canadian, and Alaskan varieties).

Academics have debated the usefulness of emphasizing a link between language and ethnic identity to propel language revitalization. Although Fishman (1991) takes an unequivocal position that ancestral language as key to cultural and ethnic identity should be the backbone for language preservation efforts, Hornberger (2006a) among others, argues that the one language–one people ideology requires much more careful nuance. The Inuit youth's positions reflect this tension. In the symposia, youth expressed to each other how the Inuit language has been a tool of belonging for some, an instrument of alienation for others. Still, knowing who they are, where they come from, and where they belong—and having a say in shaping these identities is a key youth priority. Youth's unified effort to recover the treasure (and overcome the challenges) of a shared linguistic heritage seems to have inspired them to work together and surmount the alienation some have felt.

Most Inuit youth live in communities experiencing rapid cultural and linguistic change, and this has contributed to feelings of estrangement from their roots and from their elders (even sometimes from their parents). ICYC promotes the Inuit language as a vehicle for accessing these feelings, and has included times for interaction with elders in each symposium and meeting. Youth found new confidence to approach elders following the first symposium, expressed by youth like Elizabeth Saagulik Hensley (speaking in Broberg, 2005), "This symposium has inspired me ... to communicate with people who I wouldn't normally communicate with ... to go up to elders ... It just shows that it's possible, and there's hope." This confidence was evident in ICYC General Assembly activities the following year, when youth hosted an elders' supper during which they served, sat with, entertained, and generally enjoyed elders' company. Familiarity and comfort with elders is key to language revitalization as elders are language specialists. However, youth comments suggest that elders' affirmation of youth, their actions, and abilities goes much further in supporting ICYC's goal of equipping youth to become 'healthy, confident and productive' community members.

The Inuit language is bringing youth back to their elders, and the youth are bringing the Inuit language into new areas of their lives. An ICYSIL 1 participant created an Inuktitut iPod app for children, contributing to school readiness, literacy, and Inuktitut learning (Rogers, 2012). Youth are self-publishing Inuit language rap and other lyrics on YouTube and social network sites. Canada's National Inuit Youth Council's vice-president stars in *Qanurli*, an Inuit-language television comedy that attracts interest while using Inuktitut to address youth concerns. These are just a few ways that youth are using the Inuit language to engage with each other and society.

Through organizing symposia and meetings, youth developed relationships that they can call on in reaching their goals with elders, Inuit leaders, other youth organizations, program leaders, academics, and others. Partnerships and projects have emerged on youths' own terms, with youth overcoming perceived political, dialectal, generational, occupational, and other boundaries. Empowered by their success thus far, they are moving forward together with others who listen to and support them and their agendas.

Supporting Youth Voice, Choice, and Agency

While youth are proactively assuming voice, choice, and agency in circumpolar language planning, adult responses can be helpful in creating space for this role. In the initiatives described above, four common elements support youth success:

1. The availability of youth-only spaces in which youth can discuss language issues on their own.
2. Opportunities for youth to learn from and be inspired by adult language leaders (including elders).
3. Invitations to youth to speak up and be heard by adult audiences.
4. Strong adult support that is clearly stated to let youth know adults believe in them.

Without strong statements of support for youth, their voice, choice and agency can be stifled by sometimes well-meaning critiques. At the 2010 Language Summit, for instance, youth delegates who were chosen to present the youths' discussions to the full assembly stepped back after hearing an adult comment that "if one cannot speak Inuktitut properly, one should not be presenting at an Inuit Language Summit." While devastating to the youth, such a comment reflects how some adults wish to maintain contexts where the Inuit language is needed in order to have a voice. Such comments may also reflect, in part, uneasiness with changes in the ways youth are using the Inuit language. Ultimately, the youth decided they would all stand together to present the message to other delegates, "We wish we could present in fluent Inuktitut, but this is our reality. Listen to us. Help us learn." Encouragements like those received from elders David and Lizzie Mary Angnakak at the first ICYSIL support youth's confidence to continue to speak:

> I'm missing my teeth. I don't speak properly, but I still have to speak. Even if you don't think you're speaking properly, just speak. It can be embarrassing, but forget about that. I feel satisfaction when you speak, even if it's not properly. For us, it's a pleasure. (Tulloch & ICYC, 2005)

Limitations

While the positive process and impacts of ICYC's work as agents of language planning appear evident, there are other ways of interpreting the work and outcomes, and limitations to the successes extolled here. A major challenge, glossed over above, is distance—geographic, and to some extent social, political, technological, cultural, and linguistic—especially when attempting to incorporate Russian Inuit youth. While Russian youth were well-represented at the bigger meetings, where they travelled with a full adult delegation, it proved difficult for ICYC to organize their presence in the two ICYSILs, or even in ICYC conference calls or email exchanges. While youth have met many favorable audiences, they also encounter (from community members, leaders, and others) those who challenge their voice—whether their right to speak and decide issues, or the legitimacy and usefulness of their decisions. As McCarty and Wyman (2009) highlight in their summary of research on Indigenous youth bilingualism, there is a strong need for compassion and understanding of the particular issues youth are facing. Finally, our evidence of what delegates actually do when they go back to their communities is limited. While we have records of some youth implementing action plans from the symposia, we have lost track of others. It is possible that the strong impacts we know of represent the few rather than the many. More longitudinal research is needed to broaden and deepen our understanding of ICYC's and other youths' impact on language planning. Despite these gaps, most evidence points to ICYC achieving its goal of strengthening the Inuit youth voice and positively engaging youth in planning for the future of Inuit language.

Conclusion

This study of ICYC's language planning initiatives shows this non-governmental Inuit youth organization as a middle ground between entirely grassroots or entirely policy-driven language planning initiatives. It shows Inuit youth's engagement in language planning as a collaborative, consensus-building process within a particular sociolinguistic context. As youth, through ICYC, have organized symposia, learned from each other, solicited input, made recommendations, and disseminated this information to broader Inuit and international communities, they have demonstrated and strengthened their voice, choice, and agency, affecting issues that most concern them. The work of ICYC has a very clear practical value in shaping the status of the Inuit language across the Arctic. The meetings have also increased Inuit youths' sense of identity, of belonging, of powerfulness as a capable and respectable body of language users and learners. Youth leaders learned that they're not in it alone. The study of the ICYC's work opens doors for broadening understanding agency in grassroots language planning. Inuit youth, as represented by ICYC, are an engaged speech community; the actions of their representative council are paving the way for new understandings of how Indigenous languages can be maintained and promoted. Together, they are equipping other youth and building the supportive partnerships they need to live up to the responsibility the Honourable Louis Tapardjuk highlighted in his opening speech to ICYSIL 1, of carrying the valued, but vulnerable, Inuit language into the future.

Acknowledgments

I would like to acknowledge and thank the Inuit who have offered me the privilege of being part of their language planning initiatives. Each person I have interacted with has influenced my understandings as reflected in this chapter. I acknowledge in particular Miali-Elise Coley, Greta Schuerch, and Stina Berthelsen, former leaders of ICYC, and thank them for in-depth discussions over the years of the importance and challenge of youth voice and agency. I also thank those representatives of Inuit organizations who accepted earlier versions of this chapter and distributed it to Inuit youth for comments. Finally, I am grateful to Leisy Wyman, Teresa McCarty, Sheilah Nicholas, and an anonymous reviewer for their suggestions on improvements to this chapter. Any errors and omissions are my own.

Note

1 Inuk is the singular form of Inuit (plural), the most widely used self-designation term for the indigenous group discussed in this chapter.

References

Anderson, C., & Johns, A. (2005). Labrador Inuktitut: Speaking into the future. Études/*Inuit/ Studies, 29*(1-2), 187–205.

Appadurai, A. (2000). Grassroots globalization and the research imagination. *Public Culture, 12,* 1–20.

Aylward, M. L. (2006). *The role of Inuit language and culture in Nunavut schooling: Discourses of the*

Inuit Qaujimajatuqangit conversation (Unpublished doctoral dissertation). University of South Australia, Adelaide, Australia.

Aylward, M. L., Kuliktana, M., & Meyok, R. (1998). *Report of the Kitikmeot language research project.* Cambridge Bay, Nunavut, Canada: Kitikmeot Board of Education.

Battiste, M. (2008). Research ethics for protecting indigenous knowledge and heritage: Institutional and researcher responsibilities. In N. Denzin, Y. Lincoln, & L. Smith (Eds.), *Handbook of critical and Indigenous methodologies* (pp. 497–510). Thousand Oaks, CA: Sage.

Bourhis, R. Y., & Landry, R. (2008). Group vitality, cultural autonomy and the wellness of language minorities. In R.Y. Bourhis (Ed.), *The vitality of the English-speaking communities of Quebec: From community decline to revival.* Montréal, Canada: CEETUM, Université de Montréal.

Brenzinger, M., Heine, B., & Sommer, G. (1991). Language death in Africa. *Diogenes, 39*(153), 19–44.

Broberg, R. (Producer). (2005). *Inuttut oqaatsit (Inuit languages)* [Documentary]. Available from randimut@yahoo.com

Calvet, L.-J. (1998). *Language wars and linguistic politics.* New York, NY: Oxford University Press.

Canagarajah, A. S. (2005). Introduction. In A. S. Canagarajah (Ed.), *Reclaiming the local in language policy and practice* (pp. xiii–xxx). Mahwah, NJ: Erlbaum.

Coley, M.-E., & Tulloch, S. (2008). Emerging leaders. *Horizons, 10*(1), 767–768.

Cooper, R. L. (1989). *Language planning and social change.* Cambridge, England: Cambridge University Press.

Crago, M. B., Annahatak, B., & Ningiuruvik, L. (1993). Changing patterns of language socialization in Inuit homes. *Anthropology and Education Quarterly, 24*(3), 205–223.

Crago, M. B., Chen, C., Genesee, F., & Allen, S. E. M. (1998). Power and deference: Bilingual decision making in Inuit homes. *Journal for a Just and Caring Education, 4*(1), 78–95.

Dorais, L.-J. (1990). *Inuit uqausiqatigiit. Inuit languages and dialects.* Iqaluit, Canada: Nunavut Arctic College.

Dorais, L.-J. (2010). *The language of the Inuit.* Montreal, Canada: McGill Queens University Press.

Dorais, L.-J., & Sammons, S. (2002). *Language in Nunavut: Discourse and identity in the Baffin region.* Iqaluit, Canada :Nunavut Arctic College.

Fishman, J. A. (1991). *Reversing language shift: Theoretical and empirical foundations of assistance to threatened languages.* Clevedon, England: Multilingual Matters.

Gumperz, J. J. (1968). Types of linguistic communities. In J. A. Fishman (Ed.), *Readings in the sociology of language* (pp. 460–472). The Hague, The Netherelands: Mouton.

Harcharek, J. (1992). Preservation/propagation of indigenous languages — An Iñupiaq example. In M-J Dufour & F. Theiren (Eds.), *Looking to the future: Papers from the 7th Inuit Studies Conference, Fairbanks, Alaska* (pp. 291–293). Ste-Foy, Canada: Association Inuksiutiit Katimajiit.

Hinton, L., & Hale, K. (Eds.). (2001). *The green book of language revitalization.* San Diego, CA: Academic Press.

Hornberger, N. H. (2006a). Frameworks and models in language policy and planning. In T. Ricento (Ed.), *An introduction to language policy: Theory and method* (pp. 24–41). Malden, MA: Blackwell.

Hornberger, N. H. (2006b). Voice and biliteracy in Indigenous language revitalization: Contentious educational practices in Quechua, Guarani, and Māori contexts. *Journal of Language, Identity and Education, 5*(4), 277–292.

Inuit Circumpolar Council (ICC). (2006). *Utqiagvik declaration.* Retrieved October 1, 2009, from http://www.inuit.org/UserFiles/File/2006/2006-07-09_Utqiagvik_declaration_eng.pdf/

Inuit Circumpolar Council (ICC). (2008). *Proceedings of the Arctic Indigenous Languages Symposium.* Retrieved October 1, 2009, from http://www.arcticlanguages.com/Arctic_Indigenous_Languages_Symposium_Proceedings.pdf/

Langgaard, K. (2001). Discourse practices in Nuuk, Greenland: Language usage and language attitudes of the students at the Gymnasium. *Canadian Journal of Native Studies, 21*(2), 231–272.

Lee, T. S. (2007). "If they want Navajo to be learned, then they should require it in all schools": Navajo teenagers' experiences, choices, and demands regarding Navajo language. *Wicazo Sa Review,* Spring, 7–33.

Lee, T. S. (2009). Language, identity, and power: Navajo and Pueblo young adults' perspectives and experiences with competing language ideologies. *Journal of Language, Identity, and Education, 8*(5), 307–320.

Lee, T. S., & McLaughlin, D. (2001). Reversing Navajo language shift, revisited. In J. A. Fishman (Ed.), *Can threatened languages be saved? Reversing language shift, revisited: A 21st century perspective* (pp. 23–43). Clevedon, England: Multilingual Matters.

Louis, W., & Taylor, D. M. (2001). When the survival of a language is at stake. *Journal of Language and Social Psychology, 20*(1/2), 111–151.

McCarty, T. L. (2006). Voice and choice in Indigenous language revitalization. *Journal of Language, Identity and Education, 5*(4), 309–315.

McCarty, T. L., Romero, M. E., & Zepeda, O. (2006). Reclaiming the gift: Indigenous youth counter-narratives on Native language loss and revitalization. *American Indian Quarterly, 30*(1/2), 28–48.

McCarty, T. L., Romero-Little, M. E., Warhol, L., & Zepeda, O (2009). Indigenous youth as language policy makers. *Journal of Language, Identity, and Education, 8*(5), 291–306.

McCarty, T. L., & Wyman, L. T. (2009). Indigenous youth and bilingualism—Theory, research, praxis. *Journal of Language, Identity, and Education, 8*(5), 279–290.

Morgounova, D. (2007). Language, identities and ideologies of the past and present Chukotka. *Etudes Inuit Studies, 31*(1-2), 183–200.

Nunavut Department of Culture, Language, Elders and Youth. (2011). *Uqausivut [our languages]. The proposed comprehensive plan pursuant to the Language Acts. 2011–2014.* Iqaluit, Canada: Government of Nunavut.

Patrick, D. (2003). *Language, politics, and social interaction in an Inuit community.* Berlin, Germany: Mouton de Gruyter.

Poppel, B., Kruse, J., Duhaime, G., & Abryutina, L. (2007). *SLiCA results.* Anchorage: Institute of Social and Economic Research, University of Alaska Anchorage.

Rogers, S. (2012, January 9). New Inuit language app makes learning fun for little ones. *Nunatsiaq Online.* Retrieved November 29, 2012, from http://www.nunatsiaqonline.ca/stories/article/65674new_inuit-language_app_makes_learning_fun_for_little_ones/

Schuerch, G. (Ed.). (2007). *Emerging Inuit leaders: Igniting a language movement. Final report of the 2nd Inuit Circumpolar Youth Council Symposium on the Inuit Language.* Retrieved October 25, 2009, from http://www.arcticlanguages.com/papers/2nd_ICYC_Inuit_Language_Symposium.pdf

Schuerch, G. (2008, December). Youth delegation meets at Arctic Indigenous Languages Symposium. *Arctic Future, 11,* 4, 6.

Shohamy, E. (2006). *Language policy: Hidden agendas and new approaches.* London, England: Routledge.

Spolsky, B. (2004). *Language policy.* Cambridge, England: Cambridge University Press.

Tagalik, S. (1998). *The Arviat language research project: Language beliefs as an influencing factor in the quality of oral language in Arviat* (Unpublished master's thesis). Department of Educational Studies, McGill University, Montréal, Canada.

Tollefson, J. (2006). Critical theory in language policy. In T. Ricento (Ed.), *An introduction to language policy: Theory and method* (pp. 42–59). Malden, MA: Blackwell.

Tulloch, S. (2004). *Inuktitut and Inuit youth: Language attitudes as a basis for language planning* (Unpublished doctoral dissertation). Department of Languages, Linguistics and Translation, Université Laval, Quebec City, Canada.

Tulloch, S., & ICYC. (2005). *First Inuit Circumpolar Youth Symposium on the Inuit Language. Symposium summary report.* Prepared for the Inuit Circumpolar Youth Council. Retrieved October 1, 2009, from http://www.arcticlanguages.com/papers/1st_ICYC_Inuit_Language_Symposium.pdf/

Wyman, L. (2012). *Youth culture, language endangerment and linguistic survivance.* Bristol, England: Multilingual Matters.

9

EFFORTS OF THE REE-VOLUTION

Revitalizing Arikara Language in an Endangered Language Context

Kuunux Teerit Kroupa

At the present time, the Arikara in west-central North Dakota have only a handful of passive Indigenous language speakers. A group of young adults are taking on the work of language revitalization in this critically endangered language community. Members of this group have rearranged their lives, individually and collectively, in a revolutionary way, creating a community of hope and establishing themselves as social and cultural Ree-volutionaries (a term derived from the 18th- and 19th-century term "Arikarees") who maintain and develop their vibrant Arikara culture. In this chapter, I demonstrate the critical roles young adults must play in language revitalization movements. I share a powerful narrative of young adults doing youth-focused thinking and strategizing about our approach to our work based on our ideas about engaging contemporary Indigenous youth in language reclamation. Documenting these efforts and desires in light of language revitalization is the focus of this chapter.

Community Context

Ella Waters, an elder Arikara ritual leader, represented the last generation of fluent Arikara speakers and individuals with direct knowledge of 19th-century Arikara life and thought gained from older relatives and ritual leaders. In the 1970s Mrs. Waters remarked, "We had sacred ways—all the rituals that the Arikara tribe used to perform.... Now, dust has covered all the old traditions. But now only a little is known—when someone [happens to] know something" (cited in Parks, 1991, pp. 644–645). In that statement she acknowledged that devastating forces had destroyed much of Arikara culture—a well-known phenomenon among numerous American Indian societies.

The majority of the generation that followed Mrs. Waters were sent to boarding schools, where they were separated from family and forbidden to practice Arikara cultural traditions, including speaking their heritage language. Convinced that their children needed to speak English to exist in the changing times, many parents would neither teach nor speak Arikara to their children. The next generation witnessed further loss of language and culture as Arikaras continued to attend boarding or day schools. The community faced severe social disorganization as they adapted to the newly imposed social order, causing continued cultural losses. In just a few generations, a significant number of Arikaras were forced to adapt to Western society and, as a result, had no interest in their language or their spiritual practices (Kroupa, 2011). Today, many of the young Arikara, and even some of the older people, find it hard to prioritize language in our personal lives; several wish they could speak Arikara, while others are apathetic.

However, today's generation has developed a core group of leaders who prioritize the revitalization of Arikara language and culture. Despite enduring many of the same social problems as preceding generations, these individuals have developed a strong Arikara identity that is deep-seated in traditional culture, sparked through family influence, spiritual communication (i.e., dreams), academic gain, and connections to each other. As this group matures into a collective self, a striking narrative of adaptation, learning, sacrifice, and regrouping emerges.

Today, there are new, dedicated efforts to uncover and utilize these traditions. To this end, this chapter provides a description of language revitalization efforts among the Arikara. The analysis in this chapter is rooted in the concept of "the new American revolution" (Lomawaima & McCarty, 2006; Svensson, 1981). Moving language to the center stage, Svensson (1981) describes the phenomenon as a central catalyst for Indians' "never-ending hope of and struggle for cultural autonomy" (p. 34). For several centuries, extinction and assimilation remained the only two options for Indians considered by European and U.S. authorities. Now, the Indian struggle is renewed, but, Svensson argues, this time "for an alternative, the possibility of surviving, of living, on Indian terms." Describing this new cultural option he proclaims that, "Language is the symbolic banner of this new American revolution!" (1981, p. 34). In more recent scholarship, Lomawaima and McCarty (2006) expand this theme and offer an updated working definition of the "new American revolution" by applying its importance to modern cases. Illustrating these revolutions, they focus on efforts to "protect and promote" languages in the Hawaiian, Fort Defiance Navajo, and Keres Pueblo communities. The "new American revolution," they state, is "the struggle by Indigenous communities to reclaim and retain their languages as fundamental expressions of choice and self-determination" (p. xxiv). Members of the Arikara are similarly participating in their own revolution: the Ree-volution!

Defining the Ree-volution

In the 18th and 19th centuries, the Arikaras, located along the Missouri River in what is now South Dakota, were frequently called Arikarees by French traders. Today, the name "Rees," a shortened form of Arikarees, is commonly used by Arikaras to refer to our people. The new term "Ree-volution" can be defined as a contemporary cultural revitalization movement among the Arikara; a language revival and spiritual (ceremonial) resurgence; a reorganization of the Arikara people; and a new development of an evolved belief of Arikara thought and tradition. Offered herein is a tribal case study, focusing on a group of young adults taking on the work of language revitalization in a critically endangered language community. As members of this group, I and others have rearranged our lives, individually and collectively, in a revolutionary way, creating a community of hope; we see ourselves as social and cultural Ree-volutionaries who maintain and develop our vibrant Arikara culture. Documenting our efforts and desires in light of language revitalization is the focus of this chapter.

First, a brief historical background of the Arikara people and a portrait of the White Shield community will serve to orient readers. From there, the narrative will shift to the present-day work that this small cohort of language activists has done to reclaim sources of language materials, including organizing intensive language classes as well as other activities to revive the Arikara language. By providing the following case study, this chapter hopes to document what we project to be a significant episode in Arikara history—a story that needs to be told. A second, yet equally significant goal of this chapter is to contribute to contemporary scholarly discussions concerning Indigenous language revival by highlighting the role that community context and young adult leaders play in revitalization efforts.

The Historical Setting

Arikara is a member of the Caddoan language family. Today, the form of the language that is being revitalized is a single dialect formed through historical events. In earlier times, when a numerous people comprised distinct bands and villages, the Arikara language existed in many dialectal forms (Parks, 1979).

With similar tribal roots, Arikara is closely related to the Pawnee language, although today they are not mutually intelligible. Other languages belonging to the Caddoan family include Caddo, Wichita, and Kitsai. Migrating from their Caddoan origins in the south to what is now North Dakota, the Arikara became the northernmost Caddoan speaking nation (Parks, 1996).

A once powerful nation comprised of approximately 12 groups speaking different dialects and having distinct cultural features, the Arikara maintained elaborate sets of skills and cultural practices in areas such as horticulture, commerce, and ceremonialism (Kroupa, 2011). They influenced the introduction and spread of horticultural practices among Plains tribes during a long northwestern migration up the Missouri River to what is now North Dakota. Until the late 18th century, the Arikara, along with their close relatives, the Pawnee, were among the Plains' largest and most powerful groups. The Arikara were considered "widespread and dominant" (Holder, 1970, p. 30) along the middle Missouri River region of the Plains and "dominated the Missouri Valley in South Dakota" (Wedel, 1961, p. 162). Beginning in the 1770s, smallpox epidemics swept through the Plains causing massive destruction among the settled tribes. This dreadful plague destroyed entire villages and weakened the earth lodge culture, disrupting the Arikaras' position in the power structure that existed among Plains Indians.

Cultural assault and hardship continued into the 20th century. In the 1950s the Fort Berthold Indian Reservation was divided by the construction of the Garrison Dam, which created Lake Sakakawea, flooded the bottomlands, and changed the geography of the reservation, resulting in tremendous cultural change. This trauma was exacerbated as traditional practices based on the Missouri River and horticulture were destroyed. That assault on the autonomy and cultures of the Arikara, Mandan, and Hidatsa forced the entire population to relocate to the upland prairie and establish new communities there. Fort Berthold was divided into five distinct segments: Mandaree, New Town, Parshall, Twin Buttes, and White Shield. The majority of the Arikara found their new homeland in and around White Shield. Loss of culture and self-sufficiency bred emotional and spiritual turmoil among the people. In addition to the other historical events that resulted in cultural loss, construction of the Garrison Dam led to identity crisis, depreciated self-esteem, and caused depression among numerous Arikara individuals affecting the community at large. Disturbingly, this dark historical chapter has created an intergenerational hopelessness among many individuals and families, resulting in community disorganization, a loss of ceremonial rituals and teachings, and a decline in knowledge of sacred languages.

Contemporary Portrait

Today, about 500 people reside in the White Shield community, which consists of a school, government housing for teachers and community members, and a community center. The White Shield School is a K-12 grade school. The student population is about 125 and has remained steady over the past few years. A lack of economic opportunities and access to resources has contributed to the lack of growth. Therefore, adults often relocate to New Town or off the reservation for employment or career improvement opportunities. Yet, White Shield remains the only distinctive Arikara community, hosting continuing social and cultural activities such as the annual Arikara powwow and the recently formed Mother Corn festival. Furthermore, the White Shield School is the only reservation school to offer Arikara language classes.

In the White Shield School,[1] as in many American Indian schools, there have been bilingual education programs for many years. Despite the program's duration, student heritage language learning has been and remains minimal. Numerous problems—lack of fluent speakers in the community, little or no administrative support, and insufficient time allotted to language learning— have restricted these programs' attempts to achieve significant language learning.

The first and most fundamental problem in the Arikara community is a lack of Native language speakers. If Arikara is going to be taught effectively in the school system—consisting of the White Shield Elementary and High School, and the Fort Berthold Community College (FBCC)—there must be teachers who know and speak Arikara. Furthermore, the teachers must be able to develop an array of language learning activities specific to the Arikara speech community that nurture learners and instills in them real language-speaking skills.

The lack of real opportunities for the youth to learn Arikara represents a second hindrance to language revitalization. Due to limited adult involvement, there has been a shortage of language learning opportunities for youth. Given these issues, the questions emerge: How do we bring youth into a language movement? Beyond recruiting, how do we retain and keep them interested and invested in language learning? To revitalize Arikara, it will be necessary to attract or develop youth who become *addicted* to learning Arikara. The language needs to become an important part of a new positive identity for the youth. As revitalization efforts continue among the Arikara, so does the quest to encourage our youth to become addicted to learning our language.

Another limitation to revitalization efforts is the lack of steady and supportive administrative leaders for language programming in the White Shield School. Because school leadership can play such an important role in promoting culture and language, it is important to understand why this is not the scenario that has developed in White Shield. Leadership at the White Shield School is characterized by an overall lack of consistency; there have been three superintendents in the last 4 years and the high school principal turnover rate is similar. Given such instability, it is reasonable to assume that an appropriate school culture, one which values, supports, and promotes Arikara culture and language, has not been adequately developed or implemented. Throughout the years, White Shield School administrators have continually dismissed Arikara as an important part of the curriculum; they have limited the time allotted for Arikara making effective instruction nearly impossible.

Delilah Yellow Bird, who has been the only Arikara language teacher for 18 years, opposes this lack of attention to language. She has attempted to establish language training for all teachers in the White Shield School. Her proposals have been overlooked time after time. Even more disturbing, while she has offered language resources to the school staff, no administrators have taken advantage of this potentially beneficial offer. Yellow Bird has noticed that "the teachers are not encouraged by the administration to infuse the language and culture into the classroom curriculum" (personal communication, September

28, 2012). This lack of language emphasis has characterized the situation in the White Shield School for several years. Addressing this issue, Yellow Bird provides the following insight:

> If administration would include language and culture training in their professional development I do believe that there would be a lot less behavioral problems. Last year students were disciplined for saying commonly used words in the language. Teachers wrote them up for being disrespectful and they were asked to leave the classroom and go to the principal's office. If administration would have had language and culture training I would have provided the teaching staff a list of common phrases that the students understand and that they could say to students as well.
>
> *(personal communication, September 28, 2012)*

Thus, instead of promoting and participating in language learning, the administrative staff has opted to punish language users. Yellow Bird's testimony above addresses the misunderstanding that can occur between students and staff when language is not valued in all school sectors.

During the 2011–2012 school year, the Arikara class schedule operated on a rotating basis; some grade levels had Arikara language class on even dates while the remaining grades met on odd days. Thus, students were engaged in language learning for two or three 55-minute sessions per week; equaling approximately 10 hours a month for each grade (D. Yellow Bird, personal communication, September 28, 2012). The following school year, the administration cut the already limited program offering language classes only twice a week for 30 minutes per session. Because of this shift students were only provided a total of 1-hour language instruction per week or roughly 4 hours a month (D. Yellow Bird, personal communication, September 28, 2012).

The newly implemented class schedule developed by the school's administration as well as their disinterest in language training and resources clearly demonstrates the little value they place on language learning when compared to the so-called core subjects. For the last several years, accountability in the White Shield School has been heavily centered on state and national testing; a phenomenon that has been undermining school-based Indigenous language programs across the country (McCarty, Nicholas, & Wyman, 2012). Unfortunately, these standardized tests do not measure knowledge in Arikara language or history and, because of this omission, they are often regarded as lesser important knowledge areas. The negative position of the school administration towards Arikara language and culture is erroneous given the connection between positive cultural identity and schooling achievement (Duncan-Andrade, 2007; Klug & Whitfield, 2003; Ladson-Billings, 1995). Teaching language and involving youth in the preservation of language can serve as an important component of culturally relevant pedagogy (Yazzie-Mintz, 2007).

It is daunting that the White Shield School has not been a cornerstone for promoting Arikara culture and language as it is in a unique position to serve as such. Schools can and must be part of the overall revitalization picture where that is desired by the community—schools can be "strategic tools" in those cases (McCarty, 2008). Hence there is an immediate need for consistent and supportive administration in the White Shield School in order to make significant progress in language revival. In many ways, involving the White Shield School in revitalization is necessary to the success of the Ree-volution.

Despite numerous problems, it is important for us to move forward. As difficult as it might be, our people need to overcome historical trauma and contemporary struggles, remain resilient, and focus on our future. With our language nearing extinction, the Arikara people have reached a critical period in the maintenance of our unique identity. Today's youth are unable to speak our own language, and that inability prohibits us from rightfully attaining the distinctive cultural traditions of our ancestors. Thus, we are at an urgent period in the history of our people: Will we resuscitate and maintain our language and traditions, or will we let them disappear?

Revitalization Efforts of Arikara Activists

Today, there are both Arikara and non-Arikara participants who bring a diversity of interests, skills, awareness, and passion to the effort to revitalize our language. Linguist Douglas R. Parks,[2] involved with the language program since its beginning, has witnessed an unprecedented interest and desire among various individuals and activists during this reawakening movement:

> In the late 1990s and continuing to the present I have witnessed a fundamental change in attitude in the Arikara community. A group of younger people, some still in school and some now graduated, have developed a strong desire to learn their native language and contribute to its revival. At the same time several non-Arikara students at Indiana University have also developed a serious interest in the language and have been studying it over a period of several years. All of these students have accomplished what no other younger people have ever done: they pronounce Arikara excellently—some perfectly—and, in addition to studying the language formally, they have begun to develop elementary speaking skills. Moreover, these individuals interact with each other, reinforcing not only their language learning but also sustaining their commitment and sense of purpose toward reviving Arikara.
>
> Linguists who document languages have generally had to get satisfaction out of the work as work for its own sake and for the value of the work for scientific and humanistic studies. Rarely do they have the opportunity to teach the languages in classroom situations and utilize the materials that they have compiled. Most have seen their descriptive studies languishing on a shelf in an archive or a library. Today, however, that

scenario is changing in the context of the Arikara community and here in Bloomington. Arikara parents and non-speaking elders are excited by what they see: a younger generation shaking off the apathy of the past and dedicated to reviving their native language and culture with a fervor not previously seen over the past century. This movement is gratifying to their parents and grandparents and to their linguist. It is an honor to be able to contribute to what they seek to accomplish.

(personal communication, October 1, 2012)

In the Arikara community, revitalization efforts have been less formal, meaning they have mostly occurred on individual and family levels, often going unnoticed by the larger community. Nevertheless, as grassroots efforts, they provide the building blocks for a stronger movement in the years to come. Therefore, grassroots beginnings and individual actions are crucial to the revitalization of Native languages. To show this, I will now describe such efforts among a small group of young adult language activists, including myself.

Activist Positioning

Among the Arikara, there have been four language activists who have played a major role in language recovery efforts. These active young men have dedicated themselves to learning the Arikara language and to becoming teachers of the language. These people are *Neetahkas Takaa'aahu* (Dancing Eagle), *Kunaa'u Xaawaaruxti* (Medicine Horse), *Kuunuxtawawašuxtaarit* (The Bear Who Stands Holding the Lightning), and me. In addition to us, there are many others who have expressed a strong desire to study Arikara and to develop at least an elementary competency in the language. However, we four young men have risen to positions of leadership through our efforts to revitalize our language.

Recently, there have been major advances in the revitalization of the Arikara language. In 2006, I became the first Arikara student to enroll at Indiana University in Bloomington to study under Parks. There may have been previous individuals who wished to do that, but this was the first time an Arikara took the initiative to work with Parks and demonstrate dedication to this revival movement in an academic setting.

In early 2007, Kuunuxtawawašuxtaarit visited Bloomington for several weeks in order to study Arikara. During this visit, Kuunuxtawawašuxtaarit and I met with Parks for language sessions throughout the week. After studying during the day, we would often spend the night studying the Arikara language, talking about culture and history, and discussing our aspirations for the future of the Arikara. On one occasion, we talked about being resourceful and about how language adaptation will be and has been an important strategic activity for the revitalization of the language. This activity has included creating new words for modern concepts, as well as inventing slang and word abbreviations by shortening them, as I describe in a later section below.

In 2007, Kunaa'u Xaawaaruxti came to work with Parks. During his 2-week stay, he worked intensively on language and also collected historical documents at the American Indian Studies Research Institute (AISRI). Kunaa'u Xaawaaruxti and I also spent time investigating and listening to an extensive music collection of old Arikara songs that are in the archives at AISRI. Below, Kunaa'u Xaawaaruxti discusses the significance of language revival for the Ree-volution movement.

> The importance of reviving our language is part of our commitment to represent our tribe. I want to see our language return so that our traditions become more powerful, especially in the eyes of, *Ati'ax Nacita'kux* [Our Father Above] and *Atna Neesu'* [Mother Corn]. Our language has been pretty dormant, spoken at only a few gatherings, or once in awhile by people who felt the need ... time has come to change this and bring forward what we do have. The world is changing, and the only things that are going to keep us strong are our traditions, language, culture, ceremonies, leadership, etc. It was told to us that if you keep Corn, the office of the chief, and what was revealed in the Medicine lodge, we will survive and remain strong. It is time to remember these words and live by them. Only when we are able to remember this and live by it ourselves, will our children carry it on. This is my goal, my commitment, so when the Arikara on the other side come to get me they will know my heart and know I did all I could. These things I talk about—I don't lie, I will see it happen in my time and leave room for my children to continue this work. *Nawah.*
>
> *(personal communication, September 27, 2012)*

For each of us language activists, there has been, and continues to be, a serious, developing interest in learning our language. Due to our unwavering commitment, plans were developed for organizing structured language classes.

In March 2008, I assisted in organizing the first-ever intensive Arikara language course at AISRI. This effort was intended to be the first in a series of such intensive Arikara language courses. By the end of this project, including studying the language and other efforts during one's personal time, the goal is to help Arikara tribal members become actual speakers of the language and understand its grammatical structure. In addition, they will have had instruction in second-language teaching methods. In short, they will be qualified to teach Arikara in the White Shield elementary and high schools, at Fort Berthold Community College, and for other immersion programs or classes that develop in the years to come. Equally important, they will serve as examples in the community at large: they will become motivators for other students, nonstudents, and parents to aspire to language competency.

The first intensive Arikara language course served as an important cornerstone to the revival of the language. The active Arikara participants were

Kunaa'u Xaawaaruxti, Neetahkas Takaa'aahu, and me. Parks, with the assistance of linguistic graduate students Hye-Ryoung (Heidi) Kwon, Joshua Richards, and Indrek Park, taught the course. It provided a language environment with concentrated learning by means of work with second-language teaching materials, as well as through peer interaction and practice. During this intensive language course, the participants attended a one-week class that met, at minimum, for eight hours per day. Two hours of each day were devoted to the study of grammar and pronunciation and the rest was mostly spent speaking Arikara in a guided environment. Each participant had a dictionary and grammatical sketch to serve as resources when using new vocabulary and forming new sentence structures. Everyone also had a set of materials that included practical vocabulary, conversational expressions, and other pertinent information.

In January 2009, the second Arikara language immersion class was held. The participants were Kunaa'u Xaawaaruxti, Kuunuxtawawašuxtaarit, Neetahkas Takaa'aahu, and me. During this 10-day summit, we strengthened our basic understanding and knowledge of the Arikara language by learning the basics of its structure. We also built conversational skills, which included learning a basic overview of the linguistic structure of Arikara, the verbal system, and the aspectual system (imperfective/perfective opposition) and established a stronger foundation for developing conversational skills.

Music was also a focus in this session. Reviewing and transcribing ceremonial songs acted as powerful learning tools; especially given that culturally significant words and phrases are found in these songs. As I describe in the next section, songs such as the Mother Corn songs are culturally invaluable because they represent the religious expression and ideologies of the Arikara.

Reinvigorating Language through Song and Ceremony

Song and ceremony, an integral part of contemporary Arikara cultural practices, have become platforms for language teaching and learning. Modern cultural performances express that there are those who still believe in the Arikara way and hope that the phrases in the songs will be a part of reinvigorating the language. Below is a Mother Corn ceremonial song, which is one of nearly 100 songs composed by Kuunuxtawawašuxtaarit with guidance from several spiritual powers, and is used in ceremonies today. The song below, and several others not presented here, increase awareness not only of Arikara culture but also about the language's survival.

Mother Corn Song

A	*atná neéšu*	šitaatAsištA
	Mother Corn	we love you
B	*weneekuraakIswatAt*	*naasahniš*
	We remember	the Arikara way

This song is special to the spirits and to the Mother of the Arikara because it represents the first attempt in recent times to make contact with Her. Composed in the past decade, it is a relatively new song. Yet, its wide use in language classes in the White Shield School and at the Mother Corn Festival has established it as a "new" traditional song. The significance of this song is to show our veneration of Mother Corn. However, it also demonstrates that the singer still remembers who the Arikara once were, who they are now, and *who they will always be*. This is the first time in a generation or two that the Arikara have sung in public about their love for the Mother of the Arikara people.

Song, as a domain for language learning, provides understanding about the Arikara's past and connects the Arikara people to it. When these songs are used, a cross-generational learning takes place, as old and new cultural history and teachings are preserved for the current generation and for those to come. For many youth, hearing a song in their heritage language can be the first step toward learning the language. And by creating new songs, the Arikara are strengthening their linguistic creativity and retaining their unique identity, despite devastating changes. Among the Arikara, this is most likely to occur in a ceremonial domain, such as the Medicine Lodge.

In addition to song, ceremonial activities provide a strong arena for language use among the Arikara. In May 2009, the Arikara returned to the land of their ancestors along the Missouri River in South Dakota. For the first time in more than a half-century, we built a Medicine Lodge for a ceremony. This event will be remembered as a significant moment in the history of the Arikara because it symbolizes a new beginning and hope for our people.

Present during the Medicine Lodge were the leader of the ceremony, his main assistants, and apprentices who acted as assistants and errand men. Several ritual procedures connected with the Medicine Lodge were conducted throughout the ceremony. For example, the leader opened by reciting the Arikara creation story and a prayer in the Arikara language. As the ceremony continued, the lodge echoed with constant singing and prayer. Newly created ceremonial songs, such as the one above, were sung at appropriate times throughout the day and night. In this way, the lodge represented a language arena, providing an opportunity for language access, with song and ceremony acting as invaluable cultural resources for reversing language shift.

The Arikara Medicine Lodge, given all that it represents, has proven itself to be a potent symbol in the minds of many people. The rituals that take place there declare that the universe is very much alive and that the Arikara are internally and invisibly connected to it. Today, the Arikara Medicine Lodge continues to represent a place where one can belong and be loved. It is also a place to discover one's authentic connection to self and community and to the living flow of thought, power, and life. It is representative of an Arikara worldview and of how the universe functions. At the same time, it provides a language arena where Arikara is spoken. It is an institution of learning, with an education that is not offered anywhere else.

Growing the Movement through the Use of New Technology

Like culture, our languages undergo unavoidable change. Mrs. Waters, one of the Arikara voices we hear in digital form today, undoubtedly spoke in a way that varied slightly from the way her elders spoke, just as the youth today, as they develop speaking abilities in our language, will have major observable differences due to mainstream societal influences. I hope for the revitalization of everyday spoken conversation, in all domains. To do this, our language will need to adapt and change while retaining its distinctive cultural context, as it has always done. Today's technology is an essential component of this revitalization.

In addition to spoken revival efforts, we must adapt the language for use in our daily and community contexts by utilizing new developing technologies. People are now using their Native languages on the Internet in general, and more particularly in social media sites such as Facebook, Twitter, and You-Tube. They are also using other technological devices, such as smartphones and tablets, to help the process of revitalization and preservation. Technology has been discussed by many scholars and been used in various ways in Indigenous language revival efforts (Galla, 2009; Penfield, Cash Cash, Galla, Williams, & Shadow Walker, 2006).

One consistent use of technology for Arikara language activists has been language texting. In today's society texting has become one of the primary means of communication for the large majority of youth (Paris, 2010). There-fore, it will be beneficial for language activists and educators to use texting as a tool to reinforce language use. The example below, a recent text between Neetahkas Takaa'aahu and me, is illustrative of our daily text interactions:

> Kuunux Teerit: *idodz tiče weeNAxuutaawaanú*? (bro, what you up to)
> Neetahkas Takaa'aahu: *kusu wiitA stuff* (big boy stuff)
> Kuunux Teerit: *haha … tAxi' piikaawa*! (haha … you're a stud)

This shortened dialogue provides a glimpse of our casual usage of language. It illustrates how text messaging can be symbolic and a group identity-marking feature of language. Our texts, often reflective of our personalities, are filled with jokes and humor. Using humor allows us to enjoy learning and using lan-guage in this additional way.

Technology's versatility has contributed to Arikara language learning through other methods as well. For example, by using email, users can con-nect with each other through a variety of devices without distance being a barrier. Email has allowed for the development and subsequent distribution of an Arikara "word of the day" email list. These emails, which I send out every other day, contain one Arikara word or phrase, the English equivalent of that word, and an audio clip for the listener. Each day, the new word builds upon the previous ones, ultimately providing sentences for the reader. The fact that this effort will not lead directly to fluency makes it no less important and no less a contribution to Arikara identity and to the possibility of future fluency. It is still meaningful because it builds the language learning community while assisting in the long-distance learning of Arikara sounds, pronunciation, and basic words and phrases used in everyday conversation.

Language Adaptability and Modernizing Arikara

Although controversial and frowned upon in some Native communities, it is important to continually modernize Indigenous vocabularies. If our youth are not interested in or cannot relate to the language, there will be no future for it. Thus, adaptation and creativity are essential activities that will help us to maintain and to revitalize our language. As youth culture changes, we must adapt and change with it, just as Indigenous cultures have always done. Being language activists, educators, and researchers, it is incumbent upon us to understand the interests of Native youth, and understand what kinds of messages resonate profoundly with this population. Then, we must incorporate those messages into our thinking about language teaching and learning.

It is especially important to incorporate contemporary expressions and concepts in order to engage Arikara youth, without having to revert to English. For example, the term "money" is used as modern slang in basketball; it refers to making a good shot. The Arikara word for money is *wapIsišu*. Thus, I shorten *wapIsišu* to *waap* when playing basketball—*waap* is much easier and quicker to pronounce while shooting in action. It is catchy, youth can connect to it, and, above all, the language is being spoken, albeit in a contracted form, and thus Arikara identity is reinforced.

Code-Switching: Ree-glish

The linguistic phenomenon of code switching has been discussed and described in several ways (García, 2009; McCarty, Romero-Little, Warhol, & Zepeda, 2009). Plainly stated, it is when two or more languages are used in conversation. Code switching, as discussed in scholarly literature, is generally used when referring to bi-/multilingual communities. In a study conducted by McCarty et al. (2009), the Indigenous youth studied were being raised in bi-/multilingual households and environments. As a result, many youth had developed complex communicative repertoires that included "different linguistic expertise (receptive, spoken, written) in diverse varieties of one or more Indigenous languages, English, and, in some cases, Spanish" (McCarty et al., 2009, p. 299). Thus, the youth were able to draw "upon multiple semiotic systems for different purposes in specific contexts" (p. 299).

Due to the absence of fluent speakers in the Arikara community, code switching does not occur as it does in a bilingual community. Instead, it occurs as a strategy to compensate for diminished language proficiency. Due to my inability to speak the language fluently, I use Arikara whenever possible or whenever I am able, incorporating the language into varying modern contexts and speaking domains. Thus, code switching has frequently emerged as a significant factor in my everyday language use, and in revival efforts among Arikara language activists.

To avoid confusion or scholarly conflicts with term usage, I have coined the term "Ree-glish," meaning a mixture of Arikara and English, to describe Arikara language code switching. Ree-glish is an extremely important step in the efforts to revive the Arikara language. It is essential because it requires one to begin to use Arikara. Having no fluent speakers, it is important for members of tribes like the Arikara to use all resources that they have at their disposal. Regardless of one's language proficiency, speaking level, and accuracy of pronunciation, one must use the language as often as possible and in any context. Speaking one Arikara word in an English sentence is a start; a place from which to build on language learning.

New Efforts and Opportunities for Language Teaching

As the Ree-volution progresses, we continue to seek and create new efforts and opportunities as intergenerational connections unfold. After living most his life on the Fort Berthold Indian Reservation, Neetahkas Takaa'aahu, together with his wife and three children, relocated to Bloomington, Indiana to begin advanced study of the Arikara language and music. This move demonstrated extreme courage and an unwavering commitment to the revival of the Arikara language. After completing all coursework for the Master of Arts in Anthropological Linguistics, in 2011 Neetahkas Takaa'aahu returned home to the Fort Berthold Reservation in North Dakota. He is now working as the director of the Arikara Cultural Center in White Shield. Once an empty building, he has revamped it into a community center that provides the facilities for the revitalization, preservation, and promotion of Arikara language, culture, and history. Neetahkas Takaa'aahu is also working for the Boys and Girls Club of the Three Affiliated Tribes in New Town, North Dakota as a master language teacher. The Master Apprentice project is extremely important to revitalization given its goal "to ignite the spark within our youth through a Master/Apprentice approach to revitalize the languages of the Three Affiliated Tribes; the Mandan, Hidatsa and Arikara and increase the number of speakers in our youth community" (I. Hopkins, personal communication, August 8, 2011).

In August of 2011, I worked with the Boys and Girls club to direct a language workshop of the Master Apprentice Language Project. The purpose of this 2-day language workshop was to develop language-teaching methods that are more efficient in order to revitalize the Mandan, Hidatsa, and Arikara languages. It also served to strengthen the participant's awareness of the general subject of language revitalization. Specifically, the workshop offered models and strategies for teaching in an immersion setting. It provided an overview of the principles of immersion teaching approaches and language acquisition, building off master-apprentice approaches described elsewhere (Hinton, Vera, & Steele, 2002). In particular, the Arikara, Hidatsa, and Mandan languages were used as the languages of instruction. Two master language teachers per language participated in the program. After the workshop, master Arikara teacher Neetahkas Takaa'aahu commented:

> While language revival is a huge topic across Indian country, limited interest by tribal members and lack of commitment can severely impede the progress that so many tribes seek. Language workshops, such as the one I attended at the Four Bears Casino, bring the importance of language and culture to the forefront of one's consciousness. As a language revival proponent, workshops such as these provide a much needed platform for expression, which can serve to recharge one's language batteries by examining the triumphs, challenges, and solutions that other language advocates have identified and implemented in their community.
>
> *(personal communication, August 26, 2011)*

Additionally, the workshop enabled us to take stock of our understanding of language revitalization and its challenges as we move forward in the fight to revive our language. Continued planning of proposed revitalization efforts is crucial: revitalization efforts being planned for the near future will require that the language movement continue to develop and that the current group of dedicated "masters" and "apprentices" grow into a larger community. This language workshop and the other events discussed above are steps in the right direction.

Other new efforts in 2012 have strengthened the Ree-volution movement and brought a mixture of excitement and anxiety into the Arikara community. They reveal that while there is hope, there is also a long road ahead. These recent efforts include a community-wide language assessment, a week-long language immersion camp, and the building of an earth lodge in the White Shield community.[3] In January of 2012, Neetahkas Takaa'aahu and I conducted a community-wide language assessment, through surveys and interviews, in order to assess the interest in Arikara language learning, the current status of language usage by tribal members, as well as language attitudes towards revitalization. It resulted in a more focused language action plan to further fight language loss. A part of this plan included language camps, which have been used as a means of group learning.

The most recent language camp took place in late July 2012. This week-long language camp, also conducted by Neetahkas Takaa'aahu and me, was geared towards middle and high school students. With the help of Good Earth Woman Perkins, female leader of the Ree-volution movement, we were able to enroll the White Shield youth leaders from the Tero Youth Program in language learning. This is important because we were also forming connections with other existing organizations that promote the well-being of the Arikara community. Youth participants, the majority of whom entered the class with only a handful of spoken words, left able to dialogue about food and drink; at the end of camp, these students were able to express hunger or thirst and ask for specific food and drink items with each other. More importantly, many of the youth seemed rather excited to participate in the camp. For me, this exemplified that a lack of leadership and available opportunities represent the real barriers—for the most part, youth are ready and willing to take on the challenge.

It is important to remember that "living languages are not primarily in institutions, but above them, beyond them, all around them" (Fishman, 2007, p. 175). Thus, schools cannot stand alone in the fight to revitalize our languages (Hornberger, 2008). There is a need for individual, family, and community involvement. However, without the current Arikara language activists and a few others, the community would be coasting downhill towards cultural bankruptcy; we mark the difference between a successful and a failed society. Therefore, our major contributions and successes will occur outside the walls of schools. The real changes to the Arikara community in the years to come, both short and long term, will be determined by what cultural and language activists are doing now.

The Hardest Part Still Lies Ahead

"Do not give up; but do not get your priorities wrong," Fishman declares, "because you do not get many chances in this game" (2007, p. 175). Fishman's admonition encourages language revitalization efforts but he emphasizes that such efforts need to be well organized and carefully planned. The implementation process for revitalization is essential for the Arikara, requiring strategies that are insightful and relevant and appropriate a wide array of teaching and learning tools. Promoting the Arikara language through leadership and providing the community with examples of success is critical to this process. Thus, as activists, we must promote and demonstrate the benefits of language learning as motivation for others to take up the Arikara cause. Language is important, not only because it strengthens tribal identity. Learning one's heritage language contributes fundamentally to one's overall personal development. It helps one succeed in the community and, if desired, in mainstream society.

The four language activists discussed in this chapter provide excellent examples of language and success, demonstrating how young adults are assuming substantial leadership roles in language revitalization movements. Kunaa'u Xaawaaruxti is the chief of interpretation at the Fort Union Trading Post in Williston, North Dakota. Kuunuxtawawašuxtaarit, dreamer of the Medicine Lodge, is an Arikara spiritual leader educated in ceremonies and in mainstream society, holding a master's degree in education. Neetahkas Takaa'aahu, renowned singer and leader of the drum group Yellow Face, is completing his thesis project for his Master of Arts in anthropology. His knowledge of Arikara music is extensive. Lastly, I have a master's degree in anthropology and am a Ph.D. candidate who has studied anthropology, the history of education, and Native American and Indigenous Studies. We have all established ourselves as the young leaders of the Arikara on and off the reservation, serving as role models to Arikara youth and demonstrating success through our stories. This small group, and a few others not mentioned in this chapter, are creating a foundation of promise and hope for a language revival and cultural reawakening among the Arikara.

While the four of us are successful, if the Arikara language revitalization is to continue well into the future, we must motivate others to engage in the movement and take leadership roles. Recruiting participants is not enough, as our efforts must change the way people think about revitalization—they need to *believe* in the Arikara language and culture. For youth to become more involved in the future, they must take our cause and make it their own. We must show them how they can individually contribute to the cause and that our shared belief in the Arikara language will integrate our individual contributions into a future of expanding possibilities.

Finally, revitalization will succeed when individual and group efforts grow to encompass the entire Arikara community. As Kuunuxtawawašuxtaarit states:

> It is easier for most people to allow the few to struggle while criticizing the attempts of the brave. In reality, all those who call themselves Arikara must actively seek the one collective heart and mind needed for a cultural renaissance to take place. All must become agents of change. If they do not and only criticize the others, they are no longer the courageous people that we once were and shall be again.
>
> *(personal communication, September 26, 2012)*

The Arikara possess an essential component for their language revival, a group of committed and dedicated individuals. However, we have to address more than just a nostalgic fondness for the Arikara language. We must instill a passion for language learning through an unyielding dedication that is strong enough to promote language use and to motivate others to learn and develop that language. Therefore, *all* Arikaras must become language activists, in their own right, not only to mitigate language loss but to rebuild the Arikara nation.

In this chapter, I have demonstrated the critical roles that young adults play in language revitalization movements by recounting the efforts of this core group of Ree-volutionaries. As young adults with youth-focused thinking, we create a powerful narrative as we continue to strategize how to engage contemporary Indigenous youth in language reclamation. McCarty and Wyman write that youth "recreate themselves while maintaining claims to indigeneity" (2009, p. 285). This chapter demonstrates how young adults in critically endangered language communities can also recreate themselves while maintaining their tribal identities, appropriating tools and resources to become language reclamation leaders. Through collaboration, young leaders have brought the Arikara language forward through innovative practices and the creation of new physical and virtual spaces for Indigenous languages.

Oral traditions such as song and ceremony fill these spaces. Together, these continuing oral traditions accomplish what Hopi scholar Nicholas (2009) calls "the development of an emotional commitment" to Indigenous ideals (p. 321). This emotional commitment has the power to engage youth. However, as McCarty and Wyman (2009) remind us, youth require a larger "nexus of authorizing agents" to nurture their possibilities; "they cannot be expected to act alone" (p. 287). Consequently, the Ree-volution movement involves young adult leaders who think strategically about how their roles as authorizing agents will engage and affect youth in the following generations. Yet, the central question remains: will there be youth who emerge as the future keepers of the Arikara language?

Acknowledgments

I would like to thank Leisy Wyman for the invitation to participate in such an important, high-level project. Her encouragement of my work was crucial to my effort here. I am grateful of Kuunuxtawawašuxtaarit, Kunaa'u Xaawaaruxti, Neetahkas Takaa'aahu, and Delilah Yellow Bird who have been generous in sharing their thoughts and experiences with me. I understand their struggle and commend their efforts. Let's continue to create an environment that assists in efforts of language reclamation and encourage others to maintain their Arikara heritage. I would also like to thank Teresa McCarty and Sheilah Nicholas for comments on an earlier version of this chapter. Finally, I am especially appreciative of Yesenia L. Cervera, Douglas R. Parks, and Donald Warren who provided extremely helpful close readings and gave valuable advice that made this a stronger chapter. *Nootuhnaanu. Nawah.*

Notes

1   The administrators mentioned in this section are no longer employed at the White Shield School. Their impact on the language program, however, has been felt over the last several years and is discussed herein. The White Shield School welcomed new administration during the 2012–2013 academic year. The interests, direction, and impact of the new administration are yet to be seen.

2   Douglas R. Parks is currently a Professor of Anthropology and Associate Director of the American Indian Studies Research Institute, Indiana University, Bloomington, Indiana.

3   Due to length restraints, these new efforts cannot be analyzed in detail. They are discussed at length in Kroupa (forthcoming).

References

Duncan-Andrade, J. (2007). Gangstas, wankstas, and ridas: Defining, developing, and supporting effective teachers in urban schools. *International Journal of Qualitative Studies in Education*, 20(6), 617–638.

Fishman, J. (2007). Maintaining languages: What works? What doesn't. In G. Cantoni (Ed.), *Stabilizing Indigenous languages* (pp. 186–198). Flagstaff: Northern Arizona University Center for Excellence in Education.

Galla, C. K. (2009). Indigenous language revitalization and technology: From tradition to contemporary domains. In L. Lockard & J. Reyhner (Eds.), *Indigenous language revitalization: Encouragement, guidance, and lessons learned* (pp. 167–182). Flagstaff: Northern Arizona University.

García, O. (2009). *Bilingual education in the 21st century: A global perspective.* Malden, MA: Wiley-Blackwell.

Hinton, L., Vera, M., & Steele, N. (2002). *How to keep your language alive: A commonsense approach to one-on-one language learning.* Berkeley, CA: Heyday Books.

Holder, P. (1970). *The hoe and the horse on the plains: A study of cultural development among North American Indians.* Lincoln: University of Nebraska Press.

Hornberger, N. H. (Ed.). (2008). *Can schools save indigenous languages?: Policy and practice on four continents.* New York, NY: Palgrave Macmillan.

Klug, B. J., & Whitfield, P. T. (2003). *Widening the circle: Culturally relevant pedagogy for American Indian children.* New York, NY: Routledge Falmer.

Kroupa, KT. (2011a, October). *Through Arikara eyes: History of education as spiritual renewal and cultural evolution.* Paper presented at the Annual Meeting of the Organization of Educational Historians, Chicago, IL.

Kroupa, KT. (2011b, October). *History of the Arikara as cultural evolution.* Paper presented at the Annual Meeting of the Plains Anthropological Society, Tucson, AZ.

Kroupa, KT. (forthcoming). *Ree-volution: The recovery of cultural distinctiveness* (Unpublished doctoral dissertation). University of Indiana, Bloomington.

Ladson-Billings, G. (1995). Toward a theory of culturally relevant pedagogy. *American Educational Research Journal, 32*(3), 465–491.

Lomawaima, K. T., & McCarty, T. L. (2006). *"To remain an Indian": Lessons in democracy from a century of Native American education.* New York, NY: Teachers College Press.

McCarty, T. L. (2008). Schools as strategic tools for Indigenous language revitalization: Lessons from Native America. In N. H. Hornberger (Ed.), *Can schools save Indigenous languages? Policy and practice on four continents* (pp. 161–179). New York, NY: Palgrave Macmillan.

McCarty, T. L., Nicholas, S., & Wyman, L.T. (2012). Re-emplacing place in the "global here and now" — Critical ethnographic case studies of Native American language planning and policy. *International Multilingual Research Journal, 6*(1), 50–63.

McCarty, T. L., Romero-Little, M. E., Warhol, L., & Zepeda, O. (2009). Indigenous youth as language policy makers. *Journal of Language, Identity, and Education, 8*(5), 291–306.

McCarty, T. L. & Wyman, L. T. (2009). Indigenous youth and bilingualism — Theory, research, praxis. *Journal of Language, Identity and Education, 8*(5), 279–290.

Nicholas, S. E. (2009). "I live Hopi, I just don't speak it" — The critical intersection of language, culture, and identity in the lives of contemporary Hopi youth. *Journal of Language, Identity, and Education, 8*(5), 321–334.

Paris, D. (2010). Texting identities: Lessons for classrooms from multiethnic youth space. *English Education, 42*(3), 278–292.

Parks, D .R. (1979). Bands and villages of the Arikara and Pawnee. *Nebraska History, 60,* 214–239.

Parks, D. R. (1991). *Traditional narratives of the Arikara Indians.* Lincoln: University of Nebraska Press.

Parks, D. R. (1996). *Myths and traditions of the Arikara Indians.* Lincoln: University of Nebraska Press.

Penfield, S., Cash Cash, P., Galla, C., Williams, T., & Shadow Walker, D. (2006). *Technology-enhanced language revitalization.* Tucson: University of Arizona and Arizona Board of Regents.

Svensson, F. (1981). Language as ideology: The American Indian case. *Bilingual Resources, 4*(2/3), 34–40.

Wedel, W. R. (1961). *Prehistoric man on the Great Plains.* Norman: University of Oklahoma Press.

Yazzie-Mintz, T. (2007). From a place deep inside: Culturally appropriate curriculum as the embodiment of Navajo-ness in classroom pedagogy. *Journal of American Indian Education, 46*(3), 72–93.

10

COMMENTARY

A Hawaiian Revitalization Perspective on Indigenous Youth and Bilingualism

William H. Wilson and Kauanoe Kamanā

The ʻAha Pūnana Leo began 30 years ago with the call, "E ola ka ʻōlelo Hawaiʻi!" "Let the Hawaiian language live!" (Wilson & Kamanā, 2001). We and the other founders of the non-profit were young Hawaiian language teachers in our 20s and 30s determined to save the Hawaiian language from what was then believed to be certain extinction. This volume's descriptions of language shift resulting from contemporary language discrimination link historic and present Hawaiian challenges to a broader international community. The hopes and dreams of the young people who are the subjects of these chapters are the same hopes and dreams we had as young people. Those dreams can come true!

Hawaiʻi's massive language shift began a century ago. There are numerous parallels to that shift within the cases described in this volume. In the late 1800s, everyone spoke Hawaiian, but being monolingual in Hawaiian marked one as unsophisticated. Then Hawaiian medium schools were banned, resulting in young people speaking Hawaiian with adults and Hawaiʻi Creole English with peers. The next generation could understand, but not speak Hawaiian. Finally, the generation born in the 1940s through the 1960s sometimes heard elders speaking Hawaiian but knew very little of it beyond a few words and phrases. Yet, today, as the result of a language revitalization movement that began in the 1970s and 1980s, many young people speak Hawaiian fluently. Increasing numbers are raising their children with Hawaiian as the first language of the home, as we ourselves did (Wilson & Kamanā, 2001, 2011, 2013). Later in this commentary we will describe how youth who learn Hawaiian become socialized into speaking it as their peer language, but we will begin by discussing four major themes found in chapters in this volume.

Diversity in Linguistically Healthy and Unhealthy Indigenous Communities

The chapters in this volume describe linguistic diversity in Indigenous communities. In a linguistically healthy community, the ancestral language is the regular means of community operations as well as the means of communication across intergenerational and peer-group boundaries. Fluency in other languages, including other Indigenous languages, is individual and variable from person to person. Colonial and immigrant languages may be quite widely known as second languages in an Indigenous community as has been the case with Spanish in certain communities described in this volume (e.g., Lee; McCarty et al.) and as were the languages of sugar plantation-associated immigrants in Hawai'i. Even with widespread fluency in other languages, in linguistically healthy Indigenous communities, youth grow to adulthood with full fluency in the local Indigenous language as their dominant informal peer group-language. Higher registers of the Indigenous language also constitute the "official" language used by them in their transition to, and assumption of, community-internal adult roles in Indigenous ceremonial, religious, and political life.

In cases of unhealthy linguistic diversity, community youth have widely variable fluency in the ancestral Indigenous language, and exhibit insecurity regarding their own abilities in it. Such insecurity can often be reinforced by various forms of frustration with and criticism of youth by elders. Many of the same sorts of language criticism described in this volume also occurred in Hawai'i when Hawaiian was being lost (Wilson & Kamanā, 2006). While avoiding use of the ancestral language due to this insecurity, youth may also develop a resistance toward full mastery of the colonizing language used in schooling. The result is a distinctive nonstandard dialect marking a population as what Ogbu (2003) calls a caste-like involuntary minority. Among the characteristics of such a minority are poor academic performance as evidenced by the decline in Hawaiian academic achievement associated with a historical change from Hawaiian-medium to English-medium schooling and the associated replacement of Hawaiian with Hawai'i Creole English as the peer group language of Native Hawaiian youth (Wilson & Kamanā, 2006).

Another characteristic of forcibly assimilated Indigenous minorities is an identification with other suppressed minorities. Members of small, little-known Indigenous minorities have often found that they can best communicate their resistance to the majority population power structure by expressing that resistance in an African American or Afro-Caribbean form already widely understood and acknowledged by the majority population as minority resistance. Such resistance can include the adoption of Afro-American vocabulary, phonology, body language, and other features of African American resistance language that further add to the linguistic diversity of Indigenous communities. O'Connor and Brown describe this phenomenon for Navajo. Kroupa's reference to the popularity of the African American-associated sport of basketball and the African American term "money" is another example of this and the overall phenomenon of youth adopting resistance language as part of their transition to adulthood. Native Hawaiian youth also relate to African American and Afro-Caribbean resistance genres, especially reggae music. Resistance to the majority culture through appropriation of the expressions of other oppressed groups can be the first step in the development of a consciousness that leads a language and culture revitalization movement, yet it can also mark a stalled movement in which youth are frustrated and uncertain as to what they can actually do to change what may seem like a hopeless situation.

Unhealthy linguistic diversity is also characterized by class-based language differences. Peer group use of the colonizing language characterizes the economically successful classes of the Indigenous community. Peer group use of the ancestral language or resistance dialects of the dominant language characterizes the community's least successful, least progressive, and most unfashionable subgroups. Messing (2007, this volume) draws our attention to the pervasiveness of this feature in Tlaxcala in the ideology of *menosprecio* (denigration) relative to the Mexicano language and its speakers. For the United States, Lee (2007) describes the low status of Navajo "Johns," and in this volume Lee describes young adults' fears regarding a potential negative impact of Indigenous-language use on the socioeconomic status of their children. A similar phenomenon exists relative to Hawai'i Creole English and once existed in Hawai'i relative to the Hawaiian language. Today, however, a new high-status identity of the Hawaiian language and culture has strengthened peer group use of the Hawaiian language and increased recognition that Hawai'i Creole English preserves many features of Hawaiian. High school and college courses in Hawaiian that draw attention to common features of Hawai'i Creole English and Hawaiian have served to speed learning of Hawaiian and have also resulted in an improved status for Hawai'i Creole English. There is also increasing recognition that in today's highly interconnected world, high fluency and literacy among youth in Hawaiian are always accompanied by high fluency and literacy in English and that there are unique cognitive advantages that proceed from high biliterate bilingualism.

Cultural Identity and Indigenous Languages

Messing associates the prestige of "pure" Mexicano without Spanish influence with a general Mexican population pride in pre-Western Aztec achievements. In the United States, pre-Western lifestyles are focused on by the general population when assigning Indigenous identity. The internalization of these views by Indigenous peoples affects language revitalization. Today, many Hawaiian youth seek their Hawaiianess in growing taro (a tuber with strong ties to Hawaiian culture). Nicholas describes Hopi youth who are "living their Indigenousness" as placing great importance on hand planting of corn. Wyman notes a parallel Yup'ik youth identification with the spring seal hunt. Both observe, as have we, that young people are especially eager to use the ancestral language in subsistence activities. Such activities must therefore be integrated into Indigenous language teaching and revitalization.

The close association of Indigenous language use with precontact-derived subsistence activities is part of a "two worlds" philosophy long promoted for Indigenous peoples in colonial schools. As Lee points out, under this philosophy, one's life is divided between participation in both a "culture-less" world of modernity and a "culture-based" Indigenous world tied to elders raised in the past. These elders provide the ceremonies, names, and songs that afford a means for non-Indigenous language-speaking youth to be partially enculturated into a pre-Western Indigenous world, while living primarily in the "non-Indigenous modern" world. Youth awareness of the impending end of the lives of elders, such as described by Lee and McCarty et al., can inspire youth-driven language revitalization movements, as it did in Hawai'i.

However, part of the Hawaiian Renaissance in the 1970s, out of which the Hawaiian language revitalization movement sprung, involved a bold statement by Native Hawaiian youth before their elders that they could participate in international youth culture and still be Native Hawaiian. Reminiscent of the O'Connor and Brown study of the assertion of the right of Navajo youth to participate in hip hop, part of the stance of Hawaiian youth in the 1970s involved spreading a rejection of the two worlds philosophy through Native Hawaiian identity-focused songs in English. Another part of this stance involved a new type of music with Hawaiian lyrics and a rock-inspired beat. Singing traditional Hawaiian songs in this fashion created controversy and much discussion in the Native Hawaiian community. Ultimately that discussion led to widespread agreement that it was possible for the Hawaiian language to be used in all aspects of the lives of youth and a blossoming of newly composed music in the Hawaiian language.

The movement to revitalize Hawaiian was strengthened through international contacts of young Hawaiian language activists with young Indigenous people from similar backgrounds and similar interests, in particular Māori, Rapanui (Easter Islanders), and other Polynesians. At first, these contacts were limited to meetings with students who had come to Hawai'i for university study, but subsequently grew to visits by Hawaiian to other Polynesian areas and then to the larger world. Twentieth-century and now 21st-century Hawaiian international contacts are parallel to, but less organized than, international contacts among Inuit youth described by Tulloch. Moving from youth assertion of their Indigenous identity and rejection of the two worlds philosophy to actual action is a major step. It requires much effort to successfully learn and use an endangered language; indeed it requires a lifetime dedication by some core group. The reference by Kroupa to that lifetime dedication being akin to an "addiction" is highly accurate. Such action then leads the core group back to more practical confrontations with the two worlds philosophy.

The two worlds philosophy often includes a rejection by elders and others of the creation of new vocabulary for the contemporary daily lifestyles of Indigenous youth. It may even include a rejection by elders of any use of the language by youths as inappropriate, especially if such use includes distinctive generational markers as necessarily is the case whenever a language continues to live and evolve. Yet, language is the vehicle that human groups use to maintain continuity of identity while modifying their economic systems and other features of their lives. We see this power of language in the historical movement of the Navajo from an older hunting-based life to European-introduced sheep herding fully incorporated into Navajo identity through the Navajo language. We also see this in newly coined Hawaiian terms for youth culture, including *paleoleo* (rap) and *kelekiko* (texting), in newly coined Arikara terms for playing basketball (see Kroupa), and the use of the Inuit languages for international meetings (see Tulloch).

In order to succeed, language revitalization must overcome the two worlds philosophy's placing of Indigenous languages and cultures solely in the past. One answer lies in ritual and metaphor, such as described by Kroupa relative to the intersection between language revitalization and the Arikara Medicine Lodge. Lee's interviews provide further evidence of youth recognition of the crucial roles of ceremonies and religion in connecting the present to the past, with a yearning to be able to continue those rituals through the Indigenous languages as they have always been. Nicholas gives much attention to the role of Hopi ritual and metaphor in developing Indigenous identity among young tribal members. Hopi ritual bridges the past and present by recalling the people's moving through different worlds to their contemporary situation.

Rather than a two worlds philosophy, the 'Aha Pūnana Leo has a one world philosophy of integrating new knowledge and activities into a community defined by use of the Hawaiian language. This integration, described in the Kumu Honua Mauli Ola philosophy ('Aha Pūnana Leo & Ka Haka 'Ula O Ke'elikōlani, 2009), uses ritual and metaphor within a genealogical framework similar to the Hopi movement through different worlds. 'Aha Pūnana Leo schooling includes many daily and annual school rituals, including student production of pre-Western feast foods. The focus, however, is not on preparing students to live in a subsistence economy, but on preparing them to make historical and metaphorical connections to it. These connections are crucial to a firm Hawaiian identity.

Maintaining Bonds Between Person, Location, and Language

Lee reports on the opinions of Indigenous youth that residing in an Indigenous area should be accompanied by use of the local language, while Wyman draws attention to the role of geographic mobility in language shift. Successful Indigenous-language maintenance is based on strong bonds between use of a language and a particular geographic location. Such bonds existed in all

Indigenous communities in traditional times. The analogous contemporary situation is a political unit using a minority language particular to that unit as its official language. Examples of such political units in the Americas are Canadian Québec, Danish Greenland (see Tulloch), and the U.S. Commonwealth of Puerto Rico. When a particular territory uses a language officially, there are mechanisms to teach that language to those who come to reside in the territory.

In spite of federal legislation in both Mexico and the United States according the right to use Indigenous languages officially, Native American governing bodies and Mexican townships with Indigenous communities do not generally assimilate speakers of the colonial language to the Indigenous language. Instead they often treat Indigenous language speakers parallel to immigrants, providing accommodations to assist them in participating in their own government and public functions carried out in English or Spanish. This is not true official use of Indigenous languages, but is instead transition to their replacement by dominant languages. A similar transition happened in the history of Hawai'i, yet today young Hawaiians are campaigning for full equality in official use of Hawaiian and English in government.

Language loss is so great in many Indigenous communities today that it is generally not possible to make a radical shift from use of the colonial language to use of the Indigenous language in government operations. Therefore a strategy of steps toward actualizing linguistic sovereignty must be developed. The most logical place to begin such steps is the schools. Even before schools are developed, individuals with the skills to operate schools through Indigenous languages must be developed. As no one can develop such human resources for young people, a core group must band together to do that work making themselves the target of that development. We did that in Hawai'i with the core leadership of the non-profit 'Aha Pūnana Leo (Wilson & Kamanā, 2001). An inspiring parallel example is that of the core Arikara revitalization group described by Kroupa. As with the core leadership of the 'Aha Pūnana Leo, the goal of the Arikara group is to establish education through their traditional language. Another description of such an effort is the CASLE Program for the Aanaar Saami community in Finland (Olthuis, Kivelä, & Skutnabb-Kangas, 2013).

The Role of Schools in Language Life and Death

Throughout this volume, schooling is identified as the major source of the elimination of Indigenous languages. Historically, a two worlds approach identifying schooling as non-Indigenous removed children from their Indigenous languages and identities. Even today, as recounted by McCarty et al. and by Lee, U.S. schools are often under federal and state pressure to eliminate any place for Native American languages in their curricula.

Community efforts to include Indigenous languages in schooling are currently widespread in the United States, Mexico, and Canada. Authors of this volume draw our attention to the weaknesses of such programs. Kroupa describes the woefully inadequate teaching of Arikara in the schools serving the core Arikara population. Wyman ascribes much of the language shift in her study area to lack of adequate support for Yup'ik language education. Lee awakens her readers to the fact that the Indigenous language and culture can be extensively included in the curriculum of a school and that school can still be a vehicle for language shift. Messing points out that Indigenous language teachers themselves can undermine their teaching by raising their own children in the colonial language and allowing community-internal denigration of a language to permeate Indigenous-language schooling. An overriding problem frustrating full revitalization of Indigenous languages in schools is that language revitalization efforts generally do not change the "framing" of community schools, through which colonial language privilege over the local Indigenous language is maintained (Meek & Messing, 2007).

McCarty et al. draw attention to the increased recognition of immersion as an efficient means of teaching Indigenous languages. While we certainly support immersion, it is important to understand its various models. As described in Wilson (2008), some Native American communities are uncritically adopting the Canadian-style French immersion model designed for mainstream Anglo families, and therefore framed for an outcome where English is the child's primary language rather than French. Distinctive language revitalization-focused models of immersion are required for language revitalization.

Beginning in 1983, the nonprofit 'Aha Pūnana Leo and its affiliated families have worked to redirect education, including state-operated and state-licensed education, to serve as the central institution for language revitalization using a one world approach. We have been explicit in our focus on Hawaiian language as the first priority in such schooling and built expansion through the stable base of the organization and parents affiliated with it. We have moved education through the Hawaiian language from preschool all the way through to high school. Ke Kula 'O Nāwahīokalani'ōpu'u (Nāwahī) is our most developed P-12 site. The Indigenous-language immersion model used at Nāwahī is distinct in explicitly pursuing a change from primary home use and peergroup use of English to primary use of the Indigenous language in one's peer group and the home. All instruction at all grades, preschool through 12, is through Hawaiian on a Minority Official Language Medium model (Wilson & Kamanā, 2011). Consistent with the predictions of Ogbu's (2003) theory, the replacement of English with Hawaiian as the language of the classroom has positively affected academic and standard English acquisition outcomes for Hawaiian students (Wilson & Kamanā, 2006). Nawahī has a 100% high school graduation rate, and an 80% college attendance rate.

An important part of our success has been to keep an eye on the vision and continue to move forward by conceding only things that could be overcome later. When the 'Aha Pūnana Leo moved its preschoolers into the public school system in 1987, we were told by an administrator that there would be no read-ing and writing of Hawaiian because it was an "oral" language. We refused to comply with this. If we had conceded literacy, the pressure to conduct school-ing in English would be too strong to resist. We also refused to have the teach-ing of English begin before Grade 5.

The state initially insisted on a uniform curriculum for all standard subjects using books published outside of Hawai'i, including references to flora and fauna, customs, weather, and so forth, totally foreign to Hawai'i. We agreed to this but obtained funds to translate the books ourselves, controlling the language therein. We sometimes changed the wording to explain animals or customs from a Hawaiian point of view. While "culturally incongruent," these books assured that Hawaiian would be the language of all instruction and that we had some systematic way to capture contemporary mathematics and science for the Hawaiian language (Wilson & Kamanā, 2001). Creating our own books in Hawaiian in a variety of areas would come later as we strengthened our knowledge of content areas and developed new vocabulary.

A current struggle at Nāwahī is a boycott of standardized testing and resis-tance to use of English-medium education standards over Indigenous language-medium education standards under the federal No Child Left Behind (NCLB) Act of 2001 (Wilson, 2012, in press). There is a lack of congruence between goals of the United States Department of Education that students "graduate from high school work and college ready" and standardized testing that rein-stitutes the forced assimilation of Indigenous language-speaking children (see also Wyman et al., this volume). Such forced assimilation has historically led to negative academic outcomes in the very goals that the federal government is claiming to seek. Once Indigenous populations win the struggle to the right to maintain Indigenous language integrity as the overriding feature of participa-tion in compulsory education, then such populations can focus on strength-ening academic and multilingual outcomes in Indigenous language medium schools through distinctive Indigenous pathways. Nāwahī is in a particularly fortunate position for pursuing that struggle.

Nāwahī is the main laboratory school site of Ka Haka 'Ula O Ke'elikōlani College of Hawaiian Language of the University of Hawai'i at Hilo (Ka Haka 'Ula). Ka Haka 'Ula serves as the main source of teachers and leadership at Nāwahī (Wilson & Kawai'ae'a, 2007). Like Nāwahī, it is administered and operated through Hawaiian with a fully Hawaiian-speaking faculty and support staff. Ka Haka 'Ula grew out of a small set of courses teaching Hawaiian in the university's foreign languages department and has a number of similarities with tribal colleges. Ka Haka 'Ula's courses provide idealistic college-age students an opportunity to learn Hawaiian from skilled teachers and then to use it among themselves and with fluent speakers. O'Connor and Brown include a descrip-tion of similar idealism leading to the study of Navajo in college. Lee also men-tions the positive effects of high quality instruction in widely spoken Indigenous languages at the high school and college levels. Kroupa describes a joint effort between young Arikara language activists and a university linguist to provide a high level of instruction and student research in a very small language.

At the core of Ka Haka 'Ula's programming are 4 years of daily, hour-long language-skills classes. Native speakers do not teach these language skill courses, but as described below, teach other content through the language. Language skill teachers at Ka Haka 'Ula are highly fluent second-language speakers. Unlike native speakers, these second-language speakers are very familiar with the distinctive needs of English-speaking young people seeking to master their ancestral language as a second language, a goal that they have achieved for themselves.

At all levels of language teaching at Ka Haka 'Ula there is intense teaching of Hawaiian grammar and lexicon from a somewhat purist perspective as expected by the Hawaiian elders who inspired the movement. This grammar translation approach produces student reflection and analysis of the language and culture necessary to move forward under difficult circumstances. Current best practice for the teaching of foreign languages is to use a communicative approach with a minimal focus on grammar and translation or student cultural connections to the target language. The typical goal of contemporary foreign language teaching is to produce students who have the ability to get across their thoughts and desires to non–English speakers in a foreign country, but not necessarily speak the language perfectly nor to uphold the language in its various cultural uses. There is no foreign country to turn to for Hawaiian, nor are there any foreign native speakers of Hawaiian to maintain the language in its traditional form. The students of Hawaiian must therefore become those highly skilled, culture-bearing "native speakers" themselves. Much attention to grammar allows us to revive Hawaiian in a form as close as possible to its traditional form. As described below relative to peer group use of the language, even with our attention to grammar, we produce a higher level of actual communicative use of the target language than typically found in foreign language teaching.

The teaching of Hawaiian is done within an expectation that students are fluent in both Hawai'i Creole English and Standard American English. In support of the description by McCarty et al. of Indigenous linguistic diversity as a resource, the many similarities between Hawai'i Creole English and Hawaiian allow more rapid learning and are extensively used in explaining grammar, vocabulary, and pronunciation. A heavy emphasis is also placed on the core of similarities between classical and contemporary Hawaiian culture and building a contemporary Hawaiian-speaking society based on those similarities. This process is well described by the comment of Lee's student, Doreen, regarding establishing the "energy necessary to regroup, revitalize and even, in some respects, reinvent who we are." Language revitalization involves creating your own future based on your own past.

Students enrolled in Ka Haka 'Ula's BA program begin intensive study of Hawaiian through English their first year. They transition to total use of Hawaiian in the classroom the second year, similar to recent programming developed for Aanaar Saami in Finland (Olthuis, Kivelä & Skutnabb-Kangas, 2013). In their third and fourth years, in addition to their daily language study, students take academic courses beyond Hawaiian language through Hawaiian. It is also at this stage that students learn cultural and other content from native speakers. The number of native speakers available for such teaching is now greatly reduced in Hawai'i, and Ka Haka 'Ula is adapting to that change through other programming through Hawaiian using other fluent speakers of the language. While at the undergraduate level coursework through Hawaiian is restricted to the major, at the graduate level there are more recently developed programs conducted completely in Hawaiian, including a teacher education program and two master's programs (Wilson & Kawai'ae'a, 2007). A doctoral program in language revitalization, which is open to other Indigenous language speakers, has courses taught through Hawaiian in one stream of electives for Hawaiian speakers.

The teaching of Indigenous languages, such as Hawaiian, at the college and high school levels faces the challenge of being in competition with prestigious foreign languages. As shown by Messing's description of the competition between learning Mexicano and English among Tlaxcalans, such competition can sap language revitalization of potential participants. Nāwahī has diffused such competition by bringing foreign language competence into its "one world" to further strengthen the Hawaiian language (Wilson & Kamanā, 2011). All elementary students at Nāwahī study Japanese language and Chinese characters, while intermediate and high school students have studied Chinese and Latin. This study is through Hawaiian and strengthens student awareness of Hawaiian structures as well as those of foreign languages. Furthermore, it is aligned with the Kumu Honua Mauli Ola philosophy through treating such courses as part of a "heritage language program" to honor non-Native Hawaiian ancestors (Japanese, Korean, Chinese, Portuguese, Puerto Ricans, etc.) who intermarried with Native Hawaiians and whose languages were spoken by Native Hawaiians. The goal is not full mastery of these languages in their standard forms, but learning features of the languages and their associated cultures that connect to the historic community of Hawaiian speakers and the place of those languages within that community.

English, taught at Nāwahī as an annual course beginning in Grade 5, is seen as the international language studied at the school. English study is therefore viewed as similar to foreign language study in other schools in Hawai'i. Parallel to English-medium school teaching of foreign languages through English, Hawaiian-medium Nāwahī teaches its international language, English, through its medium of education, Hawaiian. This strengthens the position of Hawaiian, yet does not diminish English outcomes. The 8 years of international language study at Nāwahī is considerably more than in the typical level of foreign (or Hawaiian) language study in Hawai'i English-medium schools. Furthermore, the content taught is at an international standard of English to allow students to fully function in any English medium university in any English-speaking country, as well as enroll in tertiary education through Hawaiian at Ka Haka 'Ula where students are expected to do some of their research through English. Nāwahī's goals for second-language outcomes in English are parallel to those characteristic of English outcomes sought in Nordic countries. Students from Nordic countries often outperform native English speakers in English composition courses at the University of Hawai'i at Hilo (Wilson & Kamanā, 2006). Indicative of Nāwahī's success in teaching English is the fact that high school students from Nāwahī have matriculated from such English medium universities as Loyola Marymount, Seattle University, the University of Northern Arizona, Stanford, and Oxford.

There is an effort within our movement to have Nāwahī and Ka Haka 'Ula students not simply learn other languages, but to have them see speaking Hawaiian as a resource in working on an international level. As with Tulloch's description of Inuit languages uniting peoples across international borders, fluency in Hawaiian allows students to connect with other Polynesian peoples whose countries use French, Spanish, or a more British-like English than that used in Hawai'i. There is also a larger benefit here—that of the "minority official language" speaker who is accustomed to successfully living life navigating linguistic and cultural diversity (Wilson & Kamanā, 2011). We believe that this strength is the reason that a number of Nāwahī graduates have proven to be exceptionally successful in living in foreign countries such as Italy and Kyrgystan, where they rapidly acquired the local language.

The Integration of Hawaiian-Speaking Youth into a Hawaiian-Speaking Peer Culture

Key to language revitalization is the reestablishment of the Indigenous language as the peer group language of youth and the subsequent families that they establish. Besides the ever expanding use of Hawaiian inside the classroom, Ka Haka 'Ula's program focuses on the use of Hawaiian outside the classroom. First- and second-year students learn vocabulary designed for use in their contemporary lives and faculty carefully scaffold use of the language with them outside, as well as, inside class. Upon entering third year, students are expected to use Hawaiian exclusively as their classmate peer-group language outside class. Fourth-year students are expected to take a leadership role in triggering the use of Hawaiian among underclassmen.

Experience using Hawaiian also occurs in social events involving the Ka Haka 'Ula community. In contrast to the descriptions of the avoidance of Indigenous languages in public in areas where the language is receding, Ka Haka 'Ula and Nāwahī use Hawaiian in all official public gatherings. While highly fluent and proper Hawaiian is admired in all contexts, speaking English rather than Hawaiian to other Hawaiian speakers is more likely to draw negative comments from others than are one's mistakes in Hawaiian. However, mistakes are corrected by teachers and advanced students— sometimes on the spot or in more discrete ways, such as by email or in meetings with teachers. Kroupa's description of their movement's development of Ree-glish, that is a mixture of Arikara and English that is constantly building toward more Arikara, is parallel in that it focuses on young adult peer group communication using a basic level of the language and then moves that peer group language toward norms documented in the language of elders.

Students at Nāwahī have a very different experience from Ka Haka ʻUla students. The choice of schooling through Hawaiian was not their own, but that of their parents. They are very much accustomed to hearing and using Hawaiian and, unlike Ka Haka ʻUla students, tend to take Hawaiian for granted. As with English-medium schools in Hilo, peer-group use of Hawaiʻi Creole English and out-of-school-derived slang comes to signify intermediate students entering adolescence at Nāwahī. However, Hawaiian skills continue to be developed through the total Hawaiian school curriculum. Students begin to move back to use of Hawaiian with peers as they mature in high school. As they do so, they strengthen their repertoire of registers of Hawaiian appropriate for different situations. All students who graduate from Nāwahī can therefore participate in the use of Hawaiian as young adults. As the movement strengthens, we expect that peer group use of Hawaiian at Nāwahī will eventually characterize students at all ages. Already, Nāwahī is distinguished from other Hawaiian immersion sites in Hawaiʻi by the widespread peer group use of Hawaiian among elementary school children.

Parallel to the description in chapters here of the language revitalization-supporting effect of international contacts, whether consciously developed as in Tulloch or through the effect of military service as in O'Connor and Brown, we have found that maturity and experiences away from Nāwahī increase (rather than decrease) the appreciation of Nāwahī graduates for their ability to speak Hawaiian and a desire to consciously participate in its revitalization. Quite a few graduates have gone on to polish their Hawaiian at Ka Haka ʻUla and are becoming leaders in the Hawaiian language revitalization movement. Most gratifying to us is the trend among graduates of Nāwahī and Ka Haka ʻUla O Keʻelikōlani to raise their children speaking Hawaiian as a first language and enroll them in Nāwahī or in a Hawaiian immersion school elsewhere in Hawaiʻi. As the ʻAha Pūnana Leo moves through its second quarter century, we expect that within a generation there will be several academically renowned schools in which the majority of children will be first language speakers of Hawaiian. There is also the potential to spread basic Hawaiian language fluency to the majority of Native Hawaiian college-educated youth in the next generation.

Conclusion

The chapters in this volume show us that while each Indigenous community undergoing language shift is distinct, there are many similarities. For communities seeking to reverse language shift, these similarities often represent challenges to overcome.

The key demographic in reversing language shift is young people ages 12 to 30. For this demographic to ensure the survival of their language, they must learn their ancestral language fluently, maintain fluency by daily peer-group use, pass the language on to their own children, protect and educate those children in strong Indigenous language-medium schools, join with Indigenous language-speaking peers to expand use of the language into higher socioeconomic domains, and then live to see grandchildren repeat and strengthen the cycle.

Not all Indigenous young people are able to reach the first step of developing fluency in the ancestral language, but if those who do reach it concentrate on developing and operating schools taught totally through their ancestral language, others of their generation can send their children to such schools to learn the language and add to the Indigenous language-speaking population. The chapters in this volume show great yearnings for ancestral language survival among youth in communities from Mexico to Alaska. Those young people should not be undervalued. They represent the hope of the future. *E ola nā 'ōlelo 'ōiwi a kākou!* Let our Indigenous languages live!

References

'Aha Pūnana Leo and Ka Haka 'Ula O Ke'elikōlani. (2009). *Kumu honua mauli ola.* Hilo, HI: Author.

Lee, T. S. (2007). "If they want Navajo to be learned, then they should require it in all schools": Navajo teenagers' experiences, choices, and demands regarding Navajo language. *Wicazo Sa Review,* (Spring), 7–33.

Meek, B., & Messing, J. (2007). Framing Indigenous languages as secondary to matrix languages. *Anthropology and Education Quarterly, 38*(2), 99–118.

Messing, J. (2007). Multiple ideologies, competing discourses and language shift in Tlaxcala, Mexico. *Language in Society, 36*(4), 555–577.

Ogbu, J. U. (2003). *Black American students in an affluent suburb: A study of academic disengagement.* Mahwah, NJ: Erlbaum.

Olthuis, L., Kivelä, S., & Skutnabb-Kangas, T. (2013). *Revitalizing Indigenous languages: How to recreate a lost working-age generation.* Bristol, England: Multilingual Matters.

Wilson, W. H. (2008). Language fluency, accuracy, and revernacularization in different models of immersion. *NIEA Newsletter, 39*(2), 40–42.

Wilson, W. H. (2012). USDE violations of NALA and the testing boycott at Nāwahīokalani'ōpu'u School. *Journal of American Indian Education, 31*(3), 30–45.

Wilson, W. H. (in press). Language assessment in Hawaiian. In A. J. Kunnan (Ed.), *The companion to language assessment vol. 4: Assessment around the world.* Malden, MA: Wiley-Blackwell.

Wilson, W. H., & Kamanā, K. (2001). "Mai loko mai o ka 'i'ini: Proceeding from a dream"— The 'Aha Pūnana Leo connection in Hawaiian language revitalization. In L. Hinton & K.

Hale (Eds.), *The green book of language revitalization in practice* (pp. 147–176). San Diego, CA: Academic Press.

Wilson, W. H., & Kamanā, K. (2006). "For the interest of the Hawaiians themselves": Reclaiming the benefits of Hawaiian-medium education. *Hulili: Multidisciplinary Research on Hawaiian Well-Being, 3*(1), 153–181.

Wilson, W. H., & Kamanā, K. (2011). Insights from Indigenous immersion in Hawai'i: The case of Nāwahī School. In D. J. Tedick, D. Christian, & T. W. Fortune, *Immersion education: Practices, policies, possibilities* (pp. 36–57). Bristol, England: Multilingual Matters.

Wilson, W. H., & Kamanā, K. (2013). E paepae Hou' ia ka pōhaku: Reset the stones of the Hawaiian house platform. In L. Hinton (Ed.), *Bringing our languages home: Language revitalization for families* (pp. 101–117). Berkeley, CA: Heyday Books.

Wilson, W. H., & Kawai'ae'a, K. (2007). I kumu; i lālā: "Let there be sources; Let there be branches": Teacher education in the College of Hawaiian Language. *Journal of American Indian Education, 4*(3), 37–53.

11

COMMENTARY

Indigenous Youth Bilingualism from a Yup'ik Perspective

Walkie Charles

Yuk eliskuni, qanruyutni-llu maligtaqukuniki nalluyagutevkenaki, tauna yuk umyuartuarkauguq.

When a person learns and follows what he is taught and does not forget them, that person is led toward wisdom. —Marie Nichols, Yup'ik Eskimo Elder [deceased].

(Tennant & Bitar, 1981, p. v)

The theme of this volume could not be more appropriate for today's conversation as we address and share young people's language issues in many of our communities where a language other than English is spoken, or has been spoken. The growing distance between heritage languages and youth has become a constant point of discourse between Elders in Indigenous communities and those who could listen. Since Western contact, the pursuit for a "better life" through formal schooling has institutionalized Indigenous youth, separating them from their homelands and broadening a space between those who speak the heritage language and those who abandoned language and culture for formal Western education's sake. It is often the descendants of early residential school students who suffer the loss of language and identity (see, e.g., Lomawaima, 1994). But the challenge is for Elders to find ways to create a language of concern so those who have the language can act as diplomatic agents for change if language revolution is evident.

The compelling stories about youth and Indigenous languages reveal an awakening of a generation who otherwise would not have a voice or the academic language with which to express their feelings, their involvement, and their concerns about being members of an ancestral language community in which English has become a pervasive venue of everyday expression. As Lee points out in this volume, "The students actually greatly respect their language, but the sociological influences surrounding their use of the language ... impede their efforts to speak." In O'Connor and Brown's chapter, Jay's efforts to create hip hop music speak to his connections to being in the military that identifies his American-ness, and his desire to create music that is heard and practiced by many youth as a way to establish an association with the modern world. Jay's efforts to glocalize hip hop while incorporating his Diné identity also tell how much of a desire he has to hold on to his Indigenous roots and to redefine his self as a young Diné man.

The efforts of the past to extinguish our home languages resonate loudly in the youths' voices in these chapters. Since Western contact and the advent of schooling, religion, and especially boarding schools, finding what it means to have an identity has become a struggle for many of our Indigenous people in the "Lower 48" (U.S. mainland) and Canadian Indigenous communities as well as in rural Alaska where Indigenous heritage languages are spoken. The generational products of the boarding school era are evident, as with many of our neighbors "outside." As Hopi people state (in Nicholas's chapter), "We are interjecting English into our Hopi. Therefore, we are speaking a truly different language."

Indigenous Alaskans are facing a similar dilemma. More and more our heritage languages lie in the minds and hearts of the Elders, and, in a very few cases, in smaller communities where economic development, such as harvesting salmon and other natural resources, seems absent. Where there is no chance for drilling oil, for example, the stronger the heritage language. In Yup'ik villages with strong economies, there seems to be more English with ancillary Yup'ik spoken to include those few who may not have acquired enough spoken English to make sense of the "business." Wyman's study, conducted over a span of 9 years, indicates a significant change in the use of the Yup'ik language in the Yup'ik village of Piniq (pseudonymn). Even in this remote Yup'ik community the effects of Western civilization have redefined the language of this Yup'ik community for youth. The "rapidly changing linguistic ecology" permeates the marrow of our youth's chances to practice and live their heritage language, and Piniq is no exception.

The chapters within this book also exemplify the desire to regain heritage languages among Indigenous youth. Tulloch, for example, identifies youth as deliberate agents of language maintenance. The young people in this chapter express how their passion to regain their heritage languages was "threatened by diminished opportunities to expand their competence and by others' judgments of their language use." Yet one realizes how critical youth feel about bringing back language to strengthen their identity as Indigenous people. One young man, Joel, is so desperate to learn that he literally finds places where his language, Yup'ik, is spoken. In Kroupa's chapter the realization of the "critically endangered language community" forces the young people to establish a movement to resuscitate the Arikara language.

Nicholas addresses a theme around which many of the chapters in this volume revolve: What role does the Hopi language play in terms of how Hopi youth define and assert their personal and social identities as members of Hopi society and as Hopi citizens in the broader sense? I would like to take this statement as a point of discussion for bringing all of the chapters together. I tell it in story form, a venue by which Yup'ik people learned about identity, survival, respect, honor, hope, and perseverance.

The Yup'ik people of Alaska populate the southwestern part of the state, and Yup'ik, one of 20 Indigenous languages in Alaska, has the highest number of heritage speakers in the state (Wyman, this volume). The common thread of this volume is familiar among the Yup'ik Eskimo people, and similar stories are heard from other Indigenous peoples in the Lower 48. Although the Yup'ik people were never forced out of their homelands, colonization by church and school was just as evident. When young Yup'ik children began leaving home to go to boarding schools in places such as Wrangell Institute and Sitka—1,500 to 2,000 miles away from their families—children learned how different they were from English speakers culturally, socially, and physically. For decades the boarding schools removed the Yup'ik children from their homes and parents and brought them to foreign locations, different lifestyles, and a culture in which they cohabitated with students from other language communities in Alaska. There they experienced ritualized rules and punishments, as well as a new diet and the elimination of their home languages. The boarding schools housed high school students as far away as Chilocco Indian School in Oklahoma, Haskell Institute in Lawrence, Kansas, Chemawa Indian School in Salem, Oregon, and Mt. Edgecumbe High School, Wrangell Institute, and St. Mary's High School in Alaska. When adolescents returned home for summer break, there was often not enough family contact. Most young men and women found seasonal work in fish canneries, fire-fighting, or commercial fishing. When the jobs were over, it was time to head back to the boarding schools.

In the mid-1970s, Rural Education Attendance Area schools were established, and school districts were developed in rural Alaska for K-12 populations in remote villages. Around the same time, a lawsuit to provide education for children in their home communities led to the development of local high schools in almost all communities of Alaska. With these changes arose challenges in rural Alaska. Although it was an emotional trauma for both the young children—sometimes as young as 5 years old—and their families, the children left for 9 months out of the year and during that time had no contact with their families except an occasional letter (if the parents were able to write, or find someone in the community to write for them). The establishment of local schools, especially high schools, became an issue.

In the fall of 1975, most adolescents didn't return to the now-familiar boarding schools because they could stay home and go to school. Parents quickly realized that they were now housing adolescents who for decades had left home in August and returned in May for summer jobs and subsistence harvesting of food, fish, and the like. In the fall of 1975, these students didn't leave; they stayed to live with their own families. This created a mixed bag of emotions for parents and adolescents. Adolescents also no longer had a sense of independence, or peer contact with students from other Alaskan villages. Many of these adolescents had been in boarding schools since they were 6 or 7 years old and now they were living at home. In most cases they had lost their ability to speak their heritage language, although they could get by using simple words and phrases (cf. Wyman, this volume). At this point it was more common for adolescents to communicate in English, creating a challenge for many Yup'ik parents, grandparents, and Elders in the community.

While this was going on at home, the new school districts contracted new teachers, most of whom had never been to rural Alaska. The new teachers began their teaching in a new environment, with children of people about whom they had very little knowledge. Most of the new teachers had not had any training in teaching students of Indigenous heritage, or working with students who had learned to survive in hostile academic institutions. The teachers struggled to find an adequate language to teach. Since the evolution of schools in rural Alaska, school officials had mandated English–only efforts. Children were taught English from the very first day they entered the school, and English was the language of instruction. Many children learned English but did not necessarily bring English home to share with their families; it stayed in the schools. The more the students learned English, the further the language distance evolved between the children and the parents and elders in the homes. From my own personal observation, the new teachers of the mid-1970s were frustrated because they wanted to teach, but felt they couldn't because of tensions from home and students. In most cases they felt inadequate to the trials of teaching in rural Alaska.

Accommodating students and parents by creating small high schools in larger villages of Alaska created many obstacles. First of all, at boarding school, the adolescent had professionals or paraprofessionals who provided guidance or discipline when needed. Now that the children and adolescents no longer attended the boarding schools, when issues of guidance and discipline arose, the parents were ill equipped to deal with them. There quickly grew a distance between parent and adolescent. "How can I talk with my child? I don't understand them. I don't know what to say to make them understand I'm trying to help, and at the same time, I'm not able to communicate with them because they only speak English, and I don't."

The new teachers faced their own predicament: "Not only am I a new teacher in the community, but I really don't know the culture. Nor do I have the adequate communicative knowledge to make sense of talking with the parents, let alone the students."

Students, on the other hand, although fortunate not to have left for boarding school, faced the challenge of being home and sharing space with younger siblings, parents, and extended families. There was also a tug between being a student as well as an older child when familial and cultural responsibilities were involved. More often than not, schoolwork became ancillary because of parents' demands to help out with chores and activities.

The feeling of not fitting into family and culture, and related confusion among the younger high school age generation was just the tip of the iceberg. A 10-day *Anchorage Daily News* series published in 1988 documented alcohol-related problems including high rates of suicide, attempted suicide, homicide, and accidents in Alaska Native villages, and related these devastating life situations to a "deeper malady" rooted in the government removal of children to boarding school, and the later return of children with "elevated aspirations, diminished prospects for advancement, and little experience in family living" (Weaver, 1988, p. 2). The series captured the situation at one point in time, tracing cultural distress and destruction to historical schooling practices and the overtaking of Native culture.

But what is the situation in communities like those above today? How are they similar or different in the Lower 48?

So What?

The chapters in this volume are compelling. They tell of struggles similar to the situation in rural Alaska as the educational system attempted to provide adequate education for Indigenous students. What binds these chapters is the fact that the authors have first-hand knowledge of the related challenges they continue to see among Indigenous youth, and in some cases, the accounts represent first-hand experiences.

What these chapters provide is a voice for the Indigenous youth vis-á-vis academics—most of us who are Indigenous to our own communities, and some of us who are products of the historical educational traumas of the boarding school era. The authors of this volume have created a language, a profound one at that, revealing the struggles that our youth continue to face as we attempt to move forward toward positive change. In this volume, the voices of Indigenous youth are heard in a way that would not have been possible in earlier years of the academy. Today, we have educational leaders—professors at universities Indigenous to the cultures of their homelands—beginning to critically address the silent voices of the youth in our communities, and creating stories that reveal their needs and how we should prepare ourselves to assist in educating for a stronger tomorrow.

The only solution is to realize how significantly our heritage languages define who we are, and, in doing so, to find ways to the "places where language is spoken" (see Tulloch, this volume). The messages of the college-age young people in many of the chapters, and the voices of other youth captured in these pages spell out the desperation to reconnect to the language of the heart. These are sincere efforts that speak volumes to other people in similar situations. As a university professor of Yup'ik, I too see a trend of young college students wanting to speak their ancestral language. I explain to the youth at the beginning of the semester that in order for them to learn Yugtun (the Yup'ik language), they have to follow some guidelines. When students enter my classroom late, they stand at the doorway and wait for me to acknowledge them, in the same way a child would enter a home of another, first waiting to be asked to come in by an adult. I share with my students that they respect the language they are about to learn by removing caps and sunglasses, shutting off their cell phones, and avoiding eating during class. When we enter the Yugtun classroom, we are there to learn and to respect the language by following protocol.

When I started teaching this way, I thought my expectations would be such that the students would ignore them. But as one student wrote in his dialogue journal, "I like the fact that you lay out expectations up front so that we could focus on the language that we are afforded to learn. I didn't learn how to speak Yugtun in my village school. All I learned in the Yup'ik class is to do arts and crafts. This class is serious, and I appreciate that."

Language and cultural shift is evident—but yet, nothing on the inside changes among Indigenous peoples and youth. Justin (Nicholas, this volume) eloquently expresses the identity that resonates among Indigenous youth:

> Since you're a Hopi [by birthright], you're brought up that way [in the language and culture of the Hopi]. [Then] you are [Hopi, and] you can't let go [simply discard it]; it's gonna be too hard.

If we can't simply let go, how do we frame our efforts to hold onto the realization that we are always going to have the essence of being Native, but move forward at the same time? I believe we start from the beginning—as a blossoming Yup'ik Elder once told me before he died—When you've taken the opportunity to listen, and the opportunity to observe, then you too will have a story to tell.

The stories in this volume are stories written after a great deal of observing and listening. They are stories of hope, stories of change, and stories of self-determination. Bringing out the passion and excitement to regain our heritages languages is critical. When facilitated properly, students show their interest and passion. The youth in these pages are revealing their desire to speak. Let's honor them by giving them the language that makes them whole. More often than not, an Elder whose first language is his or her heritage language will embrace a child in need to learn. Let's find those keepers of culture and language and bring home the song of our ancestors.

References

Lomawaima, K. T. (1994). *They called it Prairie Light: The story of Chilocco Indian School*. Lincoln: University of Nebraska Press.

Tennant, E. A., & Bitar, J. E. (Eds.). (1981). *Yup'ik lore. Yuut Qanemciit: Oral traditions of an Eskimo people. Yupiit Cayaraita Qanrutkumalriit*. Albuquerque, NM: Educational Research Associates.

Weaver, H. (1988). A generation of despair. In P. Dougherty (Ed.), *A people in peril* [Special reprint]. *Anchorage Daily News*, pp. A2, A3.

12

COMMENTARY

En/countering Indigenous Bi/Multilingualism

Ofelia García

This book advances scholarship on Indigenous language ideologies and practices in important ways. By focusing on youth, the authors, mostly Indigenous scholars, "counter" traditional ideologies about Indigenous languages and "encounter" a more dynamic Indigenous bilingualism that has remained understudied. By combining careful ethnography with interviews and longitudinal studies, the multiplicity, complexity, and ambiguity of language identities, ideologies, and practices among Indigenous youth is attested.

As with other scholarship on Indigenous languages, the authors argue here for the maintenance of Indigenous language practices. The difference here is that they acknowledge the multilayered dynamism of the bilingualism of Indigenous youth in the Americas and do not simply paint a picture of inevitable language shift and linguistic shame. Instead, they tap into the youth's language activism, as they recognize the tip toward English and the ensuing bilingualism and fluid language practices. In so doing, the authors also question traditional understandings of language policy and planning. The chapters in the book extend the lens of language policy and planning studies to focus on negotiations of minoritized groups that are mediated by relations of power (McCarty, 2004).

This volume focuses on youth. The young people whom the authors observe, interview, and interact with are at a developmental stage where recursiveness between childhood and adulthood practices is inevitable. Youth are shaping language practices that are much more dynamic than those of children under the purview of parents and teachers, or of adults who are often restricted by jobs in their language practices. Furthermore, youth's ease with electronic interactions aided through technology, as well as pop culture, gives them greater flexibility in ways of using language. For example, O'Connor and Brown's chapter documents the semiotic practices of a Navajo hip hop artist that circulate forms of popular culture in locally Diné-specific ways. Language practices in the 21st century are increasingly multimodal, and linguistic modes of meaning are intricately bound up with other visual, audio, gestural and spatial semiotic systems (Cope & Kalantzis, 2000; Kress, 2003; New London Group, 1996). This integrated discourse is also reflected in the Indigenous youth bilingual practices, as meaning and semiotic systems of both the majority and minority cultures and languages become integrated.

The contributions in this book affirm, yet break away from, some of the views espoused by the Indigenous language rights movement (see also McCarty & Zepeda, 2006; Reyhner, Cantoni, St. Clair, & Parsons Yazzie, 1999; Skutnabb-Kangas, 2000; Skutnabb-Kangas & Dunbar, 2010). The chapters, especially the one by Nicholas, insist on the importance of the maintenance and revitalization of Indigenous language practices for ecological knowledge, and yet the contributions extend the sense of traditional place by providing the possibility of an embodied space with youth activity at the center of place-making. This construction of an embodied space where youth enact global spaces in local ways is especially evident in the chapter by O'Connor and Brown.

As the "'being' Hopi by 'living Hopi'" quote that introduces Nicholas's contribution makes clear, youth's understandings of language practices go beyond traditional notions of language. Indigenous youth in this book insist on the importance of maintaining and revitalizing Indigenous language practices, often going to great lengths to do so, as in the case of the four Arikara activists in Kroupa's chapter. Other times, Indigenous youth organize transnationally into non-governmental organizations of support, as in the efforts by the Inuit youth described by Tulloch and others. And yet, there is also resistance to the discourse of authenticity that demands that Indigenous languages not be tainted by more powerful European languages such as English or Spanish out of respect for the language of ancestors. This is the case of the resistance of youth toward *legitimo Mexicano* described in Messing's chapter. To legitimize the youth's position, we need to consider how others have questioned the concept of language itself and traditional notions of bilingualism.

Makoni and Pennycook (2007) have proposed that our present conception of language was originally constructed by states that wanted to consolidate political power and missionaries eager to evangelize colonized populations. Errington (2001) has shown how missionaries and colonial officers then imposed these "invented" monolithic languages onto specific territories. Mühlhäusler (2000, p. 38) has also explained that the "notion of 'a language' makes little sense in most traditional societies where people engage in multiple discursive practices among themselves." Speaking of the Pacific region, he continues: "[t]he notion of 'a language' is one whose applicability ... in ... most situations outside those found within modern European nation-states, is extremely limited" (p. 7). Romaine (1994) concurs when describing the complex language use in Papua New Guinea: "[T]he very concept of discrete languages is probably a European cultural artifact fostered by procedures such as literacy and standardization" (p. 12).

In general, languages have been constituted separately "outside and above human beings" (Yngve 1996, p. 28) and have little relationship to the ways in which people use language, their discursive practices, or what Yngve (1996) and Shohamy (2006) call their *languaging*—language practices of people. Language is truly a social notion that cannot be defined without reference to its speakers and the context in which it is used (Heller, 2007).

In most settings throughout the world, "languaging bilingually" or what many of us, extending Williams (1994) have called "translanguaging," is the usual way of languaging (Blackledge & Creese, 2010; Canagarajah, 2011; Creese & Blackledge, 2010; García, 2009, 2011; Hornberger & Link, 2012; Lewis, Jones, & Baker, 2012a, 2012b). It is then normal and unmarked to translanguage in interactions between individuals who belong to the same bilingual culture, as Kroupa makes obvious for the Arikara. Translanguaging, or engaging in bilingual or multilingual discourse practices, is an approach to bilingualism that is centered not on the constructed notion of standard languages, but on the practices of bilinguals that are readily observable. These translanguaging practices are the normal mode of communication that, with some exceptions in some monolingual enclaves, characterizes communities throughout the world.

In the 21st century, we can no longer hold static views of American Indigenous languages as autonomous languages completely separate from English or Spanish, or other languages. If we take the perspective of the language practices of young Indigenous speakers themselves, and not of separate languages, these chapters show that the youth "language," or rather "translanguage," is being created by integrating language practices from different communities with distinct language ideologies, as they draw from different semiotic systems and modes of meaning. But these chapters also affirm the youth's loyalties toward their Indigenous cultural and linguistic practices, with their fluidities, complexities, and ambiguities.

The chapters here also document the language shift underway among different Indigenous communities in the Americas. Nicholas tells us that in 1983, most Hopi children came to school speaking Hopi, but by 2000, the shift to English was evident. Wyman documents the same in southwestern Alaska where in the decade of her study, children shifted from entering school as Yup'ik speakers to entering school as English speakers. Lee reveals that whereas 10 years ago, 90% of Navajo children arrived at school speaking Navajo, today only 10% do. Kroupa also describes the decimation of the Arikara by smallpox and the Garison Dam that divided their reservation. Although the chapters offer evidence of language shift, there is questioning of the concept of language shift itself. McCarty, Romero-Little, Warhol, and Zepeda claim that language shift is not necessarily linear or unidirectional. Messing claims that both ideological orientations and language practices can change over time. The chapter by Tull-och also makes evident that not all Inuit are focused on language; for some, the Inuit language is a tool for belonging, for others, an instrument of alienation. Yet, youth want to know who they are, have a say in shaping their identities, and empower healthy Indigenous communities.

In studying the language shift of New York Puerto Ricans, I have called this multilayered and dynamic process of shift, "*linguistic shift with vaivén*" (García, Morín, & Rivera, 2001). Linguistic shift in contemporary contexts where there is increased identity and linguistic consciousness, as is the situation of colonized minorities in the Americas, is rarely unidirectional towards language loss or shift. Instead, like the *vaivén* of sea waves, language practices come and go as the sociolinguistic environments of language socialization themselves shift. In so doing, it gives us the impression of retreat, but despite the dynamism of the surface, the ground itself is solid, although, as the ocean floor, never static. So are the linguistic practices of everyone, but especially of bilingual populations in situations of unequal power. These chapters make clear that Indigenous youth perform language practices and language ideologies that, despite their complexity, variation, and dynamism, are rich and powerful, not gloomy and weak, pointing toward the possibility of a viable future of dynamic bilingualism for the Hopi and the Navajo in the southwestern United States, Arikara in North Dakota, Mexicano speakers in Mexico, the Yup'ik in southwestern Alaska, the Inuits in North America, but also in Greenland and Russia. These youth are language activists, but their activism is not limited only to the Indigenous languages. Their activism encompasses their bilingualism, including English, and their own translanguaging practices which are claimed as also authentic and valid.

To accept this idea of promising Indigenous bilingualism for the future, one must shed the monoglossic ideologies that have limited our views of two languages as the sum of $1 + 1 = 2$. In García (2009) I propose that in the 21st century we must go beyond the traditional models of subtractive and additive bilingualism to understand the more fluid language practices of bilin-guals—their translanguaging (García, 2009). I then advance two other models of bilingualism—*recursive bilingualism* and *dynamic bilingualism*. Both begin from more heteroglossic ideologies and language practices, with bilingualism itself, and not monolingualism, as the starting point. Languages are not conceived as separate autonomous systems, but as language practices tapping all points of the continua that make up a bilingual repertoire. I see *recursive bilingualism* as that which is used in situations of reversing language shift, as in the cases in this book, where speakers take pieces of past language practices to reconstitute new practices that will serve them well in a bilingual future. Even in situations of extensive shift, as with the Arikara, there are ceremonial songs and ritual practices that subsist, and language practices of ancestors that are now available through the Web. *Dynamic bilingualism*, on the other hand, refers to the complex bilingual competence needed in some 21st-century societies. In the linguistic complexity of the 21st century, bilingualism involves a much more dynamic cycle where language use is multiple and ever adjusting to the multilingual multimodal terrain of the communicative act.

In the context of the Indigenous youth treated here in situations of progressive, although not total, language shift, we have both dynamic and recursive bilingualism. On the one hand, there is a dynamic cycle of language practices that are heteroglossic, fluid, and multiple, sometimes tipping toward English as in the case of the Navajo hip hop artist; on the other, there is attempt to revitalize language practices through recursive bilingualism, as in the efforts made by the Arikara activists. This has to do with the fact that, as McCarty et al. say, the sociolinguistic environments in which youth language socialization takes place are much more multilayered and varied than the notion of language shift, language maintenance, or reversing language shift may convey.

The concept of language maintenance itself is also contested in these chapters, for the youth are not interested in static practices tied to essentialized identities. It is *language sustainability* that these Indigenous youth desire, "the capacity [of languaging] to endure, but always in interaction with the social context in which it operates" (García, 2011, p. 7). Unlike language maintenance, the concept of sustainability contains in its core the grappling with social, economic and environmental conditions by which systems remain diverse and productive over time and into the future; it involves a dynamic relocalization in space and time (García, 2011).

One theme that cuts across the chapters in this book is that of both the limits and possibilities of schools in the sustainability of community bilingualism. McCarty et al. cite schooling as a key cause of language shift in the communities they studied, yet also see new opportunities when schooling is reimagined to capitalize on youth's fluid sociolinguistic strengths. In the Yup'ik situation, although Wyman tells us of the reduction of bilingual education programs since the 1980s, she insists that bilingual education in itself, as presently practiced, will have little to bear in the success of language retention. Messing also questions the role of intercultural bilingual programs in the maintenance and development of Mexicano. In fact, she says that because Mexicano is mostly used with people with whom there is *confianza* or trust, its introduction into schools creates an awkward sociolinguistic situation. And Lee confirms that the language shift of the Navajo youth has occurred despite Indigenous bilingual schools. This lack of faith in bilingual education for the revitalization of Indigenous languages is also the position of Kroupa, who describes a bilingual program for the last 30 years in the White Shield community that has not produced any speakers of Arikara.

The reasons for the limited effect of schools have partly to do with our conceptualizations of bilingual education programs as following either a purely subtractive or additive model. Instead, as McCarty et al. suggest, it is important to think of how bilingual schools can become more responsive to heteroglossic models of bilingualism. Despite many recent attempts to develop bilingual schools that reflect a recursive and dynamic bilingual model, schools, as products and agents of the constructed nation-state, often fail to recognize the complex language practices of bilinguals. For example, Messing tells us how linguists and educators only recognize *legítimo Mexicano*, a constructed language that takes away all syncretic elements whose source is Spanish. Wyman, quoting Jaffe (2007, p. 73) says that schools "are not set up to recognize multiple norms and mixed codes."

As described by McCarty et al., it is the different views of what constitute viable language practices that account for the different perceptions that educators and youth have about their language use. The youth are comfortable with their translanguaging, although they want to develop more complex Indigenous language practices. For the teachers, however, the notion persists that there is either a standard Indigenous language or nothing. It is monolingualism that is valued, even in bilingual education programs. These educators express a monoglossic language ideology even as they espouse bilingualism.

Salir adelante, getting ahead, is the reason given by Indigenous youth in Messing's study for favoring Spanish, but it is not Spanish monolingualism that these youth are claiming. As Wyman makes clear, bilingual practices are needed for local work in the community. To get ahead as Indigenous youth, cultural and language practices cannot be one or the other, or, as Wyman says, local or global, Indigenous or English, traditional or modern. It is by integrating all of these that Indigenous youth will get ahead. In doing so, they are affirming their past and their local lives, as they project them toward a better future in a new and generative becoming. The dynamic translanguaging of the Indigenous youth made evident in this book could be a way of tapping their activism to guard their cultural and linguistic practices carefully, but also to connect to the worldwide translanguaging practices that characterize the 21st century.

What is most important about these contributions is that the threat to Indigenous language practices is made evident and Indigenous language activism is supported. What is different is that they propose that the threat arises not only from powerful monolingual English or Spanish-speaking majorities, but also from within. The lack of understanding of the construction of languages and a monoglossic ideology that values only monolingual ways of languaging, even in Indigenous languages, also contributes to the dangerous language shift among Indigenous peoples. Educators' insistence that the youth do not speak their languages contributes to their linguistic insecurity and shame. Despite the wider societal discourse that, according to McCarty et al., marginalize Indigenous languages and their speakers, Lee tells us that these youth are not embarrassed about the language itself; they are embarrassed of "their own limited Native language ability," an attitude that can only be constructed (and deconstructed) within the Indigenous community itself, by educators and sociolinguists.

These youth's translanguaging practices are seeds for the hard work that must be done for Indigenous languages to survive. As with the affective nature of planting corn by hand that Nicholas describes, the labor of sustaining Indigenous cultural and language practices for the future is hard work. For Indigenous youth, this work could lead to the re-emergence of language practices that are different from those of the times before colonization, but in their dynamic bilingualism—their translanguaging—could lay the means to a secure future for Indigenous lifeways in the 21st century.

References

Blackledge, A., & Creese, A. (2010). *Multilingualism*. London, England: Continuum.

Canagarajah, A. S. (2011). Codemeshing in academic writing: Identifying teachable strategies of translanguaging. *The Modern Language Journal, 95*(3), 401–417.

Cope, B., & Kalantzis, M. (2000). *Multiliteracies: Literacy learning and design of social futures*. London, England: Routledge.

Creese, A., & Blackledge, A. (2010). Translanguaging in the bilingual classroom: A pedagogy for learning and teaching? *Modern Language Journal, 94*(1), 103–115.

Errington, J. (2001). Colonial linguistics. *Annual Review of Anthropology, 30*, 19–39.

García, O. (2009). *Bilingual education in the 21st century: A global perspective*. West Sussex, England: Wiley-Blackwell.

García, O. (2011). From language garden to sustainable languaging: Bilingual education in a global world. *Perspective. A publication of the National Association for Bilingual Education*, Sept./Oct. 5–10, 5–9.

García, O., Morín, J. L., & Rivera, K. (2001). How threatened is the Spanish of New York Puerto Ricans? Language shift with *vaivén*. In J. A. Fishman (Ed.), *Can threatened languages be saved? Reversing language shift revisited: A 21st century perspective* (pp. 44–73). Clevedon, England: Multilingual Matters.

Heller, M. (Ed.). (2007). *Bilingualism: A social approach*. New York, NY: Palgrave McMillan.

Hornberger, N.H., & Link, H. (2012). Translanguaging and transnational literacies in multilingual classrooms: A bilingual lens. *International Journal of Bilingual Education and Bilingualism, 15*(3), 261–278.

Jaffe, A. (2007). Contexts and consequences of essentializing discourses. In A. Duchêne & M. Heller (Eds.), *Discourses of endangerment: Ideology and interest in the defence of languages* (pp. 57–75). London, England: Continuum.

Kress, G. (2003). *Literacy in the new media age*. London and New York: Routledge.

Lewis, G., Jones, B., & Baker, C. (2012a). Translanguaging: Developing its conceptualisation and contextualisation. *Educational Research and Evaluation: An International Journal on Theory and Practice, 18*(7), 641–654.

Lewis, G., Jones, B., & Baker, C. (2012b). Translanguaging: Origins and development from school to street and beyond. *Educational Research and Evaluation, 18*(7), 655–670.

Makoni, S., & Pennycook, A. (2007). *Disinventing and reconstituting languages*. Clevedon, England: Multilingual Matters.

McCarty, T. L. (2004). Dangerous difference: A critical-historical analysis of language education policies in the United States. In J. W. Tollefson & A. B. M. Tsui (Eds.), *Medium of instruction policies. Which agenda? Whose agenda?* (pp. 71–93). Mahwah, NJ: Erlbaum.

McCarty, T. L., & Zepeda, O. (Eds.). (2006). *One voice, many voices — Recreating Indigenous language communities*. Tempe: Arizona State University Center for Indian Education.

Mühlhäusler, P. (2000). Language planning and language ecology. *Current Issues in Language Planning, 1*(3), 306–367.

New London Group. (1996). A pedagogy of multiliteracies: Designing social futures. *Harvard Educational Review, 66*(1), 60–92.

Reyhner, J., Cantoni, G., St. Clair, R. N., & Parsons Yazzie, E. (1999). *Revitalizing Indigenous languages.* Flagstaff: Northern Arizona University Center for Excellence in Education. Retrieved December 8, 2012, from http://jan.ucc.nau.edu/~jar/RIL_Contents.html

Romaine, S. (1994). *Language in society: An introduction to sociolinguistics.* Oxford, England: Oxford University Press.

Shohamy, E. (2006). *Language policy: Hidden agendas and new approaches.* London, England: Routledge.

Skutnabb-Kangas, T. (2000). *Linguistic genocide in education — Or worldwide diversity and human rights?* Mahwah, NJ: Erlbaum.

Skutnabb-Kangas, T., & Dunbar, R. (2010). Indigenous children's education as linguistic genocide and a crime against humanity? A global view [Special issue]. *Gáldu Cála: Journal of Indigenous Peoples, 1.*

Williams, C. (1994). *Arfarniad o ddulliau dysgu ac addysgu yng nghyd-destun addysg uwchradd ddwyie-ithog* [Evaluation of teaching and learning methods in the context of bilingual secondary education]. (Unpublished doctoral thesis). University of Wales, Bangor.

Yngve, V. (1996). *From grammar to science: New foundations for general linguistics.* Amsterdam, The Netherlands: John Benjamins.

ABOUT THE CONTRIBUTORS

Gilbert Brown (Navajo) has taught Diné language and culture in his native New Mexico for years. He holds undergraduate and graduate degrees in cross-cultural education, and a Ph.D. in Indigenous education from the University of Arizona. Dr. Brown's research interests include Indigenous education, Indigenous curriculum development, Diné identity, and Diné oral traditions. His work includes an analysis of the traditional conceptualization, *Diné T'aa Bi At'eego*, "a well-directed person," and the documentation of traditional narratives.

Walkie Charles is a Yup'ik from Emmonak, a coastal village on the Yukon-Kuskokwim delta in southwestern Alaska. He is an Assistant Professor of Alaska Native Language and Linguistics Programs at the University of Alaska, Fairbanks. His interests include second language acquisition and teaching the Yup'ik language. Recently appointed by Governor Sean Parnell to the Alaska Native Language Preservation and Advisory Council, he has numerous publications on Yup'ik language instruction, including recent articles in *Anthropology and Education Quarterly* and the *Journal of American Indian Education*.

Ofelia García is Professor of Urban Education and Hispanic and Luso-Brazilian Literatures and Languages at the Graduate Center of the City University of New York. Her books include *Bilingual Education in the 21st Century: A Global Perspective, Educating Emergent Bilinguals* (with J. Kleifgen), *Additive Schooling in Subtractive Times* (with L. Bartlett), *Bilingual Community Education and Multilingualism* (with Z. Zakharia and B. Otcu), *Handbook of Language and Ethnic Identity* (with J. A. Fishman), *Negotiating Language Policies in Schools* (with K.

Menken), *Imagining Multilingual Schools* (with T. Skutnabb-Kangas and M. Torres-Guzmán), and *A Reader in Bilingual Education* (with C. Baker).

Leanne Hinton is Professor Emerita of Linguistics at the University of California-Berkeley. A specialist in American Indian languages, sociolinguistics, and language loss and revival, her publications include *Bringing Our Languages Home: Language Revitalization for Families* (2013), *How To Keep Your Language Alive* (2002, with Matt Vera and Nancy Steele), and *The Green Book of Language Revitalization in Practice* (2001, with Ken Hale). She strongly supports linguistic research related to community needs and interests. In 2006, she received the Lannan Foundation's Cultural Freedom Award, and in 2012 she was awarded the Language, Linguistics and the Public Award by the Linguistic Society of America.

Kauanoe Kamanā is Director of P-12 Laboratory School Programing at Ka Haka 'Ula O Ke'elikōlani College of Hawaiian Language at the University of Hawai'i at Hilo. She is president of the 'Aha Pūnana Leo, founded in 1983 to reestablish Hawaiian medium education. She and her husband William H. Wilson raised and educated their two children totally through Hawaiian from preschool at the Pūnana Leo O Hilo through to graduation at Nāwahīokalani'ōpu'u School.

Kuunux Teerit Kroupa (Arikara) is currently working towards his doctorate degree in Cultural Anthropology, History of Education, and Native American and Indigenous Studies at Indiana University-Bloomington. He is also the Language Coordinator and Historian at the Arikara Cultural Center in White Shield, North Dakota.

Tiffany S. Lee is Dibé łizhiní (Blacksheep - Diné), born for Naałaní (Lakota). She is an Associate Professor in Native American Studies at the University of New Mexico in Albuquerque where she teaches courses on Indigenous education, research, and language revitalization. Her research involves understanding socio-culturally responsive education from the perspective of Native youth and how education is related to Native youth language activism, language reclamation, and re-articulation of cultural identity.

Teresa L. McCarty is the George F. Kneller Chair in Education and Anthropology at the University of California, Los Angeles, and the Alice Wiley Snell Professor Emerita of Education Policy Studies at Arizona State University. Her books include *A Place To Be Navajo—Rough Rock and the Struggle for Self-Determination in Indigenous Schooling* (2002); *Language, Literacy, and Power in Education* (2005); *"To Remain an Indian": Lessons in Democracy from a Century of Native American Education* (with K. T. Lomawaima, 2006); *Ethnography and*

Language Policy (2011); and *Language Planning and Policy in Native America — History, Theory, Praxis* (2013).

Jacqueline Messing is a linguistic anthropologist who studies multilingualism, identity, and ideology, and attempts to revitalize Native and heritage languages through education in Mexico and the United States. Dr. Messing is a Visiting Scholar and Adjunct Professor at Georgetown Linguistics, and Adjunct Professor of Anthropology and Latin American Studies at the University of Maryland-College Park. She has also taught at the University of South Florida and the University of Arizona.

Sheilah E. Nicholas (Hopi) is Assistant Professor of Language, Reading, and Culture at the University of Arizona, Tucson, Arizona. She is an Indigenous scholar-educator whose work focuses on Indigenous/Hopi language maintenance and reclamation, Hopi language literacy, Indigenous epistemologies and language ideologies, and cultural and linguistic issues in American Indian/ Hopi education. Her research has been published in numerous edited volumes and in *American Indian Culture and Research Quarterly* and the *Journal of Language, Identity, and Education.*

Brendan H. O'Connor is Assistant Professor of Language, Literacy, and Intercultural Studies at the University of Texas at Brownsville. He is a linguistic anthropologist of education whose interests include knowledge and identity in classroom interaction, youth language and culture, and the cultural context of schooling in the U.S.-Mexico borderlands.

Mary Eunice Romero-Little's scholarship seeks possibilities for transforming education in ways that are congruent with Indigenous epistemologies, languages, and everyday practices. A member of Cochiti Pueblo, her research on Indigenous children's early language and cultural literacy learning informs scholarship, policy, and practice in early childhood education and Indigenous language education. Dr. Romero-Little is an Associate Professor of Indigenous Language Education and Applied Linguistics in the School of Social Transformation and American Indian Studies at Arizona State University.

Shelley R. Tulloch holds a Ph.D. in Linguistics from Université Laval. Living in Cape Dorset, Nunavut, she engages in community-partnered research with organizations including the Inuit Circumpolar Council, Inuit Circumpolar Youth Council, and Nunavut Literacy Council. She is Adjunct Professor of Linguistics at the Canada Institute of Linguistics, Trinity Western University.

Larisa Warhol has a Ph.D. in Educational Leadership and Policy Studies from Arizona State University. Her research encompasses language education policy,

American Indian education policy, international and comparative education, and urban education policy contexts. Current research projects include examining the impacts of international development and education discourses on Maasai youth in Kenya. Her research has been published in the *International Journal on Bilingual Education and Bilingualism*, *Language Policy* and *Bilingual Research Journal*.

William H. Wilson is the Division Chair for Academic Programs at Ka Haka 'Ula O Ke'elikōlani College of Hawaiian Language at the University of Hawai'i at Hilo. He and his wife Kauanoe Kamanā are founding board members of the 'Aha Pūnana Leo. In 1990 he received a special award for his work in the development and passage of the Native American Languages Act from the Native American Languages Issues Institute.

Leisy T. Wyman is an Associate Professor in the Language, Reading and Culture Program at the University of Arizona. She has worked with Yup'ik youth and adults on books of Yup'ik elders' narratives (Fredson et al., 1998), and with Yup'ik educators on collaborative language planning research. Her recent works include the book *Youth Culture, Language Endangerment and Linguistic Survivance* (2012), and theme issues on youth bi/multilingualism for the *Journal of Language, Identity and Education* (with T. L. McCarty, 2009), and the *International Multilingual Research Journal* (with D. S. Warriner, 2013).

Ofelia Zepeda is a member of the Tohono O'odham Nation of southern Arizona and Regents' Professor of Linguistics at the University of Arizona. She is a recipient of the MacArthur Fellowship for her work in American Indian language education and maintenance. Her areas of teaching and research include Introduction to Tohono O'odham, Structure of the Tohono O'odham Language, and Native American Language Documentation and Revitalization. She is the director of the American Indian Language Development Institute (AILDI).

PERMISSIONS

Chapter 2 was originally published, in slightly modified form, as "Language in the Lives of Indigenous Youth," by McCarty, T. L., Romero-Little, M. E., Warhol, L., & Zepeda, O., in T. L. McCarty (2013), *Language Planning and Policy in Native America — History, Theory, Praxis* (pp. 156–181). Bristol, England: Multilingual Matters; used with permission from Multilingual Matters.

Chapter 4 has been adapted and expanded from Nicholas, S. (2009), "'I Live Hopi, I Just Don't Speak It'—The Critical Intersection of Language, Culture, and Identity in the Lives of Contemporary Hopi Youth." *Journal of Language, Identity and Education,* 8(5), 321–334; used with permission from Taylor and Francis.

Chapter 5 has been adapted and expanded from Wyman, L. T. (2009), "Youth, Linguistic Ecology, and Language Endangerment: A Yup'ik Example." *Journal of Language, Identity and Education,* 8(5), 335–349; used with permission from Taylor and Francis.

Chapter 6 has been adapted and expanded from Messing, J. (2009), "Ambivalence and Ideology Among Mexicano Youth in Tlaxcala, Mexico." *Journal of Language, Identity and Education,* 8(5), 350–364; used with permission from Taylor and Francis.

Chapter 7 has been adapted and expanded from Lee, T. S. (2009). "Language, Identity, and Power: Navajo and Pueblo Young Adults' Perspectives and Experiences with Competing Language Ideologies." *Journal of Language, Identity and Education,* 8(5), 307–320; used with permission from Taylor and Francis.

Chapter 10 has been adapted and expanded from Wilson, W. H. & Kamanā, K. (2009). "Indigenous Youth Bilingualism from a Hawaiian Activist Perspective." *Journal of Language, Identity and Education, 8*(5), 369–375; used with permission from Taylor and Francis.

Chapter 11 has been adapted and expanded from Charles, W. (2009), "Indigenous Youth Bilingualism from a Yup'ik Perspective." *Journal of Language, Identity and Education, 8*(5), 365–368; used with permission from Taylor and Francis.

Chapter 12 has been adapted and expanded from García, O. (2009), "En/countering Indigenous Youth Bilingualism." *Journal of Language, Identity and Education, 8*(5), 376–380; used with permission from Taylor and Francis.

AUTHOR INDEX

SUBJECT INDEX

activism: learning opportunities and, 7–9, 175–77, 181–83; praxis-driven youth language research, 18–19; youth language activism, 7–9, 14–17, 43–45, 210. *See also* Arikara language revitalization, counternarratives/counter-stories; Ft. Mojave language movement, Hawaiian language revitalization, Inuit language movement.

agency: xi, xviii, xx, 1–4, 12, 14–15, 18, 102, 130, 132, 136, 141–45, 149, 150, 152–53, 157, 160–66, 163–65

ambivalence: xviii, 17, 111–112, 116, 117–26

American Indian Studies Research Institute (AISRI): 176

ancestral language(s): 7, 14, 19, 140, 162, 205. *See also* Arikara language revitalization, Hawaiian language revitalization, heritage language learners, Inuit language movement.

Arctic Indigenous Languages Symposium (AILS): 156

Arikara language revitalization: xviii–xix, 1; activism and, 175–77, 181–83; code-switching and "Ree-glish" 180–81; community context, 168–69; future challenges, 183–85; historical background, 170–71; young adult activists and: Kunaa'u Xaawaaruxti (Medicine Horse), 175, 176, 177, 183; Kuunuxtawawašuxtaarit (The Bear Who Stands Holding the Lightning), 175, 177, 183, 184; Neetahkas Takaa'aahu

(Dancing Eagle), 175, 177, 181, 182, 183; language adaptability, 180; "Ree-volution", 168, 170; new technology and, 179–80; reawakening of activism, 174–75; and "Ree-volution", 168, 170; song and ceremony importance, 177–78; White Shield community and school, 171–74. *See also* Parks, Douglas, Waters, Ella, Yellow Bird, Delilah.

authenticity: 11–13, 52–53; 56, 58–61, 111, 117–18, 126, 208, 210. *See also* language ideologies

bilingual education: 1, 8, 10, 40, 92, 119–21, 171–72, 211–12. *See also* schools and schooling.

binary assumptions and false binaries: xxi, 8, 13, 38, 43, 64, 108, 212

boarding schools: xix, 37, 74, 92, 168–69, 202–5

border crossing, linguistic: 33–34, 99

Brown, Jay: xvi–xvii, 48–67, 202

Caddoan language family: 170

ceremonies: ceremonial understanding and Indigenous language, 41, 77; Hopi ritualized practices, 70, 80–81, 206

choice: Inuit Circumpolar Youth Council (ICYC) language planning and, 159–60, 163–64; language abandonment and, 93–94

class: 118–119, 124, 189